T0270994

In 1989, one-parent families comprised 17 per cent of all families with dependent children, and their number has almost doubled in the past two decades. Almost all the information we have hitherto had about them comes from 'snapshots' in cross-section surveys. This book analyses for the first time the flows into and out of lone parenthood, using demographic and employment histories from a nationally representative survey carried out in 1980. It studies how various socio-economic characteristics of women and their economic environment, such as welfare benefits, affect these flows, and how these interact to determine the attributes of the population of one-parent families, particularly their economic circumstances. The book also studies the lone parents' movements into and out of paid employment, and the effect of welfare benefits on their employment. The analyses are used to gauge the effects of alternative policies on one-parent families, their paid employment, and their living standards.

JOHN F. ERMISCH is Bonar-Macfie Professor of Political Economy at the University of Glasgow, and co-Director of the Human Resources Research Programme at the Centre for Economic Policy Research. He previously worked at the National Institute of Economic and Social Research, and as a research economist for the Department of Housing and Urban Development, Washington D.C. His previous publications include *The Political Economy of Demographic Change* (Heinemann, 1983), as well as numerous articles in learned journals and contributary volumes.

THE NATIONAL INSTITUTE OF ECONOMIC AND SOCIAL RESEARCH

Occasional Papers
XLIV

LONE PARENTHOOD

An Economic Analysis

LONE PARENTHOOD

An Economic Analysis

JOHN F. ERMISCH

The right of the
University of Cambridge
to print and sell
all manner of books
was granted by
Henry VIII in 1534.
The University has printed
and published continuously
since 1584.

CAMBRIDGE UNIVERSITY PRESS

CAMBRIDGE

NEW YORK   PORT CHESTER   MELBOURNE   SYDNEY

CAMBRIDGE UNIVERSITY PRESS
Cambridge, New York, Melbourne, Madrid, Cape Town,
Singapore, São Paulo, Delhi, Tokyo, Mexico City

Cambridge University Press
The Edinburgh Building, Cambridge CB2 8RU, UK

Published in the United States of America by
Cambridge University Press, New York

www.cambridge.org
Information on this title: www.cambridge.org/9780521412438

First published 1991

A catalogue record for this publication is available from the British Library

Library of Congress Cataloguing in Publication data
Ermisch.John.
Lone parenthood: an economic analysis /John Ermisch.
p.   cm. – (Occasional papers / National Institute of Economic
and Social Research: 44) Includes bibliographical references (p.   ) and index.
ISBN 0521 41243 9
1. Single–parent family – Great Britain.
2 Single parent family –   Economic aspects – Great Britain.
3. Single parents – Great Britain –
Social conditions.
4. Single parents – Great Britain – Economic conditions.
I. Title.   II. Series: Occasional papers (National
Institute of Economic and Social Research): 44.
HQ759.915.E76 1991
306.85′6′0941–dc20
91–8135
CIP

ISBN 978-0-521-41243-8 Hardback

To my parents

CONTENTS

LIST OF TABLES

SYMBOLS IN THE TABLES
... not available
— nil or negligible
n.a. not applicable

LIST OF CHARTS

PREFACE

This book arose from research financed by the Joseph Rowntree Foundation and the Economic and Social Research Council, for which I am extremely grateful. I would also like to give special thanks to Robert E. Wright who worked with me on a large part of the research that has made its way into this book. Some of the analyses have been published in academic journals, the *Oxford Bulletin of Economics and Statistics*, the *Journal of Human Resources*, the *National Institute Economic Review* and the *Journal of Population Economics*. I am grateful to the editors of these journals and to their anonymous referees, who have contributed to the improvement of the analysis and its exposition. I also thank Jon Barry, Brian Francis and Richard Davies for generously supplying their SABRE program for use in some of the estimation, and Fran Robinson for preparing the manuscript for publication. None of these people are, of course, responsible for the use that I have made of their help and advice.

JOHN ERMISCH
November, 1990

INTRODUCTION

Between 1971 and 1986 the number of one-parent families in Great Britain increased by nearly 80 per cent, surpassing one million. In 1989, they were 17 per cent of all British families with dependent children. Apart from the United States, this is the highest incidence of one-parent families in the world. One-parent families are often poor, because of the absence of income other than the earnings of the parent or state benefits. Their low living standards and possible adverse effects on the development of children in these families raise many social policy issues.

Almost all of the information that we have about one-parent families comes from cross-sectional surveys. These offer snapshots of one-parent families at points in time, but they leave many questions unanswered. For instance, is there a rapid turnover in the population of one-parent families, or do a few families remain one-parent families for a long period of time? Are there characteristics of parents and their families which make them more likely to become one-parent families, or to remain lone parents longer? Do state welfare benefits affect the creation and duration of one-parent families and their employment? In order to answer these questions, it is necessary to analyse information concerning flows into and out of lone parenthood.

This book does so using demographic and employment histories from a nationally representative survey carried out in 1980. It studies the creation and duration of one-parent families, and how these interact to determine the population of such families. It also studies lone parents' movements into and out of employment and the effect of welfare benefits on their employment.

The following chapter surveys the changes in the incidence of one-parent families in a number of industrialised countries and the contribution of trends in marriage, divorce and childbearing to these changes. It also looks in greater detail at the socio-economic characteristics of one-parent families in Britain.

In the third chapter, a formal model of the dynamics of one-parent families is developed. This model shows how changes in a number of demographic rates affect the proportion of families with

dependent children that have only one parent. It also forms the
basis for the empirical analysis of inflows to and exits from lone
parenthood in subsequent chapters.

In order to study the impacts of characteristics of a parent and her
family on these flows, a theoretical foundation, which suggests
which characteristics are likely to be important and the direction of
their impacts, is needed. Chapter 4 provides this. It outlines an
economic model of marriage and marital search.

Chapter 5 applies this model to the analysis of entry to lone
parenthood through marital dissolution and first births outside
marriage. The empirical results indicate the extent to which inflows
to lone parenthood are selective.

As lone parents' earnings are usually crucial in raising their living
standards, analysis of their decision whether or not to take a job is
important. Chapter 6 develops a static model of their employment
decision, and uses data from a series of ten *General Household Surveys*
(a nationally representative sample) to estimate the parameters of
the model. By providing exogenous variation in welfare benefits
over time, the time series of cross-sections makes it easier to identify
their effect on lone parents' employment separately from the effects
of children, whose age and number are the primary source of
variation in welfare benefits entitlements in a single cross-section.

More information about how differences in the probability of
being employed associated with characteristics of a lone parent and
her family come about is obtained from the study of lone parents'
movements into and out of employment in Chapter 7. This analysis
of the dynamics of lone parents' employment breaks new ground in
Britain.

Chapter 8 studies the duration of lone parenthood in Britain.
This analysis is also the first of its kind in Britain. It examines the
evidence for selective outflows from lone parenthood according to
the characteristics of the family, and it also investigates whether
welfare benefits prolong lone parenthood.

The final chapter uses the analyses of earlier chapters to gauge
the prospective number of one-parent families, and how policy
might affect it. It also simulates the effects on lone parents'
employment of different policies aimed at improving the living
standards of one-parent families.

ONE-PARENT FAMILIES IN INDUSTRIALISED COUNTRIES: AN OVERVIEW OF TRENDS

CHANGING FAMILY AND HOUSEHOLD STRUCTURE

Over the past 25 years, there have been striking changes in the composition of households and families in industrialised countries. In all countries, the archetypical western household of a couple and their dependent children has diminished in importance. For instance, such households were only a quarter of all households in Sweden and 30 per cent of households in the United States in the early 1980s, down from 36 and 44 per cent respectively twenty years earlier. In 1988, only 26 per cent of British households consisted of this traditional family. While this decline partly reflects the fall in birth rates in all industrialised countries, there generally has been only a small increase in the proportion of households containing a couple on their own, and in the case of the United States, no increase. The type of household that has been growing in importance most dramatically does not contain a family at all, but only one person.

In the early 1980s, one person households were a fifth or more of households in the industrialised countries of northern and central Europe (22 per cent in Britain, rising to 26 per cent in 1988) and North America, making up a third of Swedish households and 30 per cent of German ones. Twenty years earlier, such households were only an eighth of all households in North America, Britain and the Netherlands. In Japan, one person households rose from 6 per cent of households in 1960 to 16 per cent in 1980.

But of households containing a family, those with a one-parent family have become increasingly important over the past 25 years. In Britain, the number of one-parent families increased by 77 per cent between 1971 ad 1986, to just over a million families (Haskey 1989). As a percentage of all British families with dependent children, they have increased from 8 per cent (1971) to 17 per cent (1989). The growing proportion of one-parent families among all families with dependent children is the subject of this chapter. We start by looking at the relationship between this proportion and traditional demographic rates.

ONE-PARENT FAMILIES AND DEMOGRAPHIC RATES

The number of one-parent families at a point in time is the result of
past inflows to lone parenthood and past outflows from that state,
and these flows depend on various demographic rates. The relationship between these rates and the incidence of one-parent families
can be illustrated if we assume, for simplicity, that each mother of
dependent children has the same probability of becoming a lone
mother in any month, and each lone mother has the same probability of leaving lone parenthood in any month. If these rates of entry
and exit are constant over time, then the proportion of mothers
heading a one-parent family is approximately equal to the product
of the rate of entry to lone parenthood and the average duration as
a lone parent.[1]

The rate of inflow and the average duration depend in turn, on
traditional demographic rates. One-parent families can, of course,
be created by births outside marriage (or a consensual union) to
childless women, the death of a parent and separation of parents,
as well as divorce. As Chapter 3 demonstrates formally, a large
number of demographic rates play a role in the determination of
the number of one-parent families. These include the first marriage rate of childless women, first birth rates to women inside and
outside marriage, the marital dissolution rates of mothers and
childless women respectively, and their respective remarriage
rates.

The demographic rates of primary importance are, however, the
divorce and remarriage rates of mothers, the first birth rate outside
marriage and the marriage rate of single (that is, never married)
mothers. The other rates mentioned above help determine the
populations 'at risk' for these events (for example, the number of
single, childless women and the number of married mothers). The
terms marriage and remarriage should be taken to include the
formation of consensual unions as well as legal marriage, and
divorce should refer to marital dissolution including separation.
Most statistics however, only refer to the legal events associated
with union formation and dissolution. Thus for statistical description of trends in demographic rates in the chapter, the ideal
concepts of union formation and dissolution must be set aside. The
next section examines the trend in the number of one-parent
families in various industrialised countries, and is followed by a
discussion of the demographic rates primarily responsible for the
trend.

CHANGES IN THE NUMBER OF ONE-PARENT FAMILIES

As is common in comparisons across countries, definitions vary. According to common usage, a one-parent family is a parent with her (his) dependent children, either living as a separate household or living in the household of others (for example, with the grandparents of the children). The largest variation in definition concerns who constitutes a dependent child and whether one-parent families living in the households of others are counted. The appendix to this chapter describes briefly the definitions that lie behind the estimates of one-parent families shown in table 2.1 and the following tables. In the light of this variation in definition, caution should be exercised in comparing the incidence of lone parenthood and its rate of increase between countries.

Among the countries for which information is available in the early 1960s, there is evidence of a marked acceleration in the growth in the number of one-parent families after 1970. Indeed, there probably was a decline in the number of fatherless households in Japan between 1961 and 1967, followed by an increase during 1967–83. The rapid postwar reduction in Japanese mortality undoubtedly played an important role in this decline by reducing the number of widows with dependent children (aged under twenty in Japan's case). At the other extreme, the United States experienced fairly rapid growth in the number of one-parent families in the 1960s as well as since 1970, although the rate of increase was much faster in the more recent period.

As a consequence of fluctuations in the birth rate, there have been changes in the number of families with dependent children. Thus, it is helpful to express the incidence of lone parenthood in terms of their proportion of all families with dependent children. In the countries of northern and western Europe in table 2.1, one-parent families generally constituted about 10–15 per cent of all families in the early 1980s. This contrasts with over a quarter of families in the United States and 5 per cent in Japan. The incidence of one-parent families in the predominantly Catholic countries of Spain and Ireland is also low.

The percentage of families with dependent children having only one parent has increased since the early 1970s in all of the countries in table 2.1, but particularly in Sweden, the Netherlands, the Federal Republic of Germany and Great Britain, and most dramatically in the United States, where it has virtually doubled. Not surprisingly, these are also the countries with rapid rates of growth in the absolute number of one-parent families during the 1970s and

Table 2.1. *Changes in the incidence of lone-parent families*

		Number (thousands)	Index	As % of all families with dependent children
Belgium	1970	167	100	
	1981	213	128	12.3
France	1968	720	100	9.5
	1982	887	123	10.2
Germany	1972	707	100	8.0
	1982	927	131	11.4
Great Britain	1961	474	83	
	1971	570	100	8.0
	1984	940	165	13.0
Ireland	1975	22	100	5.6
	1981	30	135	7.1
Japan[a]	1961	1,029	164	
	1973	626	100	3.6
	1983	718	115	4.1[b]
Netherlands	1960	177	88	9.3
	1971	202	100	8.9
	1981	309	153	12.3
Sweden	1960	91	93	9.0
	1970	98	100	9.6
	1980	144	147	14.2
Switzerland	1960	99	93	11.6
	1970	106	100	10.4
	1980	124	117	12.0
United States	1960	2,786	73	11.0
	1970	3,808	100	13.0
	1984	8,544	224	26.0

[a]Indicates number does not include lone fathers.
[b]Percentage was 5.1 including lone fathers.

early 1980s. On the other hand, the increase in the incidence of one-parent families among all families with dependent children was small in France and Japan.

DEMOGRAPHIC TRENDS

A major driving force behind the rise in the number of one-parent families is marital dissolution. Table 2.2 shows the change in the number of one-parent families in a particular category relative to the *net* change in the total number of one-parent families, expressed

Table 2.2. *Percentage of net absolute increase in the number of one-parent families contributed by each sex and marital status category*

	Divorced or separated mother	Single mother	Widowed mother	Father	Time period
Great Britain	71	29	−4	4	1971–84
United States	52	39	−3	12	1970–84
Japan (lone mothers only)	131	14	−45	N/A	1967–83
Federal Republic of Germany	86	13	−25	26	1972–82
France	118	45	−54	−9	1968–82
Belgium	126	12	−26	−12	1970–81

Sources and definitions: see appendix to this chapter.

as a percentage; a negative percentage represents a fall in the number in that category, For example, of the total increase in one-parent families in Great Britain between 1971 and 1984, 71 per cent is attributable to the increase in the number of divorced or separated mothers, 29 per cent to the increase in single mothers, 4 per cent to the increase in lone fathers, and the decline in the number of widowed mothers represents 4 per cent of the net increase in the total of lone parents. Table 2.2 shows that, with the exception of the United States, the growth in divorced and separated mothers was responsible for the vast majority of the net increase in the number of one-parent families since *circa* 1970. Even in the United States, it accounted for the majority of the net increase in one-parent families, but the growing number of never-married mothers also contributed about 40 per cent of the net increase.

Clearly, mothers' divorce and remarriage rates are the primary demographic determinants of the number of divorced mothers heading one-parent families. The divorce rate, is, however, particularly important because it has risen dramatically and because the impact of the remarriage rate on the proportion of parents who are divorced lone parents rises with the divorce rate. Thus, if the divorce rate is low, changes in the remarriage rate only have a small effect on the proportion of families with only one parent.

As noted earlier, the remarriage rate is inversely related to the average length of time between divorce and remarriage. Holding this average duration of divorce constant, a rise in the divorce rate

Chart 2.1 *Divorces per 1,000 existing marriages*

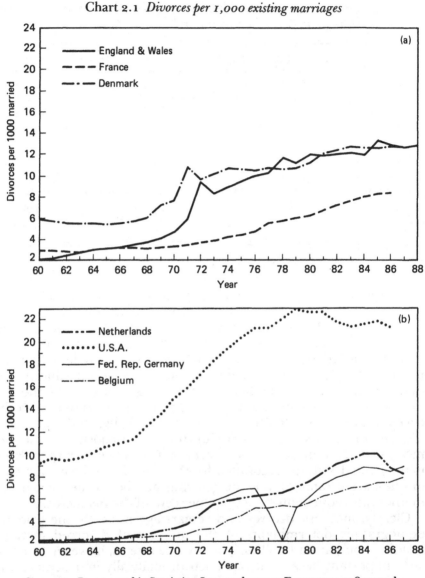

Sources: *Demographic Statistics*, Luxembourg, Eurostat, 1989; and
Statistical Abstract of the U.S., various years.

increases the number of divorced lone parents relative to all parents.
Chart 2.1 shows the divorce rate in terms of the number of divorces
in a year per 1,000 of the married population in a number of
industrialised countries. In all of these countries, there was an

acceleration in the rise in divorce during the late 1960s. Some countries, such as England and Wales and the Federal Republic of Germany, changed their divorce laws, causing sharp jumps (upward and downward) in the annual divorce rate, but the trend since the late 1960s is clearly strongly upward. The most dramatic trend is in the United States, despite the fact that it started from a much higher rate than in the European countries. There is some suggestion that the divorce rate may be levelling out in the United States and England and Wales.

Chart 2.2 measures the divorce rate somewhat differently. This measure, called the 'total divorce rate', indicates the number of marriages per 1,000 that would eventually end in divorce if the divorce rates at each duration of marriage in a particular year held throughout a person's marriage. Compared to the simple measure of chart 2.1, it controls for the composition of the married population according to marriage duration. Chart 2.2 tells a similar story to chart 2.1, showing strong upward trends in the incidence of divorce, particularly since the late 1960s. It should be noted that while the total divorce rate has a simple interpretation in terms of the proportion of marriages eventually dissolving, year-to-year changes in the timing of divorce by marriage duration produce changes in the total divorce rate. Thus, it reflects timing changes as well as the ultimate incidence of divorce, and these are particularly important if there are legislative changes, as the curve for the Federal Republic of Germany illustrates.

The longer the average length of time between divorce and remarriage (that is, the lower is the probability of remarriage), the larger is the impact of a change in the divorce rate on the number of one-parent families. Chart 2.3 shows that the remarriage rate of divorced women, expressed as the number of remarriages of divorced women per 1,000 divorced women, has been much lower in France and Germany than in the United States and England and Wales, although the difference is narrowing. Thus, changes in the divorce rate would tend to have a larger impact on the number of one-parent families in France and Germany.

A decline in the remarriage rate would reinforce the impact of rising divorce on the number of one-parent families, while a rise in this rate would moderate it. Chart 2.3 indicates that these crude remarriage rates have been declining sharply since the early 1970s in England and Wales and the United States. Some of this decline reflects an almost inevitable fall in the crude remarriage rate resulting from larger flows into the population of divorced persons, which came about because of the acceleration of the divorce rate

Chart 2.2 *Total divorce rates per 1,000 marriages*

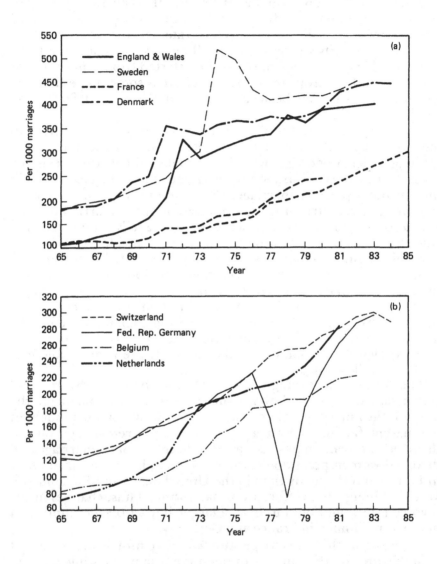

Source: Sardon (1986).

shown in charts 2.1 and 2.2. When divorces occur at a more steady rate, as they have more recently in these two countries, the crude remarriage rate is a better indicator of the underlying propensity to remarry. Thus, the fall in the remarriage rate in recent years

Chart 2.3 *Remarriage rate of divorced women*

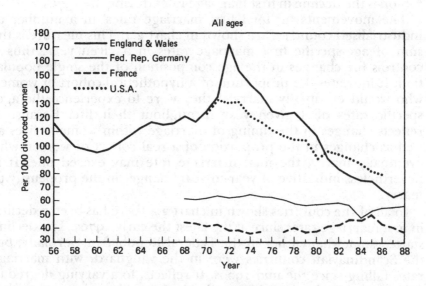

All ages

Legend:
— England & Wales
— Fed. Rep. Germany
– – – France
⋯⋯⋯ U.S.A.

Per 1000 divorced women

Year

Sources: England and Wales: *Marriage and Divorce Statistics*, London, HMSO, various years; Germany, France and the United States: author's calculations from annual statistical yearbooks.

suggests a rise in the average length of time between divorce and remarriage. In these two countries therefore, the decline in the remarriage rate of divorced persons has also been working to increase the number of one-parent families. The effect of this decline has, however, been moderated somewhat by an increase in cohabitation without legal marriage among previously married mothers. For instance, between 1979 and 1988, the percentage of divorced women who were cohabiting increased from 20 per cent to 28 per cent, and it has been shown that the median duration of cohabitation for divorced women lengthened by about six months during this period (Haskey and Kiernan 1989).

The other important source of one-parent families is births to childless women outside a marriage or consensual union. In most countries, illegitimate and legitimate birth rates (defined relative to the unmarried and married populations respectively) have tended to move together over time. Thus, relative to the mid-1960s and early 1970s, illegitimate birth rates have fallen considerably. But the number of childless women 'at risk' of producing births outside marriage has risen for two reasons. One is purely the result of the maturing of the European baby boom generations of the 1960s, who reached their 'teens' in the late 1970s and early 1980s. The other reason is the decline in first marriage rates during the 1970s.

The movements of 'total first marriage rates' in a number of industrialised countries are shown in chart 2.4. This measure is the sum of age-specific first marriage rates in a given year; thus it controls for changes in the age composition of the single population. It indicates the proportion of a hypothetical cohort of women who would eventually marry if they were to experience the age-specific rates of a given year throughout their life. Because it reflects changes in the timing of marriage within women's lives as well as changes in the proportion of a real cohort of women who eventually marry, the total marriage rate may exceed one. It is nevertheless indicative of year-to-year changes in the propensity to marry.

In all of the countries shown in chart 2.4 there has been a decline in first marriage rates since at the latest the early 1970s. The decline started somewhat earlier in the Federal Republic of Germany, but the Scandinavian countries were in the vanguard, with marriage rates falling since the mid-1960s. It reflects, to a varying degree in different countries, the rise in cohabitation without legal marriage. For instance, between 1979 and 1988, the percentage of British single (that is, never married) women aged 18–49 who were living with a man more than doubled, rising from 8 per cent to 20 per cent. For British women aged 20–29, as much as 40 per cent of the fall in the percentage of those married may be due to an increase in cohabitation, and just under half of British women marrying for the first time in 1987 had lived with their spouse before marriage (Haskey and Kiernan 1989).

At the minimum, the decline in first marriage rates in industrialised countries represents a movement toward later marriage, which has increased the proportion of young women who are single and childless, thus 'at risk' of having a birth outside marriage. This trend works in the opposite direction to that of lower illegitimate birth rates, tending to increase inflows to lone parenthood.

Changes in the percentage of births that are outside marriage reflect both changes in the illegitimate birth rate relative to the legitimate birth rate and changes in the proportion of women of childbearing age who are unmarried and therefore 'at risk' of having births outside of marriage.[2] The appendix to the next chapter shows that trends in this percentage should be suggestive of changes in the proportion of all families with dependent children headed by a never-married mother on her own. While not reflecting all the influences on this proportion, such as the marriage rate of

Chart 2.4 *Total first marriage rate per 1,000 women*

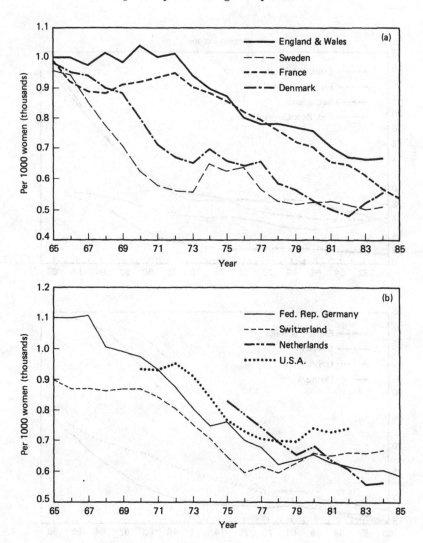

Source: Sardon (1986)

single mothers, it is a simple measure, which can be obtained for many countries, and it is shown in chart 2.5.

France, England and Wales and the United States have experienced large increases in the proportion of births outside marriage,

Chart 2.5 *Percentage of births outside marriage*

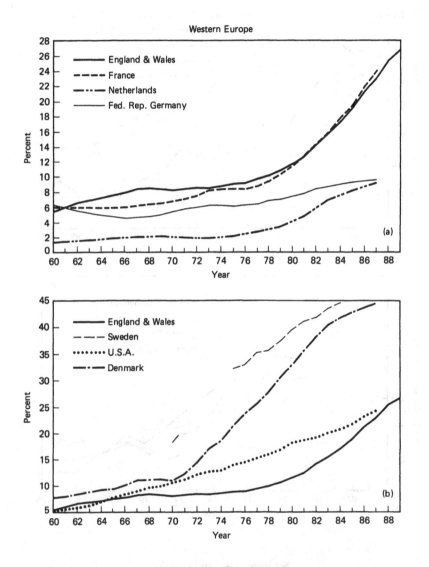

Source: As for chart 2.1.

and the proportion has also risen in the Federal Republic of Germany and the Netherlands, albeit more moderately. In England and Wales, about three-quarters of the increase in this proportion among women aged 15–29 during 1975–87 was attributable to the growth in the percentage of women of these ages who were not married. In other words it was mainly due to the fall in marriage rates, and this is probably the case in the other European countries among these as well.

In these European countries, the rate of increase in the proportion accelerated during the mid-1970s, when first marriage rates fell (chart 2.4), but in the United States there has been a fairly steady increase in this proportion since 1960. By far the largest rises in this proportion have been in the Scandinavian countries; in Sweden and Denmark over 40 per cent of births were outside of marriage in 1984, compared with about 11 per cent in Denmark and 18 per cent in Sweden in 1970.

But the dramatic increase in the proportion of births outside marriage in the Scandinavian countries is not indicative of a large rise in the incidence of single mothers bringing up children on their own. Instead it reflects the increase in childbearing within consensual unions, which is primarily a consequence of the growing importance of consensual unions, rather than an increase in the birth rate of women within such unions (see Hoem and Rennermalm 1985). For instance, despite the large fall in first marriage rates in Sweden illustrated in chart 2.4, there was little change during the 1970s in the proportion of women in their twenties and thirties living with a man, either in a consensual union or a legal marriage, but an increasing proportion of these were living in a consensual union. Between 1975 and 1983, the percentage of all cohabiting Swedish women aged 20–24 who were not married rose from 57 per cent to 79 per cent, while in Denmark this percentage increased from 18 to 25 between 1976 and 1980 (Roussel 1986). In France, the country ranking highest after the Scandinavian countries in the incidence of cohabitation without marriage during the early 1980s, this percentage only reached 17 per cent in 1983, up from 6 per cent in 1975. In starker contrast 3 and 6 per cent of cohabiting women aged 20–24 in the United States were not married in 1970 and 1980 respectively. More recent evidence indicates that, in 1987, 30 per cent of all cohabiting British women aged 20–24 were not married.

The estimates of the number of one-parent families for Sweden shown in table 2.1 take this into account (see appendix to this chapter) and exclude persons with a child who are cohabiting, whether in legal marriage or not. This is not generally the case for the other countries (for instance, the United States and the Netherlands); unmarried women with children living in consensual unions tend to be counted as one-parent families. The rise in cohabitation

without marriage in these countries means that the growth in
one-parent families is probably overstated, but since the increase in
the importance of consensual unions is not as dramatic elsewhere as
it has been in Scandinavia the overstatement is probably not large
enough to alter the general conclusions.

In order to explore the relative roles of divorce and births outside
marriage in the growth in one-parent families, analyses of the
correlation across countries between the percentage increase in
one-parent families and the percentage increases in the divorce rate
and the proportion of births that are illegitimate were carried out.
The set of countries in the analysis are England and Wales, the
Federal Republic of Germany, France, the Netherlands, Belgium,
the United States and Sweden, and the increases are measured
between the earliest and latest dates for which data are available on
one-parent families in each country. No correlation was found
between the increase in the divorce rate and the growth in one-
parent families, but a significant positive correlation was found
between the latter and the illegitimacy proportion. But it is the
United States that is responsible for this correlation. When the
United States is removed from the set of countries, there is no
correlation between the change in the illegitimacy ratio and the
growth in one-parent families (even when Sweden is excluded), but
the correlation between the growth in one-parent families and the
rise in the divorce rate is very strong, their correlation coefficient
being 0.9.

While correlations measured among a small number of countries
(6–7) will be sensitive to which countries are included, these analyses
suggest that divorce is primarily responsible for the rise in one-
parent families in the European countries, but births outside marriage also play an important role in the United States. These conclusions are consistent with the relative contributions of the different
categories of one-parent family in table 2.2, which show that, with
the exception of the United States, the increase in the number of
divorced and separated mothers accounts for most (and in three
cases all) of the increase in one-parent families during the 1970s and
early 1980s.

DEMOGRAPHIC CHARACTERISTICS OF ONE-PARENT FAMILIES

When two-parent and one-parent families are compared, one-
parent families have fewer children on average, and the children
tend to be older (that is, the youngest child is, on average, older in

one-parent families). In Britain for instance, the average number of children has fallen by a similar amount in one-parent and two-parent families, so that in 1987 the respective averages were 1.6 and 1.8 respectively. The median age of the youngest child of British lone mothers was 8.4 in 1984, compared with 7.1 for two-parent families (Haskey 1986).

A popular conception of a one-parent family is often that of a young single mother with a toddler. The reason that this view conflicts with the 'average' one-parent family is that divorced and separated mothers make up the largest proportion of one-parent families in most countries. Among the countries in table 2.2 other than Belgium (for which there is no age limit in the definition of 'dependent' children), in the early 1980s, the percentage of one-parent families headed by a divorced or separated mother varied from 45 per cent in France (for which dependent children are defined as aged under 25) to 59 per cent in Britain (during 1985–7). Between 1971 and 1986 the number of divorced and separated mothers increased by 54 per cent in Britain and among these the number of divorced mothers increased by 240 per cent (table 2.3). Demographic reasons for the growing number and changing composition of one-parent families in Britain are explored in the next chapter, and other chapters attempt to look behind these demographic reasons.

The second largest category of one-parent families in Britain and the United States is never-married mothers (23 and 25 per cent respectively in the early 1980s), but in Japan, the Federal Republic of Germany and France, widowed mothers follow divorced and separ-

Table 2.3. *Number and marital status composition of one-parent families, Great Britain, 1971–86*

	1971	1976	1981	1986
Total number (thousands)	570	750	850	1010
Per cent of all families with dependent children	8	10	12	14
Composition (per cent) Mothers:				
Single	16	17	19	23
Separated	30	25	19	18
Divorced	21	31	37	41
Widowed	21	15	14	8
Fathers	12	12	11	10
All	100	100	100	100

Source: Haskey (1986, 1989)

ated mothers in relative importance. As table 2.3 shows, never-married lone mothers have become more important in Britain, while widows diminished in importance, making up only 8 per cent of lone-parent families during 1985–7. In all countries, the vast majority of lone parents (80 per cent and over) are mothers, and in Britain lone mothers have consistently made up about 90 per cent of lone parents.

Whether the average head of a one-parent family is younger or older than the head of a two-parent family varies with the impor-tance of never-married mothers among lone parents, because they are generally younger than mothers in two-parent families. For instance, the median age of never-married mothers in Britain was 25 during 1985–7, compared with 36 for divorced mothers and 38 for heads of two-parent families (Haskey 1989). In Britain and the United States, where never-married mothers make up a larger proportion of lone parents, lone parents are, on average, younger than parents in two-parent families (35 compared with 38 in Britain), but in France, where widows are relatively more important than never-married mothers, the opposite is the case.

The demographic characteristics of one-parent families depend in part on the degree to which the flows into and out of lone parenthood vary systematically with such characteristics. For instance, focussing on divorced and separated lone mothers, most studies show that at each duration of marriage, women marrying at younger ages are more likely to experience marital dissolution. This tends to produce lone mothers that are younger than other mothers of dependent children. But, on the other hand, most studies also show that women who are older when their marriage dissolves are less likely to remarry and thus experience longer durations of lone parenthood. As a result, older mothers tend to be over-represented among lone mothers. The net effect is unclear. Because age of mother is strongly correlated with the age and number of depen-dent children, these relationships also affect the composition of lone mothers according to the number and age of their children. Clearly, to the extent that other socio-economic characteristics of parents systematically affect the probabilities of entering and leaving lone parenthood, the socio-economic characteristics of one-parent fami-lies are affected.

Chapters 5 and 8 examine how demographic and socio-economic characteristics of British women affect their entry rates to and exit rates from lone parenthood, thereby influencing the characteristics of one-parent families at a point in time. The next section examines some of these characteristics in more detail for British one-parent families.

SOCIO-ECONOMIC CHARACTERISTICS OF BRITISH
ONE-PARENT FAMILIES

The percentage of lone mothers in employment is an important indicator of the economic position of one-parent families, particularly the degree of their dependency on welfare benefits (the primary one being Supplementary Benefit, now called Income Support). Whether or not a lone mother has a job also proves to be associated with the duration of lone parenthood (Chapter 8). In contrast to most other industrialised countries, a smaller percentage of lone mothers than married mothers are employed in Britain, and the percentage employed declined markedly during the 1980s (chart 2.6). As chart 2.7 shows, the lower employment percentage for lone mothers arises because they are much less likely to take a part-time job. Indeed, they work full-time to a greater degree than married mothers, although the gap has been closing (chart 2.7).[3] With only just over 40 per cent of lone mothers employed in the mid-1980s, it is not surprising that more than 60 per cent of lone parents received Supplementary Benefit and that state benefits are the main source of income for about 65 per cent of lone parents.

One-parent families are clearly poorer than two-parent families. Evidence from the *Family Expenditure Survey*, shown in chart 2.8,

Chart 2.6 *Working mothers with a dependent child of any age*

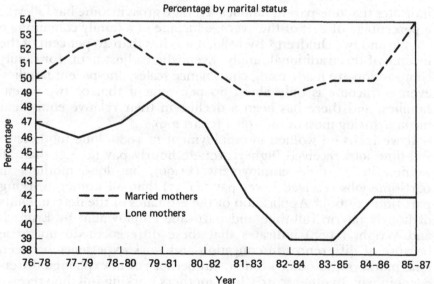

Percentage by marital status

Source: *General Household Survey*, London, HMSO, various years.

Chart 2.7 *Working mothers: percentage working full-time and part-time*

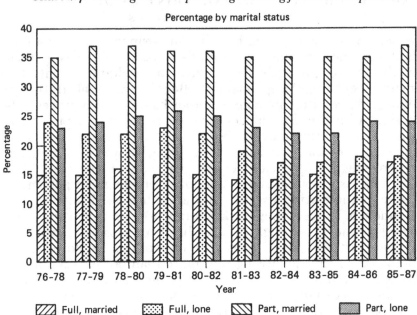

Percentage by marital status

Source: As for chart 2.6.

indicates that one-parent families' average gross income has fallen as a percentage of that of the average income of a family containing a couple and two children.[4] By 1986, it was less than 40 per cent of the income of this traditional family. Even when adjustments for family composition are made using equivalence scales, one-parent families' average income is only about 60 per cent of that of two-parent families, and there has been a decline in their relative equivalent income during most of the 1980s (chart 2.9).[5]

If we focus on women in employment in 1980, lone mothers in full-time jobs received higher average hourly pay (£1.99) than all women in full-time employment (£1.90), but lone mothers in part-time jobs received lower pay (£1.37) than all women working part-time (£1.60).[6] Application of the estimates of the determinants of hourly pay in full-time and part-time employment by Ermisch and Wright (1988) indicates that these differences do not arise because of differences in education and work experience between lone mothers and other women, but because of unexplained differences in pay. In other words, lone mothers working full time receive higher hourly pay than would be expected in light of their experi-

Chart 2.8 *One-parent families' gross income as a percentage of the income of a married couple with two children*

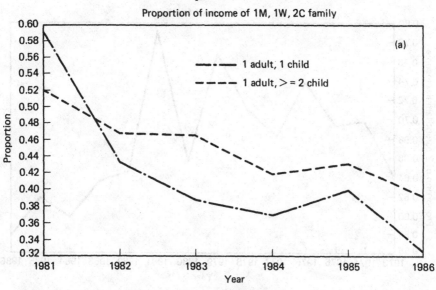

Proportion of income of 1M, 1W, 2C family

(a)

- 1 adult, 1 child
- 1 adult, > = 2 child

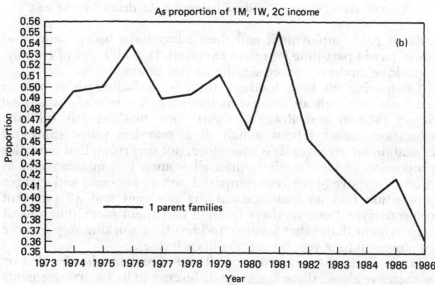

As proportion of 1M, 1W, 2C income

(b)

- 1 parent families

Source: *Family Expenditure Survey*, London, HMSO, various years.

Chart 2.9 *Average equivalent weekly household income of one-parent families as a proportion of two-parent families equivalent income*

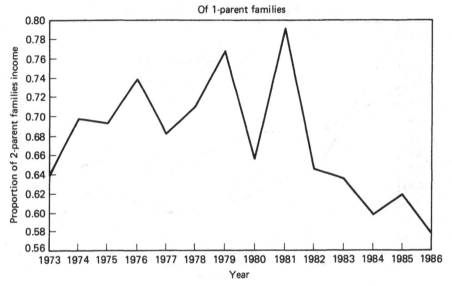

Sources: As for chart 2.8 and equivalence scales defined in the text.

ence in paid employment and their educational background, and lower pay in part-time jobs than expected. In both types of employment lone mothers worked slightly shorter hours.

Comparing all lone mothers (that is, including those not in employment) with all women in the 1980 *Women and Employment Survey* (Martin and Roberts, 1984), lone mothers left full-time education earlier (about a half of a year less post-compulsory education on average). It is, therefore, not surprising that a smaller proportion of lone mothers than all women had qualifications at A-level or above (9 per cent compared with 17 per cent) and a larger proportion had no qualifications (62 per cent and 48 per cent respectively).[7] Lone mothers in 1980 had spent more time out of employment than other women and less time working in part-time employment (one year on average in each case).

While about three-quarters of all one-parent families headed by women live alone, there is a large difference in living arrangements between never-married and previously-married mothers. Only about half of never-married mothers live alone. This percentage has been increasing at the expense of the percentage living with their parents, which has fallen to about 35 per cent. Among lone mothers heading a household only about 30 per cent are owner-occupiers, compared with over 70 per cent of two-parent families. About three-fifths of one-parent families rent their housing from local authorities (Haskey, 1989).

CONCLUSION

The incidence of one-parent families has been increasing rapidly in many industrialised countries, particularly since the early 1970s. Marital dissolution has been primarily responsible for this increase, and low remarriage rates can magnify its effect. Outside the United States, in which a quarter of families with dependent children are one-parent families, Great Britain, Sweden and Denmark had the highest incidence in the mid-1980s (about 14 per cent), with France and Germany just behind (12–13 per cent) (Roll, 1989). It is noteworthy that the United States has the highest divorce rate in the world, and the first three European countries mentioned have the highest divorce rates in western Europe, while the latter two have low remarriage rates.

In the light of the large role played by marital dissolution in the growth of the importance of one-parent families, the prospects for further increases in marital dissolution and for changes in remarriage patterns are particularly important. Chart 2.1 gave some indication that divorce rates may be levelling off in Britain and the United States, but such a tendency is not evident for the other countries in charts 2.1 and 2.2. Even in the United States and Britain, remarriage rates have been falling and, at least in Britain, have not levelled off yet. These declines do, however, reflect to some extent the rise in cohabitation without marriage among previously-married women. In sum, the demographic indicators suggest a continuing rise in the number of one-parent families headed by divorced and separated women in most industrialised countries.

Although apparently of secondary importance, particularly in countries other than the United States, the upward trend in the proportion of births outside marriage (chart 2.5) in non-Scandinavian countries suggests continuing growth in the number of never-married lone mothers. An increase in the proportion of births within consensual unions may account for a part of this trend in many countries, but by no means all of it. We return to the prospective changes in the number and composition of lone-parent families in Britain in the last chapter, after analysing the British situation in greater detail.

As elsewhere, British lone parents are relatively poor, and their living standards have recently been falling further behind those of two-parent families. In contrast to other industrialised countries, a smaller percentage of lone mothers than married mothers are employed in Britain, and over three-fifths of British lone mothers are primarily dependent on state means-tested benefits for their livelihood. Chapters 6 and 7 examine the employment patterns and welfare dependency of British lone mothers in greater detail.

The next chapter develops a formal model of the dynamics of one-parent families, and Chapter 4 provides a theoretical background for the analysis of the factors influencing the rates of entry to and exit from lone parenthood in Chapters 5 and 8.

APPENDIX
DEFINITIONS AND SOURCES

GREAT BRITAIN: A dependent child is defined to be a never-married child aged under sixteen, or under nineteen in full-time education (unless stated otherwise below 'child' always refers to a never-married child). One-parent families include those living as part of a larger household as well as those that form a single household on their own. Unmarried cohabiting couples with children are excluded. Data from Ermisch (1990).

UNITED STATES: A dependent child is one aged under eighteen. One-parent families include those living as part of a larger household as well as those that form a single household on their own. Unmarried cohabiting couples with children generally are not excluded. Data from Ermisch (1990) and Glick (1984).

JAPAN: A dependent child is one aged under twenty. Data appear to include only one-parent families that form a single household on their own. Data from Ermisch (1990).

FEDERAL REPUBLIC OF GERMANY: A dependent child is one aged under eighteen. One-parent families appear to include those living as part of a larger household as well as those that form a single household on their own. The treatment of unmarried cohabiting couples is not clear. Data from Ermisch (1990) and Schwartz (1983).

FRANCE: A dependent child is one aged under 25. One-parent families include those living as part of a larger household as well as those that form a single household on their own. It appears that unmarried cohabiting couples with children are excluded. Data from Ermisch (1990).

SWEDEN: A dependent child is one aged under sixteen. Data include only one-parent families that form a single household on their own. Unmarried cohabiting couples with children are excluded. Data from Nilsson (1985).

NETHERLANDS: No age limit is defined for a child (in 1981, 88 per cent of the enumerated one-parent families had a child aged under eighteen), but the child must never have been married nor have children of his/her own living with them. Unmarried cohabiting couples are treated as one-parent families. Data appear to include one-parent families within households headed by others. Data from Faessen (1988) and Koesoebjono (1986).

BELGIUM: No age limit is defined for a child. Data include only one-parent families that form a single household on their own. The treatment of unmarried cohabiting couples is not clear. Data from Ermisch (1990). For the sex and marital status distribution in table 2.2, a wider definition of a one-parent family is used: other persons may be living in the household and parents with previously-married children as well as never-married children are included.

SWITZERLAND: No age limit is defined for a child. One-parent families appear to include those living as part of a larger household as well as those that form a single household on their own. The treatment of unmarried cohabiting couples is not clear. Data from Blanc (1985).

IRELAND: A dependent child is one aged under fifteen. One-parent families appear to include those living as part of a larger household as well as those that form a single household on their own, although the former are likely to be undercounted. Data from Ermisch (1990).

OTHER SOURCES: Estimates of 'total first marriage rate' and 'total divorce rate' (charts 2.4 and 2.2): Sardon (1986). (Estimates of annual changes in the total first marriage rate for the United States are based on the general first marriage rate (marriages per 1,000 single women aged fourteen and over).

Data for other charts: Statistical publications of individual countries and Eurostat.

3

MODELLING THE DYNAMICS OF
ONE-PARENT FAMILIES

INTRODUCTION

Stated most generally, the number of one-parent families at a point in time depends on the history of inflows to lone parenthood and of outflows from that state. As explained in the previous chapter, the inflows arise because of marriage (and consensual union) dissolutions among mothers and fathers, births outside marriage (or a consensual union) to childless women and the death of a parent. The last source has become less important over time in Britain, and it will not be given separate consideration in the analysis that follows. Because 90 per cent of one-parent families in Britain are headed by the mother, the analysis focusses on the dynamics of 'lone motherhood'. Deaths of the father are included in marital dissolutions, but death is the reason for a small proportion of dissolutions. The outflows from lone motherhood arise because the mother enters a union with a man, either a consensual union or legal marriage, or because the youngest child becomes an adult.

In this chapter, some simplifying assumptions are made in order to derive an expression for the proportion of families with dependent children with only one parent in terms of various 'transition rates' between demographic states (for example, from never-married without a child to never-married with a child). As discussed in the previous chapter, the sources of inflow to and outflow from lone parenthood immediately point to the importance of a number of demographic rates in the determination of this proportion. The importance of the marital dissolution rate among mothers, the illegitimate first birth rate among childless women, the marriage rate of never-married mothers and the remarriage rate of mothers are fairly obvious. But 'populations-at-risk' for these events also help determine the size of the flows into and out of lone motherhood. For instance, the inflow to lone motherhood depends on the number of married mothers as well as the marital dissolution rate among mothers; inflows through births outside marriage depend on the pool of never-married childless women. These populations at risk depend, in turn, on a number of other demographic rates. This is most easily demonstrated with a fairly simple model, which is calibrated using data from the demographic histories of women collected in the British *Women and Employment Survey*.

The *Women and Employment Survey* (WES) is a nationally representative sample of women aged 16–59 in 1980. It collected marital, childbearing and employment histories from 5,320 women on a retrospective basis, and cross-checks with aggregate historical data suggest that the histories are relatively accurate. Martin and Roberts (1984) provide a full discussion of the survey and present a large number of summary statistics and analyses of women's employment. This study is the first one to use its birth and marriage history information to define and analyse one-parent families headed by women and their employment patterns. The outstanding advantage of the WES is that it is the most recent data available for analysing movements into and out of demographic states and entries to and exits from employment, and the relation between demographic and employment histories[1]. Compared with true longitudinal data, it has the disadvantage of not measuring other variables (for example income) during the demographic and employment histories (that is, at dates earlier than the interview in 1980). Other features of the WES that are relevant to particular analyses are discussed in this and later chapters at the point at which they are most relevant.

It is, unfortunately, not possible to identify consensual unions in the WES demographic histories. Thus, while we would ideally like to characterise a woman at each point in time by whether she is in a union with a man or not and whether she is a mother with a dependent child(ren), our characterisation is in terms of whether she is married or not and whether she has a dependent child(ren).

The definition of lone motherhood used here is, therefore, a mother with dependent children who is not married. A dependent child is defined as being less than sixteen years of age in the analysis. Forty per cent or more of children of the women in the WES would have left full-time education by the age of sixteen. The term 'mother' will be used to refer to women with *dependent* children.

On this definition, about 800 of the women in the WES were lone parents at least once during their lives. Starts and ends of marriages, as well as births, are dated (by month) in the survey, but there is an asymmetry. Starts of marriages generally refer to the legal date of the marriage, while ends of marriages refer to the *de facto* end as reported by the woman, rather than the date of the legal divorce. These are the dates that enter into the calculation of marital dissolution and (re)marriage rates in this chapter.

It is worth noting, however, that 10 per cent of previously married lone mothers in the WES remarried within one year, and 20 per cent remarried within two years. Murphy (1984) found that the median time between separation and legal divorce among women aged under 50 in 1980 who had experienced a separation some time in their lives was 2.5 years. Thus, it appears that in the WES a substantial number of women dated their marital dissolution closer to their legal divorce date than their date of separation from their husband. Inaccuracy in the dating of 'ends of marriages' has been reported as a general problem in retrospective surveys (for example, see Peters 1988). She notes that the unpleasant memories often associated with divorce, the fact that divorce is more in the nature of a process that an event and the ambiguity of 'when did this marriage end?' in questionnaires can contribute to inaccurate responses. These probably also play a role in explaining the apparent 'quick' remarriages in the WES.

In elaborating a fairly simple model of the dynamics of lone parenthood, this chapter serves primarily heuristic purposes. Later chapters estimate models which allow the rates of inflow to and outflow from lone parenthood to vary with the characteristics of a woman and her economic and social environment during the period in which she is at risk for these events.

A SIMPLE MARKOV MODEL

Basic model

Six states are considered: (1) single (that is, never married), no dependent children; (2) single mother; (3) married, no dependent children; (4) married mother; (5) previously married, no children; and (6) previously-married mother. States 2 and 6 correspond to lone motherhood.

We define a transition rate p_{ij} as the probability of moving from state i to state j in a month (assuming only one transition can be made in a month). This transition rate is assumed to depend only on the state that the woman occupies, making the model a traditional Markov one. We also assume, quite plausibly, that a woman cannot change marital status and motherhood status at the same time; that is, she cannot move directly between being unmarried with children to being married without children (and *vice versa*), nor directly between unmarried without children to married with children (or *vice versa*), in one month.[2] Thus, $p_{14}=p_{63}=p_{36}=p_{54}=p_{45}=p_{23}=0$. Furthermore, it is impossible to return to the single state, making $p_{jk}=0$, $j=3,4,5,6$; $k=1,2$; and it is not possible to go directly from

Table 3.1a *Markov chain transition matrix*

$$
C = \begin{bmatrix}
p_{33} & p_{34} & p_{35} & 0 & 0 & 0 \\
p_{43} & p_{44} & 0 & p_{46} & 0 & 0 \\
p_{53} & 0 & p_{55} & p_{56} & 0 & 0 \\
0 & p_{64} & p_{65} & p_{66} & 0 & 0 \\
p_{13} & 0 & 0 & 0 & p_{11} & p_{12} \\
0 & p_{24} & 0 & 0 & p_{21} & p_{22}
\end{bmatrix}
$$

where $p_{33} = 1-p_{34}-p_{35}$; $p_{44} = 1-p_{43}-p_{46}$; $p_{55} = 1-p_{53}-p_{56}$; $p_{66} = 1-p_{64}-p_{65}$; $p_{11} = 1-p_{12}-p_{13}$; and $p_{22} = 1-p_{24}-p_{21}$.

Notes: State 1 is never-married, no children; State 2 is never-married, with a child(ren) (that is, single mother); State 3 is married, no children; State 4 is married with a child(ren); State 5 is previously-married, no children; State 6 is previously married, with a child(ren) (that is, previously-married lone mother).

$$\sum_{j=1}^{6} p_{ij} = 1 \quad (i = 1,2,3,4,5,6).$$

being single to being previously married, making $p_{jk}=0$, $j=1,2$; $k=5,6$. The entire transition matrix is shown in table 3.1a.

The other transition rates relate to more traditional demographic rates as follows:

p_{34} is the legitimate first birth rate;
p_{35} is the marital dissolution rate among childless women;
p_{46} is the marital dissolution rate among mothers;
p_{53} is the remarriage rate among childless women;
p_{56} is the illegitimate first birth rate among previously married women;
p_{64} is the remarriage rate among mothers;
p_{12} is the illegitimate first birth rate among single women; ·
p_{13} is the first marriage rate among childless women;
p_{24} is the first marriage rate among single mothers.

Finally, and less familiar, p_{43}, p_{21} and p_{65} are the probabilities that the youngest child reaches adulthood (age sixteen here) for married, single and previously-married mothers respectively.

It is assumed that being single is a transient state which every woman is assumed to leave eventually. While the assumption that every woman marries is not realistic it may be a useful approximation because, on past experience around 90 per cent of British women eventually marry. The matrix of transition rates p_{ij} has been written in canonical form in table 3.1a. This matrix can be rewritten as:

$$C = \begin{bmatrix} P & O \\ R & Q \end{bmatrix}, \qquad\qquad (3.1)$$

where P is a 4×4 transition matrix composed of the top left hand corner of the matrix C in table 3.1A, and Q is a 2×2 matrix made up of the bottom right hand corner of C; O is a 4×2 matrix of zeroes and R is a 2×4 matrix from the bottom left corner of C.[3]

The estimates of the transition rates in these matrices have been estimated from the marital and childbearing histories of women collected in the WES. Under the Markov assumption, these can be estimated as the ratio of the number of occurrences of the event of interest (for example, marriage, first birth) to the total number of months of exposure to the risk of that event (these are maximum likelihood estimates). Because, as demographers would readily recognise, the transition rate p_{ij} may be dependent on the duration in state i, or on, say, the woman's age, the Markov assumption is unlikely to be correct. Furthermore, the estimation of the transition rates pools women from a wide range of birth cohorts, thereby ignoring any trends in these transition rates over time. Nevertheless, the Markov model serves a heuristic purpose, illustrating the large number of demographic rates involved in the determination of the proportion of families with dependent children headed by only one parent, and it proves to be a fairly reliable guide to how changes in these rates affect this proportion. The estimates of p_{ij} are shown in table 3.1b.

Single motherhood

Analysis of the 'absorbing chain' in the bottom two rows of C is sufficient for studying single motherhood in this framework.[4] Theorems on absorbing chains (see Kemeny and Snell, 1960, Chapter 3) make it possible to calculate from the transition rates the mean amount of time that a woman is in a given state when she starts out single and childless at age sixteen (as almost all women do). The expected duration of time spent single without children is $D_{11} = 1/(p_{12}+p_{13})$ and the expected amount of time spent as a single mother is $D_{12} = p_{12}D_{11}/p_{24}$. A woman would, therefore, expect to be single for a total of $D_{11}+D_{12}$ months. The estimates in table 3.1b indicate that $D_{11} = 92.6$ months while $D_{12} = $ four months implying an expected age at marriage of 24 years, which is consistent with past experience.

It follows that a woman would expect to spend a proportion

Table 3.1b *Estimates of transition rates* p_{ij}

	$j = 3$	$j = 4$	$j = 5$	$j = 6$
p_{3j}	0.97814	0.02098	0.00088	0.
p_{4j}	0.00191	0.99719	0.	0.00090
p_{5j}	0.01143	0.	0.98538	0.00319
p_{6j}	0.	0.00772	0.00446	0.98782
	$j = 3$	$j = 4$	$j = 1$	$j = 2$
p_{1j}	0.0102	0.	0.9892	0.0006
p_{2j}	0.	0.01405	0.	0.98595

Notes: State 1 is never-married, no children; State 2 is never-married, with a child(ren) (that is, single mother); State 3 is married, no children; State 4 is married with a child(ren); State 5 is previously-married, no children; State 6 is previously married, with a child(ren) (that is, previously-married lone mother).

$$\sum_{j=1}^{6} p_{ij} = 1 \quad (i = 1,2,3,4,5,6).$$

$\alpha_2 = D_{12}/(D_{11}+D_{12}) = p_{12}/(p_{12}+p_{24})$ of her single years as a single mother. Thus, a single woman would expect to spend 4 per cent of her time single as a single mother or, alternatively, 4 per cent of single women would be mothers. Estimates of the number of single lone mothers in 1971 and 1984 indicate that 3.7 and 5.5 per cent of single women were lone mothers in these two years. In the light of the pooling of experiences of women from different cohorts up to 1980 in estimating the transition rates in table 3.1b, the 1971 estimate would be most comparable to that from the Markov model, and these are very close to one another.

If a woman becomes a single mother, her expected duration of single motherhood is $D_{22} = 1/p_{24}$, or 71 months according to the estimates in table 3.1b. It follows that $D_{12} = p_{12}D_{11}D_{22}$, and because the expected probability of ever becoming a single mother is equal to $p_{12}D_{11}$, the time that a single woman can expect to spend as a single mother (D_{12}) is the product of the probability of ever becoming one and the expected duration of single motherhood if she becomes one. According to our estimates the probability of ever becoming a single mother is 0.055.

Table 3.2a examines the impact of different values for the transition rates on the proportion of single women who are mothers (α_2). As is clear from the expression for α_2 above, a proportionate change in the illegitimate birth rate (p_{12}) of k has the same effect on α_2 as a change in the marriage rate of single mothers (p_{24}) of $1/k$. Thus, doubling the illegitimate birth rate, or halving the marriage

Table 3.2a *Impact of different transition rates (p_{ij}) on proportion of single women who are mothers (α_2) and expected duration of single motherhood (D_{22}) (months)*

	α_2	D_{22}(months)
Base case:	0.041	71.2
Double first legitimate birth rate (p_{12})	0.079	71.2
Halve first marriage rate of single mothers (p_{24})	0.079	142.4
Double first marriage rate of childless (p_{13})	0.041	71.2

rate of single mothers, increases the proportion of single women who are mothers from 4 per cent to almost 8 per cent. When the marriage rate of single mothers is halved, this is accompanied by a doubling of the expected duration of single motherhood when a woman becomes one; when the illegitimate birth rate is doubled, it is accompanied by a higher probability of ever becoming a single mother.

Focussing on women of the main child-rearing ages, 16–44, it is also possible to compute the proportion of women aged 16–44 who are single, or equivalently, the proportion of time over these ages spent single. Denoting the proportion as s, $s = (D_{11}+D_{12})/348$, the estimates in table 3.1b indicate $s = 0.28$, which is close to the value of 0.27 calculated from marital status statistics for women aged 16–44 in 1971. The decline in first marriage rates between 1971–84 of about 40 per cent suggests a 1984 value of p_{13}, about 0.6 times its 1971 value. If the other transition rates remained constant, then $s = 0.45$, which is somewhat higher than the 35 per cent of women aged 16–44 who were single in 1984.

Finally, it is noteworthy that the rather high mean duration of single motherhood, of almost six years according to the estimated transition rates, reflects the skewed distribution of exits from single motherhood under Markov assumptions. The median duration (half of single mothers leave single motherhood before this time) implied by these estimates is only 49 months.[5] A lifetable analysis making no distributional assumptions, illustrated in chart 3.1 by the estimated survival curve for single motherhood, shows an even lower median duration of 34 months.

Previously-married lone mothers

For the analysis of previously-married lone mothers, it is sufficient to focus on the transition matrix P in (3.1) and table 3.1a. Let a_{it} be the probability of being in state i in period t ($i = 3,4,5,6$). Then, the

Chart 3.1 *Survival as lone mother*

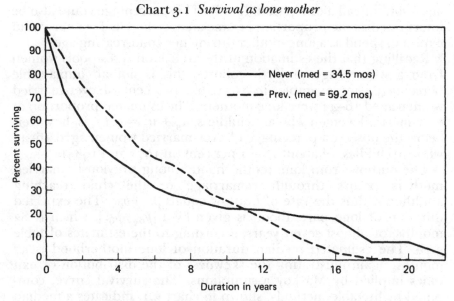

Source: Author's calculations from 1980 *Women and Employment Survey*.

Markov assumptions entail that the row vector $a_t = \{a_{3t}\, a_{4t}\, a_{5t}\, a_{6t}\}$ is given by:

$$a_t = a_{t-1} P \qquad (3.2)$$

The elements of the vector a_t, a_{it}, can be interpreted as the proportion of the population of ever-married women of child-rearing ages (say, aged 16–44) in state i at time t. Thus, a_{6t}, is the proportion of such women heading one-parent families.

Because our estimated P matrix satisfies certain regularity conditions (see Kemeny and Snell, 1960, Chapter 4), there exists an *equilibrium* vector of probabilities of being in state i, $\alpha = \{a_3 a_4 a_5 a_6\}$, such that

$$\alpha = \alpha P \qquad (3.3)$$

That is, if the proportions of women in states 3–6 are given by the elements of the vector α, then those proportions will be maintained over time. We can solve equation (3.3) analytically for α. Given our estimates of the p_{ij} in table 3.1b, the solution is

$$\alpha = \{0.085 \quad 0.821 \quad 0.026 \quad 0.068\} \qquad (3.4)$$

Thus if the estimated transition rates were maintained over a long period of time, 6.8 per cent of ever-married women of child-rearing ages would head a one-parent family. This percentage could also be interpreted as the proportion of time an ever-married woman could expect to spend as a lone mother during her child-rearing ages.

Recalling that the estimation of the transition rates pools women from a wide range of birth cohorts, this is not an implausible percentage. For example, in 1971, 6.2 per cent of ever-married women aged 16–44 were lone mothers. The estimated proportion of ever-married women who are childless, $\alpha_3 + \alpha_5 = 0.11$, is, however, below the observed percentage of ever-married women aged 16–44 who are childless of about 18–21 per cent (in 1971 and 1984).

The outflow from lone motherhood among previously married mothers occurs through remarriage or the child reaching adulthood; thus the rate of outflow equals $p_{64}+p_{65}$. The expected duration of lone parenthood is given by $1/[p_{64}+p_{65}]$, which is 82 months, or almost seven years, according to the estimates of table 3.1b. The estimated median duration of lone motherhood is 57 months, again illustrating the skewness of the distribution of exit times implied by Markov assumptions. The survival curve, computed by lifetable methods, shown in chart 3.1, indicates a median duration of lone motherhood of 59 months for previously-married lone mothers, which is very close to the estimate under Markov assumptions.

An analysis of the sensitivity of the estimate of the equilibrium proportion of ever-married women who are lone mothers (α_6) to changes in some important demographic rates is shown in table 3.2b. It shows that halving the legitimate first birth rate (p_{34}) has little effect on the proportion of ever-married women who are lone mothers, although it does substantially increase the proportion of childless ($\alpha_3 + \alpha_5$). Neither doubling the marital dissolution rate among the childless (p_{35}), nor halving the remarriage rate among the childless women (p_{53}), has much effect on the proportion of ever-married women who are lone mothers nor, somewhat more surprisingly, does doubling the illegitimate birth rate among previously-married mothers (p_{56}).

But doubling the marital dissolution rate of mothers (p_{46}) produces a large increase in the proportion of ever-married women who are lone mothers, as does halving the remarriage rate of mothers (p_{64}). In the latter case, this increase is associated with an increase in the expected duration of lone motherhood from 82 months to 120 months. In the former case, the increase in α_6 comes about because of the higher rate of inflow into lone parenthood by married mothers. Between 1971 and 1984, the divorce rate roughly doubled, suggesting a doubling in p_{46}. According to table 3.2b, 12

Table 3.2b *Impact of different transition rates* (p_{ij}) *on equilibrium probability of being in State i* (α_i)

	Equilibrium vector α			
	α_3	α_4	α_5	α_6
Base case:	0.085	0.821	0.026	0.068
Halving of legitimate first birth rate (p_{34}):	0.155	0.753	0.029	0.063
Halving of remarriage rate of childless (p_{53}):	0.081	0.804	0.044	0.071
Halving of remarriage rate of mothers (p_{64}):	0.087	0.780	0.035	0.098
Doubling of illegitimate first birth rate (p_{56}):	0.083	0.822	0.022	0.073
Doubling of marital dissolution rate of mothers (p_{46}):	0.087	0.748	0.043	0.122

Notes: State 3 is married, no children; State 4 is married, with a child(ren); State 5 is previously married, no children; State 6 is previously married with a child(ren), that is, lone parenthood.

per cent of ever-married women would be lone mothers if the other transition rates remained constant while p_{46} doubled. Estimates of the number of lone mothers indicate that about 10 per cent of ever-married women aged 16–44 were lone mothers in 1984, suggesting that the increase in divorce played the major role in the increase between 1971 and 1984 in the percentage of ever-married women who are lone mothers.

All lone mothers

The analysis of the previous sections can now be pulled together to study how the transition rates affect the proportion of all mothers who are lone mothers, which we denote as p. This proportion is a close approximation to the proportion of families with dependent children with only one parent.

$$p = [\alpha_2 s + \alpha_6(1-s)]/[\alpha_2 s + (\alpha_4 + \alpha_6)(1-s)] \qquad (3.5)$$

Closer examination of (3.5) indicates that p is increasing in α_2, α_6 and s and decreasing in α_4.

The sensitivity analysis in tables 3.2a, 3.2b and 3.2c indicates that the transition rates p_{12}, p_{24}, p_{13}, p_{46}, p_{64} and p_{34} are most important for the elements on the right hand side of equation (3.5), the α_is and s. As table 3.2c shows, the 'base case' from the estimates in table 3.1b entails that about 9 per cent of all mothers are lone mothers, which exactly equals their observed percentage in the population in 1971. Doubling the illegitimate birth rate (p_{12}) or halving the marriage

Table 3.2c *Impact of different transition rates* (p_{ij}) *on proportion of mothers who are lone mothers* (p) *and proportion of women who are single* (s)

	p	s
Base case:	0.093	0.277
Halve marriage rate of single mothers (p_{24})	0.109	0.289
Double illegitimate birth rate of single (p_{12})	0.106	0.274
Halve first marriage rate of childless (p_{13})	0.122	0.526
Halve legitimate first birth rate (p_{34})	0.095	0.277
Halve remarriage rate of mothers (p_{64})	0.127	0.277
Double marital dissolution rate of mothers (p_{46})	0.156	0.277
Double marital dissolution rate of mothers (p_{46}) and reduce first marriage rate (p_{13}) by 40%	0.172	0.446

rate of single mothers (p_{24}) raises this percentage to about 11 per cent, and halving the first marriage rate of childless women (p_{13}) raises it to 12 per cent (through its effect on s). Almost 13 per cent of mothers are lone mothers if the remarriage rate of previously married mothers (p_{64}) is halved, but the marital dissolution rate of mothers (p_{46}) has by far the largest effect on this percentage. A doubling of p_{46} raises the percentage of mothers who are lone mothers to 15.6 per cent.

Two of the major developments during the 1970s and 1980s have been the increase in the divorce rate (roughly a doubling between 1971 and 1984) and the fall in the first marriage rate (roughly a 40 per cent fall). The last row of table 3.2c shows how these changes effect p when the other transition rates are as estimated in table 3.1b. The results suggest that 17 per cent of mothers would be lone mothers. This is higher than the 14 per cent suggested by the 1984 estimates of the number of lone mothers, but clearly not way out of line. Indeed, by 1989, this percentage had climbed to 17 per cent. The overstatement partly reflects the exaggerated rise (noted earlier) in the proportion of women who are single predicted by the model (at the observed value of $s = 0.35$, $p = 0.16$).

Thus, although based on simple assumptions, the Markov model of the dynamics of lone parenthood produces quite plausible estimates of the proportion of mothers who are lone mothers. The implications of changes in particular transition rates for this proportion would appear to be reasonably approximated by using the model. It suggests that some moderate changes in other transition rates partly offset the effects of the changes in first marriage and divorce rates on the proportion of mothers who are lone mothers.

The appendix to this chapter also shows that under certain circumstances movements in the proportion of families with dependent children headed by a *never-married mother* may be roughly proportional to movements in the ratio of illegitimate births to legitimate births. This would be more likely to be the case if the ratio of the legitimate birth rate to the proportion of ever-married women who are mothers and the duration of single motherhood are relatively constant.

CONCLUSION

The analysis of the Markov model indicates that just a few transition rates have a large influence on the proportion of mothers who are lone mothers. Foremost among these are the marital dissolution rate of mothers and the remarriage rate among previously-married mothers. Although somewhat less important, the illegitimate first birth rate and the marriage rate of single mothers also affect the proportion of mothers who are lone mothers. Thus, the analysis in the following chapters studies the rates of inflow to and outflow from the two types of lone motherhood.

This chapter also suggests that the Markov model can be used to approximate the implications of changes in particular transition rates for the proportion of families with dependent children who are one-parent families. In the last chapter, the model is used to examine prospective changes in this proportion.

The analysis in subsequent chapters weakens some of the assumptions in the basic Markov model in order to capture reality better. First it allows for *heterogeneity*, which means that women with different characteristics or at risk at different times may have different transition probabilities. For example well educated women may be less likely to have a birth before marriage than poorly educated women, or the likelihood of an illegitimate birth may be higher when unemployment is higher.

It also allows for *duration dependence*; that is, variation in a woman's transition probability according to the length of time spent in the state, rather than constant (as assumed in the Markov model). Indeed, this may explain the implausibly low estimate of $\alpha_3 + \alpha_5$, the proportion of ever-married women without children, reported above. It only takes about three years to converge to the equilibrium proportions in α. That is, within three years all but 11 per cent of women are mothers. A more realistic time can be generated with

Chart 3.2 *First marriage rate and legitimate first birth rate*

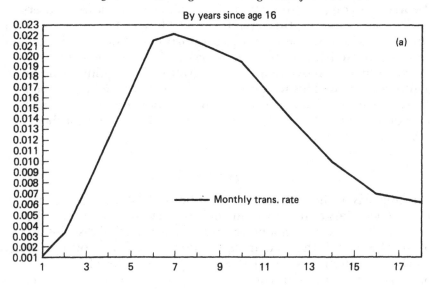

By years since age 16

(a)

Monthly trans. rate

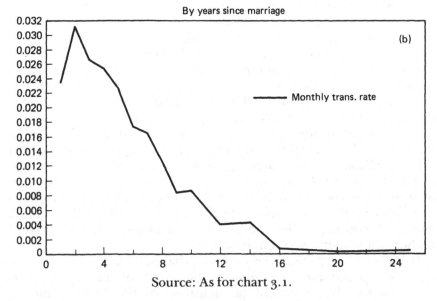

By years since marriage

(b)

Monthly trans. rate

Source: As for chart 3.1.

certain patterns of duration dependence. Duration dependence in first marriage rates may also lie behind the over-sensitivity of the proportion single to proportionate changes in p_{13}.

Consider, for example, the observed patterns of transition rates

p_{13} and p_{34} by duration of exposure. When calculating the patterns for the first marriage rate, the start of exposure to the risk of the event is taken to be sixteen years of age, and when a woman experiences the competing event of an illegitimate first birth she has been treated as 'censored' (that is, in the same way as when her observed period of exposure was ended by the interview rather than by the marriage). Chart 3.2 shows the strong relationship between the first marriage rate and the duration of exposure to risk. It also shows that the legitimate first birth rate varies considerably with the duration of first marriage (a marital dissolution has been treated as censoring in this calculation).

APPENDIX
RELATIONSHIP BETWEEN ILLEGITIMACY RATIO AND THE PROPORTION OF FAMILIES WITH DEPENDENT CHILDREN HEADED BY A NEVER-MARRIED MOTHER

The ratio of illegitimate to legitimate births is given by:

$$R = f_i u / f_1 (1-u) \qquad (3A.1)$$

where f_i is the illegitimate birth rate; f_1 is the legitimate birth rate; and u is the proportion of women of childbearing age who are unmarried. The proportion of ever-married women of childbearing age who are currently married is $\lambda = \alpha_3 + \alpha_4$, while the proportion of ever-married women of childbearing age who are mothers is $m = (\alpha_4 + \alpha_6)$. From these relationships,

$$u = s + (1-\lambda)(1-s) \qquad (3A.2)$$

and define $k = s/u$.
Then

$$R = f_i s / [f_1 (1-s)\lambda k] \qquad (3A.3)$$

If $f_i \cong p_{12}$, then

$$R = p_{12} s / [f_1 (1-s)\lambda k]. \qquad (3A.4)$$

Define the proportion of families with dependent children headed by a never-married mother as q. It follows from equation (3.5) that

$$q/(1-q) = \alpha_2 s / m(1-s), \qquad (3A.5)$$

and as $\alpha_2/(1-\alpha_2) = p_{12} D_{22}$,

$$q/(1-q) \cong p_{12} D_{22} s / m(1-s) \qquad (3A.6)$$

Thus, from equation (3A.4),

$$q/(1-q) \cong (f_1/m)(\lambda k) D_{22} R \qquad (3A.7)$$

Thus, if f_1/m, λk and D_{22} are constant, q and R tend to move proportionately. It is plausible that the ratio of the legitimate birth rate to the proportion of ever-married women who are mothers, f_1/m, is relatively constant while λk would appear to exhibit a downward trend. The duration of single motherhood may also be fairly constant. Thus, rises in the illegitimacy ratio, R, may overstate slightly the increase in q.

4

AN ECONOMIC MODEL OF MARRIAGE AND
MARITAL SEARCH

INTRODUCTION

It is clear from the demographic analysis of the previous chapter that exits from and entries to lone parenthood are often identical to decisions about marrying or dissolving marriages. The 'economic' study of marriage can, therefore, suggest potential influences on these exits and entries.

Economics is concerned with people making choices subject to constraints. It studies how choices are affected by variation in the constraints which people face, taking their preferences or tastes as given. The economic study of family formation and dissolution is no different in this respect. It is 'economic' in the sense that it focusses on the implications of constrained decision-making. As in economic analysis more generally, people making decisions do not need to think in these same terms for the analysis to provide valuable hypotheses, and it is the generation of hypotheses about how observable characteristics of a woman and her environment may affect her decisions to marry and divorce which is the main purpose of this theoretical exercise. There are undoubtedly many unobservable factors affecting marriage and divorce decisions, such as personal tastes, opportunities for partners to meet and luck. As usual, these are subsumed in the random variables in the empirical analysis.

The economic analysis of marriage does *not* presume that economic goals are paramount in marriage decisions, *nor* does it assume that traditional economic variables (for example, income) dominate marriage decisions. It focusses on constrained choices of a combination of characteristics which are the direct sources of satisfaction to a person. These characteristics include enjoyment of children, health, prestige, esteem, family life, altruism and pleasures of the senses, and there is clearly nothing particularly 'economic' about them. Preferences are defined over combinations of these characteristics. These characteristics are much smaller in number than the goods and services purchased by a household, and they cannot be purchased in the marketplace, but are produced as well as consumed by households using market purchases and people's own time. As they are 'produced' in the home, let us call these 'home commodities' for short.

Marriage is, then, viewed as a partnership in which the partners' time and purchased goods and services are combined to produce these 'home commodities'. Their 'output' is constrained by the earning capacities and other wealth of the spouses, their ability to transform time and goods into 'home commodities', the prices of goods and services and the total amount of spouses' time available. For simplicity, the weighted sum of home commodity production (weighted by their 'shadow prices'), when spouses' time and purchased goods and services are allocated efficiently, will be called 'full wealth',[1] which is divided between the partners on the basis of bargaining (see Becker, 1973 and 1981, for a full exposition). The decisions of whether to marry and whom to marry are intimately related to this constrained choice of a combination of home commodities (characteristics yielding satisfaction), as is now explained.

OPTIMAL SORTING OF MATES

The benefit or gain from a marriage is the difference between the share of full wealth obtained in the marriage and the full wealth that the person could obtain if remaining single. One important source of a gain from marriage is the fact that many personal traits are *complementary* in the production of home commodities, in the sense that the productivity in home production associated with that trait is enhanced by a similar level of that trait for the spouse. Education, intelligence, religion and race are examples of such traits, and in everyday language partners with complementary traits are usually perceived as being compatible.

For such traits, *positive assortative mating*, or the mating of likes, is optimal. In particular, persons with higher values of traits like education and intelligence gain more from marriage because of this complementarity and the mating of persons with high values of these traits with persons with large property wealth, or higher earnings (usually), also produces higher gains from marriage (see Becker, 1981, Chapter 4, for a fuller discussion). The appendix to this chapter presents some evidence that British women with higher educational attainments marry men with higher earnings.

In contrast, for traits like a person's earning capacity, which affect productivity in the labour market, negative assortative mating, or mating of unlikes, *may* be optimal, because such a mating pattern would maximise the gain from the couple's division of labour between the market and the household. Persons with values of such traits closer to their spouse's would gain less from marriage. Such traits would be substitutes in marriage.

Another source of gains from marriage and, more generally, from the formation of households with more than one person, is joint consumption economies associated with goods, like housing, which are in the nature of 'public goods' to the household. This source of gain from marriage is absent from Becker's approach, but joint consumption economies are likely to be pervasive in households. Lam (1988) shows that when these are taken account of, the optimal sorting of mates will exhibit positive assortative mating on spouses' wealth, and if the demand for household public goods increases with wages for both spouses, then there can be positive assortative mating on spouses' earning capacity in the optimal sorting.

The direction of assortative mating on personal earning capacity is determined by two (usually) offsetting forces. Lam (1988) shows that the fact that household public goods are jointly consumed generates a tendency for positive assortative mating on spouses' earning capacity because of similarity in the demands for the public goods, but home production creates a tendency for negative assortative mating because of returns to specialisation through the household division of labour. The size of these offsetting effects depends on the elasticity of demand for the household public goods, the level of consumption of these goods, and the degree of substitution of a spouse's labour supply in response to the wage of the other spouse. In particular, when the degree of substitution is low and/or the elasticity of demand for household public goods is high, positive assortative mating is more likely.

Thus, positive assortative mating may be optimal across all traits, including personal earning capacity. That certainly would be supported by the consistent finding of positive correlations for spouses' wages, even when characteristics such as age, employment experience and education are controlled (see Lam for a survey of these studies).

If there were perfect information about potential mates, or no costs associated with searching for a mate then persons would sort themselves with mates in a way which maximised their individual welfare, given their traits. The mate that a person paired off with and the welfare achieved would depend on the person's traits and on the traits of everyone else in the marriage market (that is, on both the absolute and relative level of a person's traits).

SEARCH, UNCERTAINTY AND IMPERFECT INFORMATION

There is, however, limited information about the traits of potential spouses, and both time and money usually must be spent to find a mate with satisfactory traits. In other words, it is costly to search for a mate and to obtain information about him or her. As a consequence of these costs, a person will accept a lower gain from marriage than he or she would obtain in the optimal sorting of mates discussed above.

There are two basic kinds of search. The search for a suitable partner may be called 'extensive search', and an economic model of such search produces a number of interesting hypotheses.

An economic model of extensive marital search[2]

In order to simplify the analysis, it is assumed that marriages are expected to last forever and that people live forever. These unreal assumptions can be relaxed without essentially affecting the hypotheses derived here (see Lippman and McCall, 1976). It is also assumed that if a cost of c is incurred each period, marriage offers arrive from a Poisson distribution with parameter m (m is independent of c and can be interpreted as the probability of receiving an offer). These marriage offers are defined in terms of the person's share of full wealth from the marriage, w, and the offers are assumed to be drawn from a continuous probability distribution $F(w)$.

A person searching in the marriage market for a partner is assumed to accept the highest offer; thus the return from stopping after the n-th offer (ignoring discounting for the moment) is

$$Y_n = \max[w_1, w_2, ..., w_n] - cn - S \qquad (4.1)$$

where S is the person's wealth from remaining single.

A person's objective is to find a rule for terminating search for a partner that maximises $E(Y_n)$. Let R be the offer associated with the stopping rule that maximises $E(Y_n)$, such that the person accepts the offer if $w \geq R$, and continues to search if $w < R$. R could be called the 'reservation offer', or the minimum acceptable offer. Lippman and McCall (1976) show that such an optimal stopping rule exists, and that it has this form.

The expected return from searching one more period while using this optimal stopping rule, or the value of search, is

$$V = \{m\Delta t E[\max(R,w)] - c\Delta t - S\}/(1+r\Delta t)$$
$$+ (1-m\Delta t)(V+S)/(1+r\Delta t) \qquad (4.2)$$

where r is the (instantaneous) rate of interest; Δt is the length of the searching period; and offers are received and search costs are incurred at the end of the period.

The first term on the right-hand side of (4.2) is the probability of receiving a marriage offer in the period times the discounted expected value of the best option (that is, taking the offer or continuing to search) if an offer is received, less the discounted cost of search during the period, less the discounted value of wealth if the person remains single. The second term is the product of the probability of not receiving an offer and the value of wealth at the end of the period if no offer is received, which is equal to the value of wealth if the person remains single plus the value of search in the next period.

Because R was defined to be the offer that maximises the *expected* return from pursuing the best stopping rule and V is this expected return, $V = R - S$. R is the expected wealth when the optimal stopping rule is followed, and it is the maximum expected wealth since the stopping rule was selected to maximise wealth. If $R<S$ ($V<0$), then it is not worth searching; thus equation (4.2) only holds if a person is searching. While searching, the expected gain from marriage is V.

If the time period is very small (that is, Δt approaches a limit of zero) and equation (4.2) is rearranged.

$$rV + c = m\{E[\max(R,w)] - R\} \tag{4.3}$$

Evaluating the expectation (noting that no person would accept an offer below R) and rearranging,

$$rV + c = m \int_R^{w*} (w-R)dF(w) \tag{4.4}$$

The marriage offer that a person would receive in the 'optimal sorting of mates' (if there were no search costs) would put a maximum on the offers that could be received. Thus, the upper bound of the integral in (4.4) is taken to be $w*$ rather than infinity.

The left-hand side of (4.4) is the cost of search, which is made up of two parts. The first is income foregone from remaining single one more period, which equals the product of the difference between expected marital wealth and wealth if remaining single and the interest rate ($rV = r[R-S]$), and the second is direct costs (c). The right-hand side is the expected value of the gains from further search for a partner. Equation (4.4) is a fundamental equation; it determines the reservation offer R in the optimal stopping rule.

Clearly, when this stopping rule is used, the costs of additional search are balanced by the expected gains from search.

The probability of an acceptable offer, and therefore of marriage, *conditional on receiving an offer*, is $F(w^*) - F(R)$. The probability of marriage in a small interval of time is the product of $F(w^*) - F(R)$ and the probability of receiving an offer, m. Thus the instantaneous marriage rate, or 'hazard rate' is given by

$$h(R,w^*) = m[F(w^*) - F(R)] \tag{4.5}$$

It is clear from (4.5) that the hazard function for marriage is a constant over time (given R and w^*), so that the distribution function for the time to marriage t (or age at marriage) is

$$G(t) = 1 - \exp[-h(R,w^*)t] \tag{4.6}$$

The probability of marriage before time T is, therefore,

$$G(T) = 1 - \exp\{-m[F(w^*)-F(R)]T\} \tag{4.7}$$

and the expected duration of search is $1/h(R,w^*)$.

For persons who have married, $w \geq R$; thus the density of accepted marriage offers is

$$g(w \mid w \geq R) = f(w)/[F(w^*)-F(R)]$$
$$\text{where } f(w) = F'(w), \ w \leq w^*, \tag{4.8}$$

and the expected gain from marriage is $E[w \mid w \geq R] - S$, where

$$E[w \mid w \geq R] = \int_{R}^{w^*} wg(w \mid w \geq R). \tag{4.9}$$

Mortensen (1970) uses (4.5) and (4.9) to form an expression for expected wealth before commencing to search (given $R>S$), and derives the fundamental equation (4.4) above by assuming that a person chooses the minimum acceptable offer R to maximise expected wealth. This is not surprising since choosing a stopping rule with a minimum acceptable offer R so that the rule maximises the expected return from search is equivalent to choosing R to maximise expected wealth.

The equations (4.4), (4.5), (4.7) and (4.9) and the fact that $R = V+S$ make it possible to derive hypotheses about the impacts of direct search costs (c), the arrival rate of marriage offers (m), wealth from remaining unmarried (S) and the maximum offer in the 'optimal sort' (w^*) on the reservation offer (R), the duration of search ($1/h(R,w^*)$ or $G(T)$) and the expected gain from marriage ($E[w \mid w \geq R] - S$).

Thus, to summarise, the costs of continuing marital search include direct expenditure of time and money on searching (for example, dating a number of people) and the income foregone by remaining single rather than marrying the best available mate. The expected benefit from continuing to search is the expected increase in full wealth from finding a preferable partner, which depends on the arrival rate of offers and the distribution of offers potentially available to the person. A person maximises his or her expected full wealth, and therefore stops searching, when the expected benefit from continuing to search equals the cost of continuing to search.[3]

Impacts of parameters (c, S and w) on the reservation offer R

From total differentiation of equation (4.4),

$$\partial R/\partial c = -1/[h(R,w^*) + r] < 0 \tag{4.10}$$

$$\partial R/\partial S = r/[h(R,w^*) + r] > 0 \tag{4.11}$$

$$\partial R/\partial w^* = m(w^*-R)f(w^*)/[h(R,w^*) + r] > 0 \tag{4.12}$$

$$\partial R/\partial m = (rV+c)/m[h(R,w^*) + r] > 0 \tag{4.13}$$

Thus, higher direct search costs lower the reservation offer (the expected marital wealth while searching) while higher single wealth, marital wealth in the optimal sort and arrival rate of marriage offers raise the reservation offer R.

Impacts of parameters on the duration of search

The expected duration of search is the reciprocal of $h(R,w^*)$. The impacts of R, m and w^* on $h(R,w^*)$ are derived, and using equations (4.10) and (4.11), the impacts of the parameters c and S can be derived. Total differentiation of equation (4.5) yields

$$\partial h(R,w^*)/\partial R = -mf(R) < 0, \text{ thus } \partial h/\partial c > 0 \text{ and } \partial h/\partial S < 0 \tag{4.14}$$

$$\partial h(R,w^*)/\partial w^* = mf(w^*)\{1 - [mf(R)(w^*-R)]/[h(R,w^*) + r]\} \gtrless 0 \tag{4.15}$$

$$\partial h(R,w^*)/\partial m = h(R,w^*)/m - f(R)[r(R-S)+c]/[h(R,w^*) + r] \gtrless 0 \tag{4.16}$$

From differentiation of (4.7)

$$\partial G(T)/\partial R = T\exp(-hT)[\partial h/\partial R] < 0 \tag{4.14a}$$

$$\partial G(T)/\partial w^* = T\exp(-hT)[\partial h/\partial w^*] \gtrless 0 \tag{4.15a}$$

$$\partial G(T)/\partial m = T\exp(-hT)[\partial h/\partial m] \gtrless 0 \tag{4.16a}$$

Equations (4.14) and (4.14a) show that higher search costs raise $h(R,w^*)$ and $G(T)$ and reduce the duration of search, while higher single wealth has the opposite effects. While a casual inspection of equation (4.5) would suggest that a higher arrival rate of marriage offers would raise $h(R,w^*)$ and $G(T)$, equation (4.16) shows that this need not be the case, because a higher m also raises the reservation offer, R. In other words, while the person may be more likely to receive an offer, he/she is less likely to accept it, making the net effect of m on $h(R,w^*)$ and $G(T)$ ambiguous.

The impact of the arrival rate on duration will depend on the distribution of offers. If, for instance, w had a uniform probability distribution (that is, $f(w) = 1/d$, where d is a constant, $d>1$), then $h(R,w^*) = m(w^*-R)/d = r(R-S)+c$, so that when $w^*-R>1$, (4.16) implies $\partial h(R,w^*)/\partial m>0$; that is, a higher arrival rate reduces the duration of search. Equation (4.16) also indicates that this would also be the case when m is large.

The impacts of marital wealth in the optimal sort (w^*) are also ambiguous, depending upon whether $[mf(R)(w^*-R)]/(h+r)$ is less than or greater than unity. If, as above, w had a uniform distribution,

$$[mf(R)(w^*-R)]/(h+r) = [m(w^*-R)/d]/(h+r)$$
$$= h/(h+r)<1 \text{ for } r>0 \qquad (4.17)$$

Thus, $\partial h/\partial w^* >0$ and $\partial G(T)/\partial w^* >0$, and higher wealth in the optimal sort reduces the duration of search. This is also true if the distribution of w is unimodal and w^* is less than the mode (this can be shown by noting that in this case $wf(w) > Rf(R)$ for $R<w\leq w^*$, and by using the equilibrium relationship (4.4)). These distributional assumptions are sufficient conditions for higher wealth in the optimal sort to reduce the duration of search; it may also be true for other distributions, but no general statement can be made.

Impacts of parameters on the expected gains from marriage among married persons

Differentiation of equation (4.9) yields

$$\partial E(w \mid w \geq R)/\partial R = f(R)[E(w \mid w \geq R) - R]m/h(R,w^*) > 0 \qquad (4.18)$$

$$\partial E(w \mid w \geq R)/\partial w^* = \{[w^* - E(w \mid w \geq R)]f(w) + f(R)[E(w \mid w \geq R) - R][\partial R/\partial w^*]\}m/h(R,w^*) > 0 \qquad (4.19)$$

Higher marital wealth in the optimal sort raises the average gain from marriage among the married ($E(w \mid w \geq R) - S$), while higher search costs and a lower arrival rate of marriage offers reduce it.

Higher wealth if remaining single raises the average wealth within marriage. It is not, however, clear whether it raises or lowers the average gain among the married. This will depend on the distribution of w; for instance, if w has a uniform distribution or a unimodal distribution with w^* less than the mode (thus $f(w) > f(R)$ for $R<w\leq w^*$), it can be shown that higher single wealth lowers the mean gain from marriage among the married (this follows because higher S raises R more than it raises $E(w : w\geq R)$, and equation (4.20) shows that the rise in R is less than the rise in S).

The expected gain from marriage while searching, $R-S$, decreases with S. This is clear from equation (4.11), from which

$$\partial(R-S)/\partial S = r/(h+r) - 1 < 0 \qquad (4.20)$$

Impacts of parameters on the likelihood of searching

As noted earlier, if a person is searching, his/her expected wealth is R; if not searching, it is S. Thus, a person would search if and only if $S \leq R \leq w^*$. Parameters which raise $R-S$ therefore raise the likelihood that a person will search for a partner. Equation (4.20) has shown that higher single wealth reduces the likelihood that a person would search. Equations (4.10), (4.12) and (4.13) indicate that persons with higher search costs or a lower arrival rate of marriage offers are also less likely to search, but persons with higher marital wealth in the optimal sort are more likely to search.

Summary of predictions from the model

It has been shown that persons with the same full wealth from remaining single ('single wealth'), but higher search costs (for whatever reason), search for a shorter time (equation (4.14)), accept a lower marriage offer (equations (4.10) and (4.18)) and obtain a smaller gain from marriage. For such persons, there is a larger deviation between the welfare that they would obtain in the optimal sorting of mates and that actually received; in other words, a larger 'mismatch'.

Given search costs and single wealth, persons who would gain more from marriage in the optimal sorting of mates receive a better marriage offer (equation (4.19)) and gain more from marriage. While less than optimal such persons make a better match in terms of the gain from marriage.

Among persons with the same search costs those with a higher single wealth search longer (equation (4.14)) and obtain a better marriage offer (equations (4.11) and (4.18), but tend to gain less from marriage. The appendix to this chapter presents evidence that there is a positive association between the duration of search and the size of the marriage offer.

Finally, persons otherwise identical who receive marriage offers at a higher rate per period, obtain a higher marriage offer when they marry (equations (4.13) and (4.18)), and gain more from marriage. Thus, such persons make a better match. It is not, however, clear whether their duration of marital search is shorter or longer; the higher arrival rate of marriage offers tends to shorten the duration, but a higher arrival rate also increases the minimal acceptable offer, which lengthens the duration of search (equations (4.13) and (4.16)).

Intensive search

The second type of search begins when an acceptable partner is found, and it involves obtaining more information about this particular person. This 'intensive search' improves the reliability and accuracy of expectations about a particular match. Thus, it would have the effect of reducing the variance in the distribution of realised full wealth in marriage. Higher intensive search costs (for whatever reason) would shorten this learning period and/or reduce the information obtained, thereby leading to a higher variance in the actual outcomes regarding full wealth in marriage.

The two kinds of search are directly related to one another because those skilled at one kind are likely to be also skilled at the other and because the value of a person's time affects the costs of both types of search. Smaller expected gains from marriage, owing to less extensive search, and less reliable expectations, owing to less intensive search, tend, therefore, to go together. Thus, the variance in realised gains from marriage and the expected gains from marriage are likely to be negatively correlated.

APPLICATION TO THE ANALYSIS OF MARRIAGE AND MARITAL DISSOLUTION

The analysis of marriage, or remarriage, is concerned with if and when a match is made. The model can be used to predict how various observable characteristics of a woman and her environment affect the likelihood of searching for a(nother) mate and the probability of receiving an acceptable marriage offer in any given time interval.

A woman will only search for another mate if the minimum acceptable marriage offer that can be expected exceeds the expected wealth if she remains unmarried ('single wealth'). It has been shown that the probability of that occurring is higher the lower is single wealth, the lower are her search costs, the higher is the arrival rate of marriage offers and the higher is the woman's gain from marriage in the optimal sorting of mates. Characteristics of the woman which affect these variables influence the probability of searching for another mate.

Given that the woman is searching, the likelihood of (re)marrying in any given interval of time depends on the probability of receiving an acceptable offer in that interval. The latter probability is higher for a woman with higher search costs and lower wealth if remaining unmarried (equations (4.10), (4.11) and (4.14a)). The arrival rate of marriage offers has an ambiguous effect on this probability (equations (4.16) and (4.16a), as does the woman's gain from marriage in the optimal sort, with their effects depending on the distribution of offers. For instance, it was shown above that if offers followed a uniform distribution, a higher gain from marriage in the optimal sort would increase the probability of receiving an acceptable offer in the interval and if the uniform distribution had $w^*-R>1$ or the arrival rate is large, then a higher arrival rate of offers would also increase this probability.

Observable characteristics of a woman can be related to the concepts of search costs, single wealth, rate of receipt of marriage offers and the expected gain from marriage in the optimal sort, thereby making it possible to derive some predictions concerning how these characteristics may influence the marriage hazard rate and the probability of (re)marrying within any given number of years.

Analysis of marital dissolution is conditional on a match having been made. Search costs, single wealth, the arrival rate of offers and the gain from marriage in an optimal sorting of mates come into the analysis through their effect on the size of the marriage offer which was accepted and the expected gain from marriage. The next section derives hypotheses about the effects of observable characteristics related to these concepts on the probability of a woman's marriage dissolving.

MARITAL DISSOLUTION: HYPOTHESES

The dissolution of marriage is unlikely to be the realisation of some lifetime plan, but rather a consequence of disappointed expectations. The high rates of dissolution in the first few years of marriage support this view: since there are emotional and financial costs of divorce it is reasonable to suppose that people would not enter a marriage which they expect to dissolve within a few years. Thus, marriages dissolve primarily because of outcomes not expected at marriage; that is, because of surprises!

Within the conceptual framework of this chapter, the breakup of a marriage occurs when the gain from the present marriage disappears. It arises because new information becomes available, leading to a reassessment of the expected gain from the present marriage. It is more likely that new information will reveal that the gain from the present marriage has disappeared when the expected gain at the start of marriage is low or when the variance of outcomes is high. Thus, a lower expected gain or higher variance increases the likelihood of marital dissolution. (See Becker, Landes and Michael, 1977, for the first application of this framework to the analysis of divorce.)

While it is not possible to measure the expected gain from marriage for individuals, it can be related to a number of observable personal characteristics using the framework outlined above. In recent years, contract theory has also been applied to analysis of the decision to divorce and its implications for behaviour before and after any divorce (Weiss and Willis, 1985, and Lommerud, 1989). While providing new insights, these analyses do not generate any hypotheses about marital dissolution that can be examined with the available data. Thus, the hypotheses about how personal characteristics may affect the probability of marital dissolution are developed primarily from the framework outlined earlier in this chapter.

Consider, for instance, how *age at marriage* may affect the probability of marital dissolution. According to the economic model of search for a marital partner, persons with high search costs, for whatever reason, will both accept a lower marriage offer, thereby gaining less from marriage and making a poorer match, and also marry earlier. This suggests an inverse association between the age at marriage and the likelihood of marital dissolution.

Furthermore, less extensive search before marriage also raises the likelihood that random search after marriage will reveal a better match. Or, to put it another way, persons marrying later are likely to have collected more information about themselves, their mates and the marriage market prior to marriage; because they are better informed, it is less likely that new information would lead to a revision of expectations about their mate and the gain from their current marriage.

There are also other factors which suggest a negative association between age at marriage and likelihood of subsequent dissolution. Young persons may be overly optimistic about their present offer relative to the distribution of potential marriage offers. Thus, if they accept the present offer, it is likely that a better offer will materialise after marriage. In addition, unanticipated developments after marriage may be more likely among those who marry young because they are less settled in their careers before and after marriage than those who marry at older ages.

On the other hand, as people age their marriage market shrinks, causing their minimum acceptable marriage offer to fall. People marrying relatively late in their lives are likely, therefore, to have lower expected gains from marriage and to make a poorer match. Thus both early and late marriage could be associated with a bigger chance of marital dissolution.

A *pre-marital pregnancy* (which is not terminated) usually makes the mother less appealing to men other than the father of the child. Thus, the expected value of additional extensive search for a mate is likely to be low. Because of the burden of child care, the costs of searching extensively after the birth are high. Search for a mate is limited in consequence, and these women tend to accept a lower marriage offer and a lower expected gain from marriage.

Intensive search also tends to be curtailed because of the desire to legitimate the child. This makes it more likely that new information will cause a revision of expectations about the gain from the match. Along with the lower expected gain from marriage, such revisions make it more likely that the gain from marriage will disappear and the marriage will dissolve.

Women who have received more *education* are likely to be more productive in the home (Michael, 1973). Thus education is a trait for which positive assortative mating is likely to be optimal; better educated women would marry better educated men. Women with higher educational achievements would, therefore, tend to gain more from marriage, for any given division of labour.

But education also increases a woman's earning capacity and participation in paid employment. Earlier in the chapter it was argued that negative assortative mating may be optimal for spouses' earning capacities because this maximises the advantage of the marital division of labour between the home and the market. In that men usually have higher earning capacities, a higher earning capacity for the woman is associated with lower benefits from the division of labour and a lower expected gain from marriage, all else being equal. Furthermore, because it raises the cost of children, a higher earning capacity for the woman lowers the demand for children. Since children are an important source of the gain from marriage it lowers the expected gain from marriage for this reason as well.

When joint consumption economies are taken into account, there can, however, be positive assortative mating on spouses' earning capacities. Thus, the net effect of a woman's educational achievements on her expected gain from marriage and the likelihood that her marriage breaks down is not clear.

When it is easier and *less costly to dissolve* a marriage legally, there is less incentive to make a lengthy search in order to avoid a mismatch. Shorter search entails the acceptance of a lower marriage offer, and it makes it more likely that random search after marriage will reveal a better match. Indeed, search within marriage becomes a better search strategy when marital dissolution is easier and less costly. Thus, easier dissolution raises the likelihood of dissolution.

In Britain, the Divorce Reform Act (1969) amended the grounds for divorce. Irretrievable breakdown of the marriage, including two years separation of the partners with consent and four years without consent, became the sole criterion for divorce. These easier grounds for divorce came into effect in 1971, and would have affected the likelihood of marital breakdown at all durations among marriages since 1971 and at the higher durations for marriages contracted earlier.

Investments of time and money which are much less valuable outside the present marriage have been called 'marital-specific capital' by Becker (1981). The most important of these are knowledge about the idiosyncracies of one's spouse and children from the marriage. Children come into this category because it is difficult for both spouses to enjoy their children if the marriage breaks up; one spouse is likely to have less contact with the children. Almost by definition, marital-specific capital discourages dissolution.

Because marital-specific capital tends to increase with the *duration of marriage*, the likelihood of marital breakdown is expected to decline with duration, all else being equal. There is, however, also a 'selection effect' associated with duration. Women with a higher risk of a marital breakdown (for whatever reason) dissolve their marriages earlier, leaving those facing a lower risk and creating a tendency for the risk to decline with duration of motherhood.

As an important part of marital-specific capital, *children* inhibit marital dissolution. Thus childlessness is likely to be associated with a higher risk of dissolution, and larger families with a lower risk.

But there are probably also other effects of children and patterns of childbearing on marital breakdown, which are associated with unanticipated developments after marriage. Rapid childbearing after marriage may produce unexpected financial strains, and it may impede the process of learning about one's spouse. Larger than normal families are often likely to be the result of unexpectedly high fertility (perhaps due to excessive fecundity). Childlessness could reflect a fertility impairment which was not anticipated at marriage. The new information provided by these unexpected developments may lead the couple to revise their expectation about the gain from the particular marriage.

As the concern here is with entry to lone parenthood, the empirical analysis focusses on couples with children. Thus, we do not discuss the impact of childlessness on the risk of marital dissolution. Analysis in Ermisch (1986) shows it raises the risk, but not more than pre-marital conceptions increase it.

A *woman's occupation* is not well defined because of occupational mobility over her life. The empirical analysis below uses a woman's last job before her first birth as a benchmark. Because of the importance of downward occupational mobility after childbearing, particularly associated with return to part-time work (see Martin and Roberts, 1984, Chapter 10), this benchmark is more likely to be indicative of a woman's potential occupational status and the earning capacity associated with that status.

Again, whether there is positive or negative assortative mating on spouses' earning capacities depends on whether joint consumption economies or gains from specialisation dominate. Thus, it is unclear whether the expected gain from marriage increases or decreases with earning capacity and occupational status.

When both spouses are in paid employment, a conflict can, however, arise when the geographic locations of the best earning opportunity for each spouse do not coincide. If the gain from marriage is not sufficient to compensate the spouse who has to compromise in terms of earning opportunities, the marriage would dissolve. The closer is the woman's earning capacity to her husband's (which generally means the higher it is), the more likely that the conflict can only be resolved by dissolution of the marriage (Mincer, 1978).

Higher earning capacity also tends to be associated with higher wealth from remaining unmarried, or 'single wealth'. While higher single wealth produces a longer search and a better marriage offer (for given search costs), it also tends to reduce the expected gain from marriage. Since it raises the cost of time, higher earning capacity could also be associated with higher search costs, which would also lower the expected gain from marriage.

Earning capacity is directly related to *experience in paid employment* ('work experience' for short) (see, for example Wright and Ermisch, 1988, Ermisch and Wright, 1988, Joshi, 1984, and Joshi and Newell,

1986). But, in addition, work experience *before marriage* is also likely to be associated with better search opportunities and more marriage offers through more contacts. All else being equal, better opportunities entail a more efficient extensive search and lower search costs, thereby a better marriage offer and a higher expected gain from marriage. More marriage offers also increase the expected gain from marriage. Intensive search may also be more efficient, and the better search is likely to produce more reliable expectations. Women are, therefore, less likely to be disappointed after marriage, particularly in the early years of marriage when lack of information about difficult to assess attributes makes dissolution more likely.

Participation in paid employment after marriage, particularly during parenthood, could also affect the risk of marital breakdown in important ways. It is likely to provide new information about earning capacity, which may affect marital dissolution differently from pre-marital work experience.[4] It may also be associated with better search opportunities within marriage, which lower the cost of search within marriage and may increase the number of new marriage offers, making it more likely that a better marriage offer is received.

There may, however, also be aspects of 'reverse causation' associated with participation in paid employment. Women who perceive a higher risk of dissolution (for whatever reason) may be in paid employment more after marriage in order to 'insure' themselves financially if divorced. Thus, causation could flow, in part, from a higher risk of marital breakdown to more employment after marriage.

Finally more participation in paid employment by the woman could be the result of financial strains arising from her husband's low earnings, which would be associated with a low gain from marriage. Thus, the wife's employment may be just an indicator of low husband's earnings (which cannot be measured in the empirical analysis that follows).

The economic environment may also affect the risk of dissolution. For example a large number of studies indicate that high male unemployment rates in the community are associated with a higher risk of marital dissolution (see Bishop, 1980, for a survey of the evidence). The *husband's unemployment* is not likely to have been anticipated by the wife at the time of marriage, making it likely that there is a downward revision in the gains from marriage. Thus, a higher unemployment rate in the economy may increase the risk of marital dissolution. On the other hand, a higher rate may indicate poor alternative sources of income for a woman, which helps maintain the gains from marriage.

General changes in *women's pay relative to men's* over time, such as those stimulated by the Equal Pay Act in Britain during the first half of the 1970s, could also change the expected gain from marriage. As women, on average, receive lower pay than men, when this ratio is higher the benefits from the conventional marital divison of labour is lower. Higher women's relative pay also increases a woman's wealth when unmarried. The resulting lower gains from marriage tend to raise the marital dissolution rate. On the other hand, higher women's relative pay increases the similarity of spouses' demands for household public goods, which enhances the gains from sharing public goods in marriage.

Increases in real *welfare benefits* available to lone parents when out of employment would also tend to raise a woman's wealth when unmarried, thereby reducing the gain from marriage and raising the probability of marital dissolution. For instance, it has been contended, with varying degrees of supporting evidence, that the amount and form of assistance to poor American families through Aid to Families with Dependent Children (AFDC) and through the Negative Income Tax Experiments (NITE) have affected the risk of marital dissolution (see, for example, Groeneveld, Tuma and Hannan, 1980, Moffitt, 1988, Cain and Wissocker, 1986, and Bishop, 1980).

The next chapter uses these hypotheses to structure and interpret the empirical analysis of marital dissolution among mothers.

APPENDIX
SOME EMPIRICAL EVIDENCE ON SEARCH AND
MARRIAGE OFFERS

There tends to be positive assortative mating between husband's earnings and most personal traits of a woman. Only those traits that mainly increase a woman's productivity in the labour market may be negatively sorted with husband's earnings, and it was argued in the text that there is likely to be positive assortative mating on these traits as well because of joint consumption economies. Thus, most traits are complementary to husband's earnings, and the 'gain from marriage' tends to be positively correlated with husband's earnings (see Becker, 1981, Chapter 4). Husband's earnings should, therefore, be directly related to complementary traits of his wife and, because longer search for a partner tends to be associated with better marriage offer (see equations (4.14) and (4.18) in the text), they should also be directly related to the duration of search.

A regression analysis was carried out to test these hypotheses using a sample of women from the Women and Employment Survey. The data in the survey on husband's earnings relates to earnings in 1980. Older women

Table 4A.1 *Gains from marriage, assortative mating and payoff to search*
Dependent variable: husband's gross earnings in 1980
(Women who have married only once and whose husband's earnings are reported only)

| | Regression[a] | |
	Coefficient	t-value
Constant	5242.1	3.65
Post-comp. ed. None		
1 year	320.2	0.75
2 years	866.6	1.58
3+ years	2,451.2	2.94
Age at marriage (years)	62.5	0.88
DoB−513(months)	−2.552	3.43
SQ(DoB−513)	−0.04235	2.65
Standard error	10,639.7	
Adj. R²	0.010	
F-statistic	3.976	
N	1,828	

[a]Standard errors of coefficients adjusted for heteroscedasticity in the random disturbance term of the equation; chi-squared statistic for test of homoscedasticity = 1,467 (6 degrees of freedom). DoB is the woman's date of birth in terms of months since January 1900.

in 1980 would have an older husband, who would be higher up his age-earnings profile, thereby having higher earnings in 1980 than a similar man earlier in his career. In order to control for these cohort differences in husband's observed earnings in 1980, two cohort trend variables, a woman's date of birth in months since January 1900 (denoted as DOB) and its square, are included as regressors in an equation for husband's earnings. The sample was restricted to women married only once who reported their husband's gross earnings.

The other regressors are a set of dichotomous variables for years of education beyond the minimum school-leaving age (years of 'post-compulsory education') and age at marriage. The latter is a measure of the duration of search for a partner.

The results in table 4A.1 suggest positive assortative mating with respect to educational attainments. Women who stayed on in education longer married a husband with higher earnings. As expected, husbands of women from more recent generations tend to have lower earnings in 1980.

While marrying later in life, and presumably searching longer for a husband, tends to pay off in terms of a husband with higher earnings and a larger gain from marriage, the impact of age at marriage is not statistically significant at conventional levels; indeed the t-value is less than one. But this outcome may arise because it is improper to assume that age at marriage is uncorrelated with unmeasured characteristics captured in the error term of the equation. If a woman has unmeasured characteristics which make her attractive in the marriage market, she will tend to marry a husband with higher earnings and marry sooner in her life. The analysis here has failed to control for these unmeasured characteristics; thus the estimate of the impact of marriage age on husband's earnings in our equation would understate the true payoff of search. Boulier and Rosenzweig (1984) also found age at marriage to have an insignificant impact on husband's earnings in an ordinary least squares regression but when they treated it as an endogenous variable in a system of equations and estimated its impact using 3-stage least squares, its impact was significantly positive.

ENTRY TO LONE PARENTHOOD: ANALYSIS OF MARITAL DISSOLUTION AND PRE-MARITAL BIRTHS

MARITAL DISSOLUTION AMONG MOTHERS

The hypotheses developed at the end of the last chapter are now used to structure the empirical analysis of marital dissolution among mothers. In the analysis, the period during which a mother is at risk for a marital dissolution starts from the date of her first birth. Women whose first birth preceded marriage have been excluded, as their first entry into lone parenthood is analysed later in the chapter. The data is from the demographic and employment histories collected in the 1980 *Women and Employment Survey* (WES), discussed in Chapter 3. The distribution of the lengths of time to marital dissolution from this date are modelled, taking into account the large proportion of women whose marriages do not dissolve before the date of interview in 1980 or before the youngest child reaches the age of sixteen, after which the mother can no longer become a lone parent according to the definition used here. The analysis is confined to first marriages because the risk of dissolution may be different in subsequent marriages. Nevertheless, the bulk of time that women are exposed to the risk of dissolution occurs in first marriages.

In order to focus on more recent developments and also to reduce computational costs, the analysis is confined to marriages starting in 1960 or later. The *marital dissolution hazard* is the probability of a woman's marriage dissolving in a month conditional on being a married parent up to that time. Chart 5.1 shows the 'raw' marital dissolution hazard rate per month, by duration of motherhood, or equivalently, age of the oldest child, during the first ten years of motherhood.[1] The top panel shows a centred twelve-month moving average rate, and the bottom panel shows the average rate for each year.[2] The horizontal line at approximately 0.0012 is the estimated marital dissolution rate if the rate were constant over the first ten years of motherhood. While there are quite large fluctuations in the hazard, the chart suggests an increase in the marital dissolution hazard as the duration of motherhood increases. This need not, however, be the case when the hazard is allowed to vary with characteristics of a mother and her family and over calendar time.

Chart 5.1 *Marital dissolution raw hazard rate*

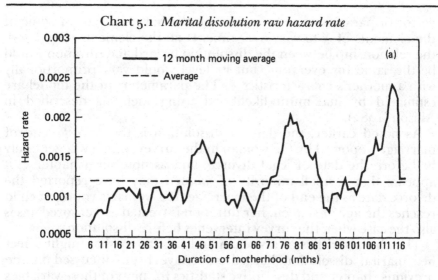

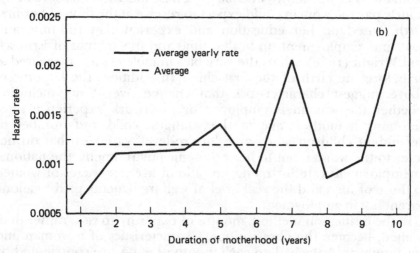

Source: Author's calculations from 1980 *Women and Employment Survey*.

Empirical analysis that allows for such variation employs the so called *proportional hazards model*. The hazard rate at duration of parenthood t, $h(t,X)$, is given by

$$h(t,X_t) = \lambda(t) \exp(X_t\beta) \tag{5.1}$$

where $\lambda(t)$ is a function of duration 'at risk'; X_t is a vector of characteristics of the mother and her family at duration t; and β is a

vector of parameters to be estimated. We have allowed for some of
the elements of X to vary over time. If all the elements were fixed,
the relationship between the dissolution hazard and duration would
be the same for everyone, but its level would vary proportionally
with a mother's characteristics X. The parameters of the model are
estimated by maximum likelihood using methods described in
Allison (1982).

As noted earlier, the date of dissolution is the *de facto* 'end of
marriage' reported by the woman in the survey, which will generally
be before the date of legal divorce, but, as noted in Chapter 3, it
appears that a small minority of women may have reported the
divorce date as the end of the marriage. If a woman's youngest child
reaches the age of sixteen, her duration is treated as 'censored' (as is
also the case when the survey intervenes before dissolution).

The characteristics of a woman and her family that might affect
her marital dissolution hazard rate have been discussed in the
previous chapter and descriptive statistics for most of these variables
from the WES are shown in table 5.1 These include a measure of the
hourly pay the woman could expect to receive at the time of her first
birth, based on her education and experience in full-time and
part-time employment up to that time and the analysis of Ermisch
and Wright (1988). All of the variables in table 5.1 are measured at
or before the birth of the first child. In addition, the hypotheses
above suggest characteristics that change over time, including
whether the woman is employed or not, work experience since
becoming a mother, age of the youngest child and number of
dependent children, and some 'macro-level' variables that do not
refer to the woman but to her economic environment: the national
unemployment rate for men, the ratio of average wages of women
to those of men and the real level of welfare benefits paid to a lone
parent not in employment.

In the estimation method, months of exposure to risk, rather than
women, become the observations. Characteristics of a woman and
her family are 'attached' to each month of exposure contributed by
her, as are macro-level variables that vary with calendar time.

In this type of model, the pattern of duration dependence, $\lambda(t)$,
must be specified. As a compromise between flexibility and the
number of parameters to be estimated, it was assumed that, given
the values of the explanatory variables, the hazard is constant within
each of ten duration segments, but can vary between the segments.
These segments were constructed so that each contributes about a
tenth of the monthly 'exposures to risk'. Continuous functions of
duration (for example, $\log(t)$) are also considered.

Table 5.1 *Descriptive statistics for explanatory variables[a]*

Variable	Mean	Standard deviation
Age at marriage (years)	21.56	3.37
Timing of first birth:		
Conceived before marriage	0.221	
More than 8 but less than 18 months after marriage	0.235	
18 or more months after marriage	0.544	
Months between marriage and first birth	26.88	24.09
Highest educational qualification:		
A-level or above	0.182	
O-level or above	0.186	
Other qualification	0.170	
No qualifications	0.463	
Years of education beyond the minimum school-leaving age	1.31	1.90
First birth in 1971 or later	0.495	
Year of first birth *minus* 1900	70.83	5.36
Woman's occupation in last job before her first birth:		
Professional	0.150	
Other non-manual	0.483	
Manual	0.343	
No job	0.023	
Expected log of woman's hourly wage at time of first birth	0.465	0.224
Months in paid employment before first birth	81.06	47.20

[a] The analysis is based on a sample of 1982 women who married for the first time during 1960–80 and had a child; 253 (12.8 per cent) of these marriages dissolved.

There are of course, unmeasured attributes of a woman, her husband and her family that can affect her risk of marital dissolution. It is well known that failure to control for these unobserved differences between women in the estimation of the model biases estimated hazards towards negative duration dependence and biases parameter estimates towards zero (for example, Lancaster, 1979). The large computational costs involved in estimating models with such unobserved heterogeneity precluded such estimation for the large samples used here.[3]

Results for macro-level variables
The macro variables are measured annually, and they are allocated to women's months of exposure to risk occurring in that calendar year. The indicator of women's relative pay is the logarithm of the

ratio of average women's to men's hourly wages (for adults of each
sex working full-time in manual occupations). As measures of
women's unemployment rates are not very reliable in Britain, the
male unemployment rate is the sole measure of the unemployment
rate in the economy used in the analysis.

Real welfare benefits vary both over time, as benefit rules and
rates change, and over women because benefits vary with the
number of children. They are constructed by computing the
amounts of Supplementary Benefit, including payments for housing, that lone mothers with different numbers of children would
receive in each year (computed from Department of Health and
Social Security, 1984), and these amounts are allocated to women's
months of exposure according to the year that they occur and the
number of children the woman has in that month. There has been
an upward trend in real benefits for each family size.

None of these macro variables appear to be stationary time series,
and their trends over time make them strongly correlated with one
another. This can make it difficult to estimate the impacts of these
variables on marital dissolution with any precision. It also may make
the estimated effect of any one variable strongly dependent on
which of the other macro variables are included in the equation.

The macro variables never proved to be statistically significant.
Indeed, their coefficients never exceeded their respective standard
errors. Thus, there is no evidence that welfare benefits, unemployment nor women's relative pay in the economy affect the risk of
marital dissolution. In particular, the failure to find that higher
welfare benefits encourage dissolution probably reflects the low level
of benefits relative to the share of income in marriage going to a
mother and her children. The discussion of the results focusses,
therefore, on models that exclude the macro variables other than
time trends.

Impacts of a mother's characteristics on her dissolution risk

The estimation started with a general model including all of the
variables in table 5.1 plus variables indicating a woman's current
employment status, or her experience in paid employment during
motherhood, number of dependent children and age of her youngest child. Then more parsimonious models, which eliminated particular variables and regrouped categories of categorical variables,
were estimated and these restrictions were tested using likelihood
ratio tests. Table 5.2 shows the estimates of the parameters (β) and
their standard errors for two statistically acceptable restricted ver-
sions of the general model.

Table 5.2 *Hazard models of marital dissolution*

Variable	Model 1		Model 2	
	Coefficient[a]	Relative risk[b]	Coefficient[a]	Relative risk[b]
Age at marriage	−0.455 (0.158)	0.38	−0.443 (0.157)	0.39
Age at marriage squared	0.0080 (0.0031)		0.0078 (0.0031)	
Premarital conception	0.253 (0.145)	1.29	0.226 (0.145)	1.25
2-child family	−0.259 (0.134)	0.77	−0.249 (0.134)	0.78
Expected log wage at motherhood	−0.672 (0.500)	0.86	−0.782 (0.503)	0.84
Year-1900	0.0500 (0.0169)	1.25	0.0504 (0.0169)	1.25
Mother in employment	0.396 (0.136)	1.49		
Proportion of months in employment			0.782 (0.195)	1.26
log duration	0.023 (0.073)		0.028 (0.072)	
Constant	−4.464 (2.227)		−4.675 (2.221)	
Model chi-square	80.60		87.11	

[a] The reference categories are first birth not a premarital conception, a one child or 3 or more child family, mother not in employment (model 1 only); standard errors in parentheses.
[b] Refers to the risk of being in the particular category of a categorical variable relative to the reference category, or the relative risk associated with a standard deviation higher value of a continuous variable. The means and standard deviations of variables that do not vary over time are in Table 5.1. The means (and standard deviations) of time-varying variables, over months of exposure, are as follows:

Proportion of months in employment	0.212 (0.300)
Year-1900	74.02 (4.48)
Mother in employment	0.350
2-child family	0.429

The risk of dissolution for a woman with characteristics A relative to a woman with characteristics B, or her *relative risk*, at a given duration of lone parenthood is defined as the *ratio of their hazard rates* (that is, $\exp[(A-B)\beta]$). In table 5.2, the relative risk of being in a particular category of a categorical variable (relative to the reference category) or associated with a standard deviation higher level of a continuous variable (for example, age at marriage) is computed. A relative risk above one indicates a higher risk than the reference category (or a standard deviation lower value) while below one indicates a lower risk.

These estimates show that *age at marriage* has a strong influence on the risk of marital dissolution. Women who marry at younger ages face a higher risk up to about the age of 28, after which a later age at marriage increases the risk. This result is consistent with the hypotheses set out earlier.

The Divorce Reform Act would tend to raise the dissolution hazard for marriages still intact after 1970. Although not shown in table 5.2, the coefficient of a dichotomous variable (D) taking on the value of unity in months of exposure to risk of dissolution occurring in 1971 and later (and zero before 1971) indeed indicates a much higher risk of marital dissolution in 1971 and later.[4] The Act could, however, also alter the trend rate of increase in the dissolution rate; thus the following model was estimated:

$$\log[h(t,X_t)] = \log[\lambda(t)] + (X_t\beta) + \gamma_1 D + \gamma_2 y + \gamma_3 D(y-70) \qquad (5.2)$$

where y is the year of exposure to risk. A change in trend would be indicated by a statistically significant estimate of γ_3, where γ_2 is the annual trend rate before 1971.

The results suggest that the period after 1971 saw a continuation of the trend observed in the 1960s: that is, the hypothesis that $\gamma_1 = \gamma_3 = 0$ is easily accepted ($\chi_2^2 = 0.15$). An upward trend in the dissolution risk during 1960–80 of about 5 per cent per annum appears to be an acceptable description of the data. When, however, the sample is confined to the first ten years of motherhood and is split between women at risk during the period 1960–70 and those at risk in 1971 and later, the estimated trend rate of increase in the dissolution risk is higher in the latter period. The coefficient (and standard error) of year of exposure is 0.0688 (0.0308) in the latter period in contrast to 0.0287 (0.0721) during 1960–70.[5] While both coefficients are within one standard error of a 5 per cent per annum increase, it appears that the Divorce Reform Act probably contributed to a steeper upward trend in dissolution risk after 1971.

As the earlier discussion of hypotheses suggests, women who *conceived their first child before marriage* (identified as births occurring within eight months of the date of marriage) face a higher risk of dissolution. The more limited search for a partner in these circumstances makes it more likely that a poor match is made, so that the risk that the marriage subsequently dissolves is higher. The analysis does not, however, indicate that *early childbearing within marriage* (a birth 8–17 months after marriage) is associated with a significantly higher risk of dissolution.[6]

Mothers of the modal size family of two children are less likely to have their marriage dissolve than mothers of one or of three or more children, resulting in a U-shaped relationship between family size and dissolution risk.[7] Murphy (1984) came to similar conclusions for British women and Hoem and Hoem (1988) obtained a similar finding for the dissolution of conjugal unions (including both legal marriages and consensual unions) in Sweden. Larger families than 'normal' may be unanticipated and they may also produce financial strains, leading to a revision of the expected benefits from the marriage. The one-child family could, however, be partly the outcome of a perceived high risk of marital dissolution, which leads to the postponement of a second child until the marriage appears more secure. Such behaviour would produce a positive association between the risk of dissolution and the incidence of one-child families.

Although not statistically significant at 0.05 level, the coefficient of the woman's potential wage at her first birth suggests that women with higher earning capacity are less likely to dissolve their marriage. This suggests that, because of joint consumption economies, positive assortative mating on spouses' earning capacities may be optimal, so that higher women's earning capacity raises the expected gain from marriage.

As noted earlier, however, the measure of expected earning capacity at motherhood reflects the woman's educational attainments and experience in paid employment up to that time. For the reasons suggested earlier, these could have direct effects on dissolution independent of earning capacity. When the potential wage is replaced by a woman's educational attainments and her work experience before motherhood, it is clear that the negative association between the potential wage and marital dissolution arises primarily because more experience in paid employment before motherhood, which raises the expected wage, has a negative impact on the risk of dissolution.[8] This is consistent with more experience in paid employment being associated with better search opportunities for a partner, which raise the marriage offer and the expected gain from marriage. There is not a clear relationship between educational attainments and marital dissolution.[9]

The first model of table 5.2 shows that a mother who is employed has a much higher risk of dissolution. This relationship could arise because employment affords better opportunities for receiving a

Table 5.3 *Work status and marital dissolution*

	Coefficient[a]	Chi-square[b]
Present work status	0.396 (0.136)	8.53
Work status 3 months earlier	0.218 (0.136)	2.57
Work status 6 months earlier	0.135 (0.133)	1.03
Work status 12 months earlier	0.122 (0.130)	0.88

[a] Standard error in parentheses; in addition to the particular work status measure, each specification includes the other variables in model 1 of table 5.2.
[b] Chi-square for test of hypothesis that parameter is zero (1 d.f.).

better marriage offer, or because women in jobs feel better able to support themselves if their marriage dissolves.

But this relationship could also reflect a tendency for women to date the 'end of the marriage' at the time they return to employment. Chapter 7 indeed shows that inflows into full-time employment increase sharply in the month the marriage ended. Thus, the relationship between employment status and dissolution could measure the employment response to dissolution rather than the other way around.

To reduce the chances of measuring such a response to dissolution, in a series of re-specifications of the first model in table 5.2, employment status is measured three, six and twelve months before the particular month of exposure. As table 5.3 shows, the strong positive association between being in a job and the risk of dissolution quickly disappears, with the association between employment status and the risk of dissolution weakening as the lag on employment status is increased.[10] Even at a three-month lag, the association is not statistically significant at the 0.05 level. At the higher lags, it is clearly not statistically significant. Thus, it appears that this association is picking up employment changes in anticipation of dissolution.

The association between marital dissolution and a measure of participation in paid employment that covers the entire period of motherhood is more likely to be indicative of the effect of participation in paid employment on dissolution, rather than the converse. In the second model in table 5.2, the proportion of months that a woman has spent in paid employment since becoming a mother replaces present (or lagged) work status. Its coefficient is four times its standard error.

It indicates that mothers who have spent a larger proportion of their time in paid employment face a much higher risk of marital dissolution. Women who have worked more since their first birth may have higher earning power than is predicted by the measure of their expected wage at motherhood; thus, with a better ability to support themselves, they may be more willing to dissolve an unhappy marriage. Also, their employment may provide better opportunities for meeting another partner who compares favourably with their present one.

As noted earlier, however, more participation in paid employment by the mother could be the result of financial strains, which both encourage the mother to work and destabilise the marriage. Thus a mother's employment may just be an indicator of financial strains on the marriage. There could also be some reverse causation. Women who perceive that they are in a shaky marriage, with a high risk of splitting up, may participate more in paid employment as a financial 'insurance' in the event of their divorce.

After taking account of these characteristics of a mother and the family and of trends in marital dissolution, the risk of dissolution does not vary much with the duration of motherhood. Model 4 in table 5.4 excludes log duration from model 2. When it is compared with a model containing nine dichotomous duration variables, the exclusion of all nine is statistically acceptable at significance levels of 0.05 or less ($\chi^2_9 = 15.82$).[11] Examination of the coefficients of these duration variables, however, suggests model 3 in table 5.4, which produces the highest value of the likelihood function of any of the many specifications tried.

In this model, the dissolution risk is constant over the second to tenth years of motherhood, but is 45 per cent lower during the first year after a birth.[12] Although the coefficients of dichotomous variables for the eleventh and later years of motherhood suggest a lower risk, this could reflect the upward trend in dissolution, because only women married in the 1960s could have had durations of this length. Note that the coefficient of the trend variable is higher when these duration variables are in the model (compare model 3 with models 1, 2 and 4), thereby acting to offset the effects of the long duration variables. In model 4, which excludes all duration variables, the coefficients of variables other than the trend differ very little, although most are larger in size and more precisely estimated in model 3.

Thus, it appears that, abstracting from time trends, for a woman

Table 5.4 *Hazard models of marital dissolution*

Variable	Model 3		Model 4	
	Coefficient[a]	Relative risk[b]	Coefficient[a]	Relative risk[b]
Age at marriage	−0.423 (0.158)	0.41	−0.439 (0.157)	0.40
Age at marriage squared	0.0075 (0.0031)		0.0078 (0.0031)	
Premarital conception	0.235 (0.146)	1.26	0.227 (0.145)	1.25
2-child family	−0.267 (0.131)	0.77	−0.237 (0.131)	0.79
Expected log wage at motherhood	−0.925 (0.501)	0.82	−0.797 (0.496)	0.84
Year-1900	0.0624 (0.0166)	1.32	0.0531 (0.0154)	1.27
Proportion of months in employment	0.802 (0.192)	1.27	0.797 (0.191)	1.27
Child aged less than one year	−0.597 (0.200)	0.55		
Period since first child: 121–149 months	−0.574 (0.235)	0.56		
150 or more months	−0.527 (0.219)	0.59		
Constant	−5.461 (2.276)		−4.817 (2.191)	
Model chi-square	105.44		86.95	
Degrees of freedom	10		7	

[a] The reference categories are first birth not a premarital conception, a one child or 3 or more child family, no child aged less than one (model 3 only), and 120 months or less after first child (model 3 only); standard errors in parentheses.

[b] Refers to the risk of being in the particular category of a categorical variable relative to the reference category, or the relative risk associated with a standard deviation higher value of a continuous variable. The proportion of months of exposure in which a child is less than one is 0.213.

with given characteristics, it is acceptable to view her marital dissolution rate as virtually invariant to the time she has spent as a married mother, which contrasts with what we may conclude from the raw dissolution hazard in chart 5.1, which reflects the time trend in dissolution. The main exception to this is a much lower risk of marital dissolution in the first year after giving birth. Other models,

Table 5.5 *Hazard models of marital dissolution*

Variable	1960–70		1971 and later	
	Coefficient[a]	Relative risk[b]	Coefficient[a]	Relative risk[b]
Age at marriage	−0.294 (0.107)	0.36	−0.046 (0.041)	0.86
Premarital conception	0.218 (0.331)	1.24	0.343 (0.189)	1.41
2-child family	0.097 (0.313)	1.10	−0.276 (0.169)	0.76
Expected log wage at motherhood	0.193 (1.449)	1.04	−1.945 (0.632)	0.65
Year-1900	0.0287 (0.0721)	1.07	0.0688 (0.0308)	1.21
Proportion of months in employment	1.190 (0.430)	1.40	0.888 (0.246)	1.30
Child aged less than one year	−0.759 (0.383)	0.47	−0.442 (0.238)	0.64
Constant	−3.264 (5.299)		−10.179 (2.480)	
Model chi-square	36.13		69.45	
Degrees of freedom	7		7	
Number of exposures	53878		110813	
Number of events	44		147	

[a] The reference categories are first birth not a premarital conception, a one child or three or more child family, and youngest child aged one or more; standard errors in parentheses.
[b] Refers to the risk of being in the particular category of a categorical variable relative to the reference category, or the relative risk associated with a standard deviation higher value of a continuous variable.

which tested for a different risk for a child aged 0–4, did not indicate that a pre-school child had a significant impact on the risk. A lower risk appears to be confined to the presence of very young children.

Finally, it is possible that the ease of divorce after 1970 may have changed the relationships between characteristics of women and their families and the risk of marital dissolution. To examine this the sample is confined to the first ten years of motherhood and is split between women at risk during the period 1960–70 and those at risk in 1971 and later. Table 5.5 shows the estimated parameters for

these two groups of women. The alteration of the trend in dissolution has already been discussed. While the relatively small number
of dissolutions in the 1960s sample must qualify the comparison, a
woman's potential wage at motherhood and the number of children
had virtually no impact on dissolution risk in the 1960s, in contrast
to the 1970s, when a woman's potential wage had a particularly large
impact. But age at marriage had a much smaller effect in the 1970s
than earlier.[13] On the other hand, the proportion of months worked
since becoming a mother has a strong and similar positive impact in
both periods.

PRE-MARITAL BIRTHS: HYPOTHESES

The probability of a pre-marital birth can be partitioned into the
product of two probabilities: the probability of becoming pregnant
outside marriage and the probability of having a birth outside
marriage conditional on being pregnant. On the plausible assumption that few pre-marital conceptions are planned, the former
probability depends on whether a young woman is sexually active
and her contraceptive practice if active. Sexual activity tends to
increase with age, but contraceptive knowledge and efficiency of
practice also may increase with age. The latter are probably also
better for women with higher levels of education. While family
background also influences sexual and contraceptive behaviour, the
WES data contain relatively little information about a woman's
family of origin. The characteristics of a young woman and her
environment other than her age that can be observed from the WES
data would appear to mainly influence the second probability.

Thus, we are primarily concerned with a woman's decision
concerning how to resolve a pre-marital pregnancy. Should she
abort, or marry the father before the birth, or have the baby without
marrying? There are clearly costs to taking the last course of action.
As dropping out of education entails a considerable loss in future
earnings, young *women in education* tend to face a higher opportunity
cost of having a child than other young women, particularly women
who are not in a job either. As the rate of return to an additional
year of education is probably higher for those with less education,
younger women face a higher opportunity cost. Thus, the likelihood
of an abortion would be higher and the probability of having a baby
without marrying lower for women in education, but the latter
probability would tend to increase with a woman's age.

While perhaps not as high as for women in education, the
opportunity cost of childbearing would be higher for women in a job

than for women who are neither in a job nor in education. *Women in a job* would have a higher probability of abortion and a lower probability of having a child outside marriage, but not as low as for women in education.

So far the discussion has emphasised the choice of whether to abort or not. The probability of having a child outside marriage is also affected by the decision whether to marry or not among women having the child. By providing financial support independent of her own or a husband's earnings, higher *welfare benefits* for young single mothers would make it more likely that a young pregnant woman has the child without marrying.

As noted earlier, higher *women's pay relative to men's* reduces the gains from the traditional marital division of labour and raises potential earnings as a single mother. Thus, increases in women's relative pay could discourage a young pregnant woman from marrying the father, thereby increasing the likelihood that she has the birth without marrying. On the other hand, higher women's wages would tend to raise the opportunity cost of a birth because it would increase foregone wages arising from the employment interruption associated with the birth. Although higher wages have an income effect when the mother returns to work, the cost effect is expected to dominate. The evidence from analysis of general first birth rates certainly indicates that the cost effect dominates (Ermisch, 1988). Higher women's real wages would, therefore, discourage pregnant young women from having the child.

Another element of the economic environment faced by single women is the *unemployment rate* in the economy. Higher unemployment could reduce the perceived prospects of getting a job for young women out of employment and thereby reduce the cost of a pre-marital birth. Higher unemployment may also be associated with a poorer marriage market, making it less likely that a pregnant woman marries. Both of these influences suggest that the probability of a birth outside marriage may increase wth the unemployment rate.

EMPIRICAL ANALYSIS OF PRE-MARITAL BIRTHS

In the WES data, pregnancies that are aborted are not identified. Only the product of the two probabilities above, the unconditional probability of a pre-marital birth, can be analysed empirically. As with marital dissolution, this probability is expressed in terms of the monthly 'hazard' of a premarital birth. Assuming that being in education, being in a job, welfare benefits, the unemployment rate

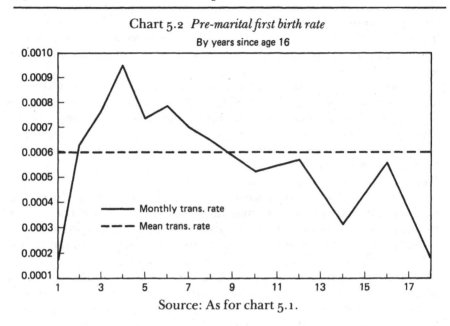

Chart 5.2 *Pre-marital first birth rate*

By years since age 16

Source: As for chart 5.1.

and women's relative pay do not affect the probability of becoming pregnant in the opposite direction to their effect on the probability that a pregnant woman has a birth outside marriage, the hypotheses in the preceding section also apply to the hazard of a pre-marital birth.

The analysis assumes that exposure to the risk of a pre-marital birth starts when the woman reaches the age of sixteen. With the exception of two births, all illegitimate births in the WES data occurred after the age of sixteen. A woman is treated as 'censored' if she marries or if the interview occurs while she is single and childless. Months beyond her sixteenth birthday is the duration variable in this analysis.

The 'raw' hazard rate of a pre-marital birth by age is shown in chart 5.2. The rate peaks at age twenty and then falls. Analogous to the analysis of marital dissolution, estimation of a proportional hazards model allows us to consider the impact of factors other than the woman's age on the pre-marital birth hazard. The hypotheses above suggest that whether a woman is in full-time education ('educational status'), whether she is employed or not ('work status'), welfare benefits, the unemployment rate and women's average relative pay may affect the hazard rate. In order to capture the influence of these variables around the time of pregnancy they are measured nine months before the month in which a woman is at risk for a birth. Welfare benefits are measured as the real amount of Supplementary Benefit that a mother of one child would receive in that month, and women's average relative pay and the unemployment rate are the same as in the analysis of marital dissolution.

In addition to a measure of current educational status, a woman's educational background may also influence the hazard of a pre-marital birth. As women who remain in education beyond the age of sixteen are at risk of pre-marital birth before completing their education, it is not appropriate to measure educational background in terms of the qualifications or years of post-compulsory education that a woman eventually receives. One simple measure of educational background, which avoids these problems, is whether a woman left school before the age of sixteen.

There may be a time trend in the probability of a pre-marital pregnancy arising from trends in sexual activity and contraceptive practices among young women. Changes in the cost and availability of abortion, perhaps related to the Abortion Act (1967), which legalised abortion from April 1968, could produce a trend in the probability of a birth outside marriage to pregnant young women. Thus, the analysis allows for time trends in the hazard of a pre-marital birth. In order to focus on more contemporary developments (and also to reduce computational time), the analysis is confined to women who reach their sixteenth birthday after 1960, which approximates the era of the contraceptive pill. There are 2,555 women in the analysis, and 149 of them have a pre-marital birth.

Tests for a shift in the pre-marital birth hazard and a change in its trend after abortion was legalised in 1968 did not indicate that these occurred.[14] Thus, only a linear trend in the logarithm of the hazard rate is employed in the models of the pre-marital birth hazard shown below.

Because of the strong trends in the macroeconomic variables and in welfare benefits, it proves difficult to disentangle their effects from time trends in the pre-marital birth rate arising from other sources. Estimates of models with different specifications for these trended variables are shown in table 5.6. Fortunately, estimates of the parameters associated with the woman-specific variables do not vary much across specifications. These are discussed first.

Effects of women's characteristics
As hypothesised, women in education are much less likely to have a pre-marital birth than other women. Women in jobs are about four times more likely than those in education to give birth before

Table 5.6 *Models of the pre-marital birth hazard*

Variable	Model 1	Model 2	Model 3	Model 4	Model 5
Left school before 16	0.637 (0.182)	0.629 (0.184)	0.624 (0.182)	0.620 (0.183)	0.650 (0.183)
In full-time education	−2.162 (0.417)	−2.163 (0.418)	−2.169 (0.417)	−2.172 (0.418)	−2.118 (0.417)
In employment	−0.770 (0.236)	−0.779 (0.236)	−0.782 (0.236)	−0.786 (0.236)	−0.768 (0.236)
Duration (mos)	0.013 (0.009)	0.014 (0.009)	0.014 (0.009)	0.013 (0.009)	0.0155 (0.009)
Duration squared/100	−0.0185 (0.0078)	−0.0189 (0.0078)	−0.0188 (0.0078)	−0.0184 (0.0078)	−0.0198 (0.0078)
log (Welfare Benefit)	3.832 (1.493)	2.857 (2.109)	3.194 (1.416)	1.844 (2.039)	
log (Unemployment rate)	0.379 (0.400)	0.731 (0.463)	0.809 (0.290)		0.530 (0.433)
Year-1900		0.012 (0.058)		0.084 (0.037)	0.073 (0.038)
log (Women's relative pay)	1.263 (0.788)				
Intercept	−16.924 (3.776)	−16.086 (3.726)	−16.202 (3.700)	−17.631 (3.627)	−12.375 (2.327)
Chi-square (d.f.)	115.02 (8)	112.63 (8)	112.53 (7)	110.06 (7)	110.75 (7)
R^a	0.204	0.202	0.204	0.201	0.202

Note: 2,555 women contribute 156,975 months of exposure to risk of a pre-marital birth and 149 pre-marital births.
[a] The R-value is the square root of a 'pseudo-R^2', adjusted for degrees of freedom. More specifically,

$$R^2 = [-2\log(L_o/L\beta) - 2p]/[-2\log(L_o)] \text{ and } R = \sqrt{R^2}, \text{ where}$$

L_o is the value of the likelihood function when the model only includes an intercept; L_β is the value of the likelihood function when the model also includes explanatory variables with parameters ß; and p is the dimension of ß (i.e. the number of explanatory variables).

marriage, but only half as likely as women who are neither in education nor employment.[15] The risk of a pre-marital birth for women in education is about 10 per cent of that of women in neither education nor employment.

An American study of how teenage pregnancies were resolved in the mid-1970s found that girls enrolled in school up to the point of their pregnancy or later are less likely to have the baby and remain single (Leibowitz, Eisen and Chow, 1986). It also found that self-supporting teenagers (that is, not receiving financial aid from parents, family or friends) are less likely to become single mothers. These results are generally consistent with the analysis here, although the American study suggests that being self-supporting reduces the risk that a pregnant girl becomes a single mother more than school enrolment does, contrary to what the present analysis suggests.

Women who left school before their sixteenth birthday are about 1.8 times more likely to have a pre-marital birth than other women. In 1972, the minimum school-leaving age was raised to sixteen. Thus, it is possible that the impact of leaving school before sixteen is partly a cohort effect, but the coefficient hardly changes when a set of three five-year cohort dummy variables are included in the model. As a set, these dummy variables are not statistically significant. Thus, in conjunction with the effects of their current education and employment status, the analysis implies that women with lower educational attainments are more likely to become a single mother.

The models also indicate that all else being equal, the risk of a pre-marital birth increases with a woman's age until about her nineteenth birthday and then declines, which is similar to the raw hazard. The initial rise in the pre-marital birth rate with age supports the hypothesis that the opportunity cost of a pre-marital birth falls with age, but the age pattern could also reflect changes in sexual activity and the use of contraceptives with age, and in the declining phase, unobserved differences between women (that is, an increasing proportion of women at risk are those who are less likely to have a pre-marital birth). While the models in Table 5.6 use a quadratic duration specification, a similar age pattern is obtained from the coefficients of a step-wise duration specification with ten six-month steps.

Effects of women's economic environment

The first model in table 5.6 includes all three macro variables.[16] The direction of the effect of welfare benefits is as hypothesised, and its coefficient is well determined. While the unemployment rate also has the predicted positive impact on the risk of a pre-marital birth, its coefficient is less than its standard error. The estimated positive coefficient of women's relative pay only makes economic sense if its impact on the gains from marriage dominates its effect on the opportunity cost of a pre-marital birth.

It is, however, somewhat implausible that this latter effect does not dominate. The measured effect of relative pay could, therefore, be purely spurious, and this interpretation is supported by the statistical insignificance of relative pay in model specifications which omit welfare benefits.[17] Thus, the remaining specifications in table 5.6 focus on the estimated effects of the unemployment rate and welfare benefits in models without women's relative pay.[18]

In the second model, which replaces women's relative pay by a simple trend, none of the trended variables is statistically significant at levels below 0.10, but the trend variable only has a chi-square value of 0.05. The third model drops the trend, and both welfare benefits and unemployment are statistically significant at the 0.025 level or less.[19]

This is the preferred model. After adjusting for degrees of freedom, it does as well as the first model in terms of explanatory power (see R value). As hypothesised, higher unemployment and higher welfare benefits raise the risk of a pre-marital birth.

In order to explore the robustness of the estimated effects of unemployment and welfare benefits, each is replaced in turn by a simple trend. The fourth model includes welfare benefits along with a linear time trend. The upward trend in the pre-marital birth risk of 8.4 per cent per annum is statistically significant ($\chi_1^2 = 5.29$). Although higher welfare benefits are again estimated to increase the probability of a pre-marital birth, the coefficient is below its standard error.[20] When welfare benefits are replaced by a linear trend (model 5), the estimated impact of unemployment is no longer statistically significant ($\chi_1^2 = 1.50$), and there is evidence of a significant upward trend of 7 per cent per year.[21]

There is a danger that the education and employment status variables are just reflecting unobserved traits of young women; thus their coefficients may not represent 'structural effects' of educational and employment status on pre-marital births. In other words, we may only be measuring the tendency for young women who are predisposed to leave education early or to be out of employment to also be predisposed to have children before marriage. If so, our statistical conditioning on these variables is improper, and we have not maximised the correct likelihood function.

In order to see how the estimated impacts of welfare benefits and the other macro variables are affected, we estimate a 'reduced form' model which excludes the education and employment variables. The results for a series of models comparable to those in table 5.6 are shown in table 5.7. In these models there is a stronger duration pattern, now peaking at age 20, but our conclusions about the effects of the macro variables are similar. The estimated impacts of

Table 5.7 *Models of the pre-marital birth hazard*

Variable	Model 1A	Model 2A	Model 3A	Model 4A	Model 5A
Duration (mos)	0.0251	0.0254	0.0254	0.0250	0.0263
	(0.009)	(0.009)	(0.009)	(0.009)	(0.009)
Duration squared/100	−0.0249	−0.0251	−0.0250	−0.0247	−0.0256
	(0.0079)	(0.0079)	(0.0079)	(0.0079)	(0.0079)
log (Welfare Benefit)	2.936	2.191	2.400	1.199	
	(1.480)	(2.109)	(1.408)	(2.031)	
log (Unemployment rate)	0.365	0.690	0.739		0.535
	(0.396)	(0.461)	(0.281)		(0.432)
Year-1900		0.008		0.077	0.054
		(0.058)		(0.036)	(0.038)
log (Women's relative pay)	1.081				
	(0.788)				
Intercept	−15.418	−14.764	−14.843	−16.227	−11.868
	(3.732)	(3.708)	(3.668)	(3.605)	(2.288)
Chi-square (d.f.)	50.79	49.01	48.99	46.71	47.91
	(5)	(5)	(4)	(4)	(4)
R^a	0.131	0.128	0.131	0.201	0.130

Note: 2,555 women contribute 156,975 months of exposure to risk of a pre-marital birth and 149 pre-marital births.
[a] The R-value is described in table 5.6.

welfare benefits and unemployment are, however, smaller than in table 5.6, as is the estimated upward trend.

Table 5.8 provides a better idea of the size of the effects of welfare benefits and unemployment in the different model specifications. Using lifetable calculations, it shows the percentages of women having a pre-marital birth before the ages of 22 and 26 under different stationary conditions, taking account of the competing risk of marriage while childless. Ten per cent higher (than the mean) welfare benefits raises these percentages for the reference woman by at most 1.7 percentage points, and perhaps by as little as one point. A doubling of the unemployment rate represents an increase from the mean unemployment rate to that experienced in 1980 (5.8%). It raises the percentage of women having a pre-marital birth before the age of 26 by 2–4 percentage points, depending on the

Table 5.8 *Impacts of welfare benefits, unemployment and education on the percentage of women having a pre-marital birth before their 22nd and 26th birthdays*

	Percentage of women having a pre-marital birth before:	
	age 22	age 26
(1) Reference woman[a]		
Models 3 and 4	4.8	5.7
Model 5:	4.7	5.6
(2) 10 per cent higher real welfare benefits		
Model 3	6.5	7.3
Model 4	5.7	6.8
(3) Doubling of unemployment rate		
Model 3	8.2	9.7
Model 5	6.7	8.0
(4) Left school before 16	8.7	10.3
(5) Neither in school nor working	10.1	11.9
(6) Neither in school nor working, left school before 16	18.0	21.0
(7) In school until 22nd birthday, working thereafter	1.2	2.2

[a] Reference woman: left school at sixteen, working thereafter, facing mean values of real welfare benefits and unemployment rate (2.9%) throughout.

model. Thus, even when statistically significant, the effects of welfare benefits and unemployment are not dramatic.

The strong effects of school-leaving are also illustrated in table 5.8. At the extreme, only about 2 per cent of women who remain in school until their 22nd birthday and then take a job would have a pre-marital birth before their 26th birthday. In sharp contrast, one-fifth of women who leave school before sixteen and who never have a job would have a pre-marital birth before 26.

The analysis suggests, therefore, that higher welfare benefits and higher unemployment moderately encourage single women to decide in favour of becoming a single mother.[22] It also indicates that increases in unemployment and real welfare benefits over this period have contributed to an upward trend in the risk of a pre-marital birth of about 10 per cent per annum.[23]

CONCLUSION: SELECTIVE INFLOWS TO LONE PARENTHOOD

The analysis has shown that a number of characteristics of a woman and her family affect the likelihood that she becomes a lone parent through marital dissolution. Put differently, they are factors which 'select' women into lone parenthood. To what extent do these selection factors influence the economic circumstances of one-parent families?

There is evidence that, in Britain, women who marry younger, particularly as teenagers, tend to come from the least advantaged family backgrounds and educational and occupational careers (Kiernan, 1986). Thus, if their marriage dissolves they would tend to be in poorer economic circumstances. The high risk of marital dissolution among women marrying young tends, therefore, to produce one-parent families in poor economic circumstances. Women who conceived their first child outside marriage also tend to come from poorer backgrounds, and it has been shown that such mothers are more likely to dissolve their marriage. It has also been found that, given their other characteristics, women with lower earning power at motherhood are more likely to dissolve their marriage. A tendency for selection factors to produce lone mothers in poor economic circumstances is reinforced if more participation in paid employment as a mother, which raises the risk of dissolution, is indicative of a couple's poor financial situation. On the other hand, women who have worked more since becoming a mother would tend, *ceteris paribus*, to have higher earning power. While mothers of three or more children, who would tend to be worse off financially, are more likely to have their marriage end than mothers of two, one-child families are also more likely to become one-parent families.

It is not possible, therefore, to say conclusively whether the woman's characteristics that affect her risk of marital dissolution select women for lone parenthood who are better or worse off than average. There are, however, a number of indications that it may select those in poorer economic circumstances, which would reinforce the economic plight of lone mothers.

The picture is clearer for entries to single motherhood. Women who have left education earlier are more likely to become single mothers, particularly if they are not employed. As women with lower educational attainments have lower earning power, and not being in a job may also be indicative of poor earning capacity, pre-marital births tend to occur among women least able to support themselves and their baby. All else being equal, the risk of a pre-marital birth peaks at the age of nineteen; thus these single mothers are quite young as well.

There is no evidence that higher welfare benefits encourage

marital dissolution. Although the effects are not large, higher welfare benefits do, however, increase the likelihood that a young woman has a birth outside marriage.

APPENDIX

Table 5.A1 Models of the pre-marital birth hazard

Variable	Model 6	Model 7	Model 8	Model 9	Model 10
Left school before 16	0.626 (0.183)	0.618 (0.181)	0.651 (0.183)	0.656 (0.183)	0.624 (0.183)
In full-time education	−2.178 (0.418)	−2.188 (0.416)	−2.120 (0.417)	−2.111 (0.417)	−2.120 (0.417)
In employment	−0.777 (0.236)	−0.781 (0.236)	−0.765 (0.236)	−0.762 (0.236)	−0.784 (0.236)
Duration (mos)	0.013 (0.009)	0.013 (0.009)	0.015 (0.009)	0.0156 (0.009)	0.018 (0.009)
Duration squared/100	−0.0181 (0.0078)	−0.0179 (0.0077)	−0.0195 (0.0078)	−0.0198 (0.0078)	−0.0210 (0.0079)
log (Welfare Benefit)	3.832 (2.382)	4.203 (1.146)			
log (Women's relative pay)	1.642 (0.779)	1.793 (0.544)	0.913 (0.673)	0.663 (0.758)	0.628 (0.747)
Year-1900	0.014 (0.051)		0.095 (0.023)	0.073 (0.038)	
log (Unemployment rate)				0.350 (0.480)	1.110 (0.293)
Intercept	−18.327 (3.726)	−18.821 (3.282)	−12.983 (1.901)	−11.924 (2.381)	−7.538 (0.706)
Chi-square (d.f.)	114.20 (8)	114.12 (7)	110.95 (7)	111.48 (8)	107.65 (7)
R	0.203	0.205	0.202	0.201	0.199

Note: Model 6 in table 5A.1 replaces the unemployment rate by a linear trend, but it is not statistically significant ($\chi_1^2 = 0.07$), while the coefficients of real welfare benefits and women's average pay relative to men's are positive and fairly well-determined. Model 7 drops the linear time trend, and the positive impacts of women's average relative pay and welfare benefits on pre-marital births are each statistically significant at the 0.001 level or less. The exclusion of a more complicated trend from model 6, analogous to equation (2) in footnote 2, is also acceptable: the hypothesis that $\gamma_1 = \gamma_2 = \gamma_3 = 0$ cannot be rejected: $\chi_3^2 = 2.30$. Models 8, 9 and 10 exclude real welfare benefits; model 8 also excludes the unemployment rate, and model 10 also excludes the trend variable.

Table 5A.2 *Means and standard deviations of explanatory variables for analysis of pre-marital births (calculated over months of exposure to risk of a pre-marital birth[a]*

	Mean	Standard deviation
Left school before 16	0.393	
In full-time education	0.260	
In employment	0.689	
In neither education nor job	0.051	
Duration (months)	43.286	36.371
log (Real welfare benefit)	2.746	0.112
log (Unemployment rate)	1.065	0.419
log (Women's relative pay)	−0.458	0.126
Year-1900 (yr)	71.489	5.173
Month in 1968 or later (D)	0.711	

[a] 156,975 months of exposure to risk of a pre-marital birth, contributed by 2,555 women. 'Raw mean monthly hazard' is 0.00095.

6

LONE PARENTS' EMPLOYMENT AND
WELFARE BENEFITS

It was noted earlier (Chapter 2), that, in contrast to other industrial-ised nations, the employment rate for lone mothers in Great Britain is lower than for married mothers, and it declined during the 1980s. About 60 per cent of lone parents receive welfare benefits from Supplementary Benefits (now called Income Support), which is the main system of support for poor people not in employment. A key policy issue is how to raise the low living standards of a large proportion of lone-parent families while reducing their dependence on means-tested state benefits. This chapter investigates the impact of variation in the level of benefits within the Supplementary Benefit system on employment, and compares this way of supporting lone mothers with other ways, such as benefits that are not means-tested, child care subsidies and higher maintenance payments from fathers.

In the first section of the chapter, a model of lone parents' decisions concerning whether to take a job or not is developed. This model allows us to examine how the benefit system, fixed costs of employment, children's requirements in terms of time and goods and the cost of child care outside the home affect employment decisions. The model is a static one which refers to decisions in a 'planning period', which we take to be the same as the period for assessment of welfare benefit payments. The number and ages of children play a key role in all of these influences on work decisions. The model is then estimated using micro-data on female lone parents from a series of ten *General Household Surveys* covering the period 1973–82.

THEORETICAL FRAMEWORK

A theoretical model provides a framework for conducting and interpreting the empirical analysis. In this particular instance, the theory also generates some testable hypotheses about behaviour that probably are not readily apparent without it.

Children create demands for purchased goods and services and for time, and these vary with the age of a child. It is assumed that

$$X_C = \alpha(N_1,...N_{15}), \text{ and} \qquad (6.1)$$

$$L_C = \beta(N_1,...N_{15}), \tag{6.2}$$

where N_j is the number of children aged j at the start of the period, and X_C and L_C are minimum goods and time requirements respectively made by children over the period. It is assumed that α_j and β_j, the marginal demands for goods and time made by a child aged j, are exogenous. While the possibility of substitution between time and goods in the care and rearing of children is ignored, this does not alter the main conclusions.

A novel feature of the model is that it assumes that time for child care and rearing can be purchased outside the household, although it is not a perfect substitute for the mother's time,

$$L_c = H + h(M), \; 0 < h'(M) < 1, \; h''(M) < 0,$$
$$h(0)=0, \; (h'(M)=dh/dM) \tag{6.3}$$

where H is the amount of the mother's time devoted to children, M is the amount of time purchased on the market, and $h(M)$ is a function converting purchased time into units equivalent to mother's time. It appears reasonable to suppose that as more child care time is purchased, additional purchased time becomes a poorer substitute for mother's time; thus the assumption that $h''(M) < 0$. Children require a minimum amount of mother's time, k, where k depends on the number of children of each age, analogous to (6.2). Thus, a weak inequality constraint is added to the model,

$$H \geqq k; \quad \text{also}, M \geqq 0. \tag{6.3a}$$

Mother's utility U depends on her leisure time, L, and purchased goods and services, X,

$$U = g(X,L). \tag{6.4}$$

The function $g(\cdot)$ is assumed to be concave. The quantities X and L could include expenditures of goods and time on children above the minimum requirements.

All of the variables refer to total amounts during the period for assessment of benefits (weekly). The mother faces a budget constraint during this period of

$$w(T-L-H) + Z + S = X_c + X + pM + \delta FC, \tag{6.5}$$

where T is the total amount of time available to the mother during the period; w is her net wage rate if she is in paid employment; Z is non-labour income; S is welfare benefit payments; p is the market price of time for child care; FC is fixed costs of employment, such as travel-to-work costs and fixed elements in child care costs, $\delta = 1$ if

$T-L-H > 0$ and zero otherwise; and the price of purchased goods and services is taken to be the numeraire.

The British benefit system

Supplementary Benefit (SB) and Family Income Supplement (FIS) were the main welfare benefits received by lone mothers in Great Britain during the period of analysis, 1973–82. The SB 'guarantee' level of benefit (that is, entitlement at zero income) varies with the age and number of children, and actual housing costs are also reimbursed by SB. The first £4 of earnings and all reasonable work expenses are disregarded in the benefit calculation but a 100 per cent tax rate is applied to higher earnings and other income.[1] The FIS scheme was designed to increase the income of poor people in employment. A lone mother must work at least 24 hours a week to be eligible. If she does, she receives a payment of $FIS = 0.5(C - w_g E - Z^*)$, where C is the FIS benefit scale (based on the number of children), w_g is her gross hourly wage, E is hours worked, and Z^* is her gross non-labour income other than Child Benefit or One Parent Benefit.[2]

Let B be the SB guarantee level and Z be her other non-labour income. Because non-labour income reduces SB payments pound for pound, it is clear that a woman with $Z > B$ will never receive SB. Initially, we shall assume that $B > Z$ ('eligible for SB'), as will be the case for most lone mothers. Chart 6.1 illustrates two budget constraints.[3]

Lone mothers with lower non-labour income and/or lower wages would be more likely to face a range of working hours in which they could receive FIS. Such a woman's budget constraint is shown in the top panel of chart 6.1. This woman's hourly pay is assumed to be equal to the lower quartile of the women's hourly wage distribution in 1979. The budget constraint for a woman wth median hourly pay is shown in the bottom panel. Clearly, she would be unlikely to receive FIS if she takes a job, and mothers earning even higher hourly pay would not be eligible for FIS (the third 'kink' in the budget constraint would disappear). Preferences would be represented by indifference curves, $g(X,L) = $ a constant, which slope upward from left to right.

In each case, it is clear from chart 6.1 that most lone mothers eligible for SB when out of employment choose either not to work, to work only a few hours, or to work 24 or more hours ('full-time' for short). Most lone mothers probably face fixed time costs of employment (for example, commuting) or fixed money costs not disregarded in the benefit calculation, and employers may only offer

Chart 6.1 *Lone mother's budget constraint*

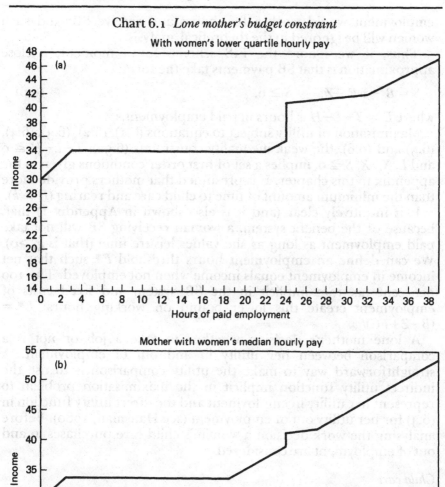

With women's lower quartile hourly pay

(a)

Hours of paid employment

Mother with women's median hourly pay

(b)

Hours of paid employment

jobs at a minimum number of hours. In these circumstances, it is likely that they would only have a choice between working 'full-time' or not at all, and SB benefits would only be received by lone mothers not in employment.[4] Only women with very low fixed costs of employment would work a few hours and receive SB, and such women will be ignored in the theoretical analysis.

Thus, if we ignore the FIS scheme for a moment, a close approximation is that SB payments take the form:

$$S = B - wE - Z, \qquad S \geq 0, \tag{6.6}$$

where $E = T - L - H$ is hours in paid employment.[5]

Maximisation of utility subject to equations (6.1), (6.2), (6.3), (6.4), (6.5) and (6.6), the weak inequality constraints (6.3a), $T - L - H \geq 0$ and $L, X_c, X, S \geq 0$, implies a set of first order conditions given in the appendix to this chapter. It is presumed that mothers provide more than the minimum amount of time to child care and rearing ($H > k$).

It is intuitively clear (and it is also shown in Appendix I) that, because of the benefit system, a woman receiving SB will not take paid employment as long as she values leisure time (that is $g_L > 0$). We can define an employment hours threshold E^* such that net income in employment equals income when not employed. The 100 per cent tax rate implicit in the SB system and fixed costs of employment create this lower bound on working hours: $E^* = (B - Z + FC)/w$.

A lone mother's decision whether to take a job or not is a comparison between her utility in and out of employment. A straightforward way to make the utility comparison is to use the indirect utility function implicit in the maximisation problem to represent her utility in employment and the direct utility function in (6.4) for her utility out of employment (see Hausman, 1980). Before analysing the work decision a woman's child care purchases in and out of employment are considered.

Child care

Equations (6.7a) and (6.7b) in the appendix to this chapter entail that when a lone mother is not in paid employment (and receiving SB)

$$p/h'(M) \geq \mu/\lambda \tag{6.8}$$

The variable λ can be interpreted as the marginal utility of income, while μ is the 'shadow price' associated with the constraint on mother's time.

When the mother is not in paid employment, μ/λ is her opportunity cost of time. As our focus is on women with low non-labour income ($Z < B$), her cost of time when not in a job is likely to be low, making it likely that it does not exceed p/h' (0). In this case she does not purchase child care.

When the mother participates in paid employment, the value of her time equals her market wage, and w replaces μ/λ in (6.8). Then, if her wage is high enough relative to the price of child care, she also purchases child care and (6.8) becomes $h'(M) = p/w$. Thus, the mother adjusts her purchases of child care, M, so that the marginal contribution of an extra hour of M equals the ratio of the price of child care to the value of the mother's time.

While it is clear that some mothers obtain child care from a child's grandparent or neighbours without making a monetary payment, there is often some other exchange 'in-kind' for the child care, or the availability of such care could produce constraints on the mother's allocation of time. For simplicity, these costs are expressed as a monetary price in the model. The 'price' is likely to be much smaller for such women.

The employment decision

If lone mothers not in employment do not purchase child care, then, from (6.3), $L_c = H$. Their income when not employed is B. Thus, their utility is, from (6.4), $U^o = g(B-X_c,T-L_c)$. When employed, their utility is given by the indirect utility function $U^w = V(w,p,Z-FC-X_c,L_c)$. A lone mother works if $U^w > U^o$, or

$$V(w,p,Z-FC-X_c,L_c) > g(B-X_c,T-L_c). \tag{6.9}$$

Wages clearly do not affect utility when the mother does not have a job, while the properties of the indirect utility function entail that $\partial V/\partial w > 0$. Fixed costs of employment also only affect women in jobs, and $\partial V/\partial FC < 0$. Thus a higher wage offer and a lower fixed cost of employment make it more likely that a lone mother takes a job.

Similarly, if, as argued above, women do not purchase child care when they are not in a job, then its price does not affect their utility when out of employment, while $\partial V/\partial p < 0$. A higher price of child care would, therefore, reduce the probability of taking a job. The conclusion would be the same if purchases of child care are relatively small when not employed. Then the size of $\partial U^w/\partial p$ exceeds that of $\partial U^o/\partial p$, and the likelihood that a lone mother takes a job is higher at a lower p. Thus, child care subsidies would tend to raise the probability that a lone mother takes a job.

Welfare benefits and the employment decision

Continuing the focus on women eligible for SB ($B > Z$), the effect of a small change in benefits is considered. As $U^o = g(B-X_c,T-L_c)$, $\partial U^o/\partial B > 0$, while $\partial V/\partial B = 0$, because women do not simultaneously

work and receive SB benefits. Thus, from (6.9), a higher SB
guarantee reduces the probability that a lone mother takes a job.

As $\partial V/\partial Z > 0$, while $\partial U^o/\partial Z = 0$ because of the 100 per cent tax
rate in the SB system, higher income from sources other than
employment or benefits (for example, child maintenance from the
father) increases the likelihood that the lone mother takes a job.[6] In
other words, higher non-labour income does not affect a mother's
income when she is not employed, because the benefit system taxes it
away pound for pound, but it does increase her income when she
has a job. As a consequence, mothers with higher non-labour
income are more likely to take employment.

Among women who would be eligible for FIS if they take a job,
the FIS scale, C, is a parameter of $V(\cdot)$. As $\partial U^o/\partial C = 0$ and $\partial V/\partial C > 0$
for these women, higher C raises the probability of taking a job. The
FIS represents a 'notch' subsidy to working more than 24 hours.[7]

Now consider the case of a lone mother whose non-labour income
exceeds her SB benefit guarantee (that is $Z > B$). If she does not
work and does not purchase child care, her utility is $U^o =
g(Z-X_c, T-L_c)$, and $\partial U^o/\partial Z > 0$. Although $\partial V/\partial Z > 0$ as well, because
total income is higher when there are earnings (goods are relatively
abundant) the marginal utility of income is lower when in employ-
ment than when not in a job, so that $\partial U^o/\partial Z > \partial U^w/\partial Z$. Thus, higher
non-labour income reduces the probability of taking a job among
women not affected by the benefit system.

This contrasts with the positive effect of Z on the probability of
working among women eligible for SB when out of employment.
The contrast provides one test of the impact of the benefit system on
work decisions: the effect of non-labour income should differ in
sign between women with $B > Z$ and women with $Z > B$. In addition,
the SB guarantee (B) should not affect the probability of taking a job
among women with $Z > B$.

Effects of children

The effect of having a child aged j on the probability of taking a job
is complex because the child affects both time and goods
requirements L_c and X_c. Larger goods requirements reduce utility in
and out of employment, but as goods are relatively scarce when not
in a job, $\partial U^o/\partial X_c$ is larger in absolute value than $\partial U^w/\partial X_c$, so that, all
else being equal, higher X_c raises the probability of working. Higher
child care time requirements also reduce utility in and out of
employment. Time is, however, relatively scarce when a woman is in
a job, making it likely that $\partial U^o/\partial L_c$ is smaller in absolute value than
$\partial U^w/\partial L_c$. Thus, higher L_c tends to reduce the probability of taking a
job, all else being equal.

Young children tend to have larger time requirements and older children larger goods requirements. Younger children would tend, therefore, to reduce the probability of taking a job, and older children would tend to raise it. A larger number of children would increase both X_c and L_c, thereby having an ambiguous effect on the probability of their mother working, which would depend on their age composition.

As noted earlier the SB guarantee (B) primarily varies with the age and the number of children. It is plausible that fixed costs of employment also vary with the age and the number of children. For instance organising child care and delivering the children to their respective care places and schools may create large fixed costs of employment. Cogan (1981) and Hausman (1980) both find indirect evidence from American data that fixed costs of employment increase with the number of pre-school children. In the empirical analysis below, fixed costs and the influences of L_c and X_c are proxied by a set of dichotomous variables for the age of the youngest child and the number of other children.

The associations of benefit entitlement, child care time and goods requirements and fixed costs of employment with the number and ages of children can make it difficult to identify the effect of benefits from a single cross-section. Pooling data from different benefit periods introduces exogenous change in benefit entitlement arising from annual changes in the real value of the SB guarantee and occasional changes in the rules defining the allocation of benefit.[8] During our study period, the real value of the SB guarantee (B) increased by about 7 per cent on average (excluding housing cost entitlements), and in late 1980 the guarantee formula's relative weights for children of different ages changed.

ESTIMATION OF THE MODEL

The data used in the estimation are from the *General Household Survey* (GHS). It is a yearly random sample of households in Great Britain carried out by the Office of Population Censuses and Surveys (see OPCS, 1981). More specifically, a pooled cross-section of ten *General Household Surveys*, covering the period 1973–82, constructed by Bamford and Dale (1988), is used. The advantages of a time series of cross-sections for identifying benefit effects have been discussed, and the pooled sample also is much larger than could be obtained from any single cross-section. The GHS data does not, however, provide reliable information about the amount of SB and FIS benefits received, nor about housing costs, which are an important element in benefit entitlement, and this particular compilation of ten GHS's does not provide information on hours worked. The *Family Expenditure Survey* is better in all of these respects, but a number of these would also have to be pooled as in Walker (1990), to obtain a large enough sample and improve the identification of benefit effects.

A lone mother is defined as a woman whose youngest child is aged less than sixteen or if the youngest child is still in full-time education, aged eighteen or less. The analysis is restricted to female-headed households containing only the mother and dependent children.[9] Accounting for missing information, the sample consists of 2,062 women, of whom 966 were employed. Among the workers, 54 per cent worked full time, where full-time employment refers to working more than 30 hours per week, or in the case of teachers more than 25 hours per week.

Thus, while less important than among married mothers in employment, 70 per cent of whom worked part-time during this period, part-time employment is important among lone mothers. As noted earlier, the data do not provide working hours, but Walker's (1990) analysis shows a fairly uniform distribution of hours among lone mothers working part-time, and my own analysis of the 249 lone mothers in the *Women and Employment Survey* comes to a similar conclusion. In particular, there is no clustering of women around 2–3 hours per week (the first kink in the budget constraint), nor at 24 hours, when they could receive FIS. In the context of the theoretical model, this suggests that both measurement error in hours and heterogeneity in preferences and fixed costs play a role in the observed distribution of hours (see Moffitt, 1986).

In the data, we cannot determine whether lone mothers receive SB or not. Administrative statistics (*Social Security Statistics*, various years) indicate that during the sample period 14 per cent of lone mothers receiving SB reported some earnings. The theoretical model predicts that only mothers who face low fixed costs of employment would work while receiving SB, and a 1982 study of lone parents receiving SB and working part-time indeed showed that 78 per cent had no child care costs and 53 per cent incurred no travel-to-work costs (Weale *et al.*, 1984). Thus, 14 per cent of lone mothers receiving SB being in part-time employment is not inconsistent with the predictions of the model when there is a distribution of fixed costs of employment in the population. Furthermore, in a dynamic context, lone mothers who expect to receive SB for only a short time may not want to give up their part-time jobs. The distribution of fixed costs of employment and these dynamic motives among lone mothers are reflected in the distribution of the stochastic component in the empirical analysis.

The SB guarantee level (B) for each woman is calculated from the benefit schedules prevailing in the month that the woman was interviewed. It is expressed in 1982 pounds per week (as are all other amounts). A family's SB entitlement also includes actual expenditures on rent and rates (property taxes). There is not, however, sufficient information in the data to account for these. If we could observe housing costs, that would also produce variation in benefit entitlements, which, as in Walker (1990), would help identify benefit effects if, as is likely in Britain, housing costs are exogenous.

Non-labour income from private sources $(Z*)$ includes income from pensions, rent from property, interest payments and maintenance payments. In addition, lone mothers receive Child Benefit and One Parent Benefit (CB).

Non-labour income from private sources plus Child Benefit and One Parent Benefit is the non-labour income variable, $Y*=Z*+CB$, that is compared with the SB guarantee to determine whether a woman would be eligible for SB or not when not in a job. Because we do not know her rent (or mortgage payment), this was excluded from her SB entitlement even though SB would cover housing costs. Thus, our comparison of her estimated SB guarantee (B) with total non-labour income $(Y*)$ can misclassify some women who are eligible for SB as ineligible, but all who are classified as eligible should be so, subject to any reporting errors in non-labour income from private sources. The eligible group consists of 1,785 women (47 per cent of whom are employed) while the not eligible group consists of 277 women (49 per cent employed).

In the data, three-fourths of employed lone mothers deemed to be eligible for SB if they did not work have other non-labour income $(Y*)$ plus weekly earnings in excess of the SB guarantee. Among the remaining quarter, some may be receiving SB and have part-time earnings, and others may not claim SB because FIS brings their income above the SB guarantee, or because of stigma, ignorance, or earnings that are only low temporarily.[10]

The appropriate non-labour income and net wage variables in the model of work decisions depend on whether a woman is eligible for FIS or not if she takes a job. Income and national insurance (social security contribution) thresholds are such that women receiving FIS would also pay national insurance contributions and income tax at the basic tax rate. It is clear from chart 6.1 that for women with a broad range of hours in which they could receive FIS, the main work choice is whether to receive SB and not take a job, or take a job and receive FIS. Denoting the marginal tax rate (including national insurance) as t and personal tax allowances as A, their net wage in a job is $(1-0.5-t)w_g$ and their 'virtual non-labour income' (that is, where the FIS segment of the budget constraint would intersect the vertical axis if extended) is $Y_1 - FC$, where $Y_1 = 0.5C + tA + CB + (1-0.5-t)Z^*$, and where CB is Child Benefit (or Family Allowance) plus One Parent Benefit.[11]

The maximum hours a woman can work and receive FIS is denoted as $MHR = (C-Z^*)/w_g$. Thus, women with low values of non-labour income from private sources (Z^*), and/or low gross wages, will have higher values of MHR and a broader range of hours in which they could receive FIS. They would therefore, be more likely to be receiving FIS if they take a job.

We distinguish two types of women: (1) those who would receive FIS when they take a job and (2) those who would not. Women in the latter group will have low values of MHR, and the tax thresholds and 'breakeven working hours' for SB are such that these women would pay national insurance contributions and tax at the basic tax rate when they take a job. Their budget constraint would look like the bottom panel of chart 6.1 without the small FIS kink, where their net wage when employed is $w_g(1-t)$ and their virtual non-labour income is $Y_0 - FC$, where $Y_0 = tA + CB + (1-t)Z^*$. Thus, in (6.9) above, w is replaced by the appropriate net wage, $w_g(1-0.5-t)$ or $w_g(1-t)$, and Z is replaced by Y_0 or Y_1.

Into which of these two groups a woman would fall depends on her preferences as well as her gross wage and Z^*. But, as an approximation, MHR is calculated for each woman and used to classify her into one of the groups. Once classified, she receives the appropriate values for the net wage and virtual non-labour income. Note that this assignment is based solely on exogenous variables; although it produces errors in variables problems, these already exist (for example, because of the use of a predicted wage). In order to explore the sensitivity of the estimates to different classifications, two critical values for MHR are considered. One corresponds to classifying the top 30 per cent of the distribution of MHR to the group of women who would receive FIS if they took a job, and the other puts the top 50 per cent of the distribution into this group. The latter critical value is clearly too low, but it is used only to explore the sensitivity of the parameter estimates to the classification.

Tax allowances (A), including child tax allowances when they were in force, FIS scale amounts (C), Child and One Parent Benefit (CB) and tax rates (t) were assigned to each woman on the basis of the rules in force in the particular month that she was observed. Non-labour income from private sources is likely to primarily represent maintenance payments for most women. As these are generally paid net of (husband's) tax when court-ordered or are free from tax when voluntary, Z^* and $(1-t)Z^*$ are assumed to be identical.

A woman's gross wage is measured as the prediction from a wage offer equation estimated from lone mothers observed in full-time employment during 1973–82, allowing for possible sample selection bias (Heckman, 1979). The estimation is restricted to women in full-time employment because hours are not included in the data. The prediction refers to weekly earnings, and the estimated earnings equation is given in table 6A.1 at the end of this chapter.

The possibility that lone mothers may find it more difficult to find a job when unemployment is higher is also considered. The regional-level total unemployment rate in the month that the woman is observed is included as an explanatory variable. In addition, a set of dichotomous variables indicating the region in which the woman resides are included (eleven regions). The excluded category is residing in Greater London. It is hoped that these variables capture regional differences in costs of living.

It is well known that women's labour force participation rates may vary with age because of differences between cohorts or evolutionary changes over the life cycle (for example, see Heckman and MaCurdy, 1980). Therefore, the woman's age, measured in years, along with its square, are included in the model.

Two linear functions are specified to approximate the difference in utilities in and out of employment for the 'eligible' ($Y^*<B$) and 'non-eligible' ($Y^*>B$) mothers. Variation in preferences and in fixed costs of employment is incorporated by making the difference in utilities a random variable that follows a logistic distribution. The parameters of the models are estimated by maximum likelihood (see Maddala, 1983). Descriptive statistics for all variables are given in table 6A.2.

PARAMETER ESTIMATES

Table 6.1 reports the parameter estimates for the logit employment models. Column 1 shows the results for all lone mothers. In this model, two interactions are included. A dichotomous variable (D) was created which takes on a value of one if the woman is *not* eligible for SB and zero if she is eligible, This variable was interacted with virtual non-labour income (that is, $D \cdot Y_i$) and the SB guarantee ($D \cdot B$). Both interactions are statistically significant at conventional levels,

Table 6.1 *Logit estimates of the probability of being in employment, female lone parents, Great Britain, 1973–82*

Variable	(1) All women	(2) Eligible	(3) Not eligible
Age[a]	0.0746 (1.46)	0.0821 (1.48)	−0.0724 (0.46)
Age^2	−0.00120 (1.83)	−0.00128 (1.80)	0.000391 (0.19)
Youngest child:			
Age < 1	−2.918 (5.83)	−2.830 (5.46) ⎫	−2.296[b] (4.01)
Age 1–2	−1.793 (8.56)	−1.805 (7.86) ⎭	
Age 3–4	−1.383 (7.51)	−1.322 (6.54)	−1.847 (3.76)
Age 11–15	−0.171 (0.97)	−0.218 (1.15)	0.568 (1.12)
Age 16–18	−0.181 (0.52)	−0.352 (0.92)	0.949 (1.04)
Number of other children:			
One	0.145 (0.73)	−0.073 (0.34)	1.164 (1.98)
Two	−0.088 (0.25)	−0.205 (0.54)	−0.766 (0.74)
≥ Three	0.273 (0.46)	−0.136 (0.22)	1.155 (0.62)
Unemployment rate	−0.0874 (4.57)	−0.0943 (4.58)	−0.0550 (0.99)
Net earnings	0.0820 (15.55)	0.0881 (15.20)	0.0531 (3.52)
Virtual non-labour income	0.0506 (8.36)	0.0560 (8.56)	−0.0123 (2.23)
SB guarantee level	−0.0581 (3.43)	−0.0491 (2.77)	−0.0584 (1.17)
Not eligible• non-labour income	−0.0635 (7.57)	—	—
Not eligible• SB guarantee level	0.0666 (5.03)	—	—
Region:			
North	1.845 (6.33)	1.930 (6.17)	1.295 (1.54)
Yorkshire/Humberside	1.199 (5.03)	1.189 (4.58)	1.042 (1.56)
North West	1.230 (5.52)	1.261 (5.22)	0.878 (1.41)
East Midlands	0.934 (3.61)	0.719 (2.56)	2.169 (2.80)

Table 6.1 (*cont.*)

Variable	(1) All women	(2) Eligible	(3) Not eligible
Region:			
West Midlands	0.889 (3.76)	0.914 (3.58)	0.763 (1.11)
East Anglia	0.013 (0.04)	−0.092 (0.27)	0.636 (0.88)
South East	1.055 (5.40)	1.067 (4.96)	1.040 (2.04)
South West	0.802 (3.27)	0.683 (2.54)	1.423 (2.12)
Wales	0.702 (2.35)	0.625 (1.89)	1.287 (1.67)
Scotland	1.024 (4.37)	1.036 (4.09)	0.871 (1.33)
Constant	−3.943 (3.65)	−4.749 (4.10)	2.064 (0.62)
−2.ln$L$	2,146.6	1,801.6	315.8
N	2,062	1,785	277
$\bar{P}$	0.469	0.465	0.491

[a] The reference categories for the binary variables are youngest child age 5–10; no other dependent children; and residing in Greater London.
 Asymptotic t-ratios in parentheses.
[b] Youngest child less than age three.

and they confirm the theoretical prediction that non-labour income has a positive effect (0.051) on the probability of employment for eligible mothers and a negative effect (−0.013) for the non-eligible. In addition, benefit entitlement has a negative effect (−0.058) in the sample of eligible mothers, but it is virtually zero in the non-eligible sample (0.009).

The other two columns in table 6.1 allow all coefficients to differ between the two groups of mothers. A likelihood ratio test of the hypothesis that the only parameters that differ between groups are those for SB guarantee and non-labour income (as in column 1) cannot reject it at significance levels of 0.05 or less ($\chi^2_{23} = 31.4$).

In both specifications, a higher SB guarantee lowers the probability of employment among mothers eligible for SB. In the specification in which all parameters can differ, the SB variable also has a negative coefficient for non-eligible mothers, but it is not significantly different from zero at conventional significance levels. As

noted earlier, some eligible mothers have probably been misclassi-
fied as ineligible, and this, along with the relatively small sample of
non-eligible mothers, probably accounts for the negative coefficient
with a high standard error associated with the SB guarantee. The
results from the statistically acceptable specification in column 1
certainly suggest that the SB guarantee does not affect the probability of employment among women who are not eligible for SB
because of high levels of non-labour income.

Both specifications also indicate, as predicted by the theoretical
model, that higher non-labour income *raises* the probability of
employment among lone mothers who are eligible for SB, because
of the 100 per cent tax rate in the SB system. In line with standard
labour supply models (with convex budget constraints), an increase
in non-labour income *lowers* the probability of employment among
lone mothers who are not eligible for SB.

As predicted, lone mothers who can command a higher wage have
a much higher probability of being in employment after other
relevant factors are held constant. It is also not surprising that lone
mothers in high unemployment environments have much lower
probabilities of being in employment.[12] Moffitt (1983) also found
that a higher unemployment rate substantially reduced lone
mothers' labour supply. The size of the unemployment effect does,
however, appear to be implausibly large, and I return to this issue
below. Estimates of the elasticities of the probability of employment
with respect to the variables of primary interest are shown in table
6.2.

The set of regional dummy variables are statistically significant (as
a block) in both equations. With the exception of East Anglia, the
coefficient signs are all positive, indicating that lone mothers residing outside Greater London have higher employment probabilities
when other factors, including wage and unemployment rates, are
held constant. This may reflect the interaction of regional differences in housing costs with benefit entitlements. Mothers in London
have higher SB entitlements because of higher housing costs; thus,
all else being equal, they are less likely to find it beneficial to take a
job. Fixed costs of employment, particularly commuting costs, are
also likely to be higher in London, thereby discouraging employment.

In line with most other studies of women's labour supply, the
parameters indicate that lone mothers with younger children have
much lower employment probabilities. This effect is strong for
children of pre-school age (that is, less than age five), but it appears
to 'level off' after the age of five.[13].

Table 6.2 *Elasticities of the probability of employment*

With respect to: Variable	(1) All women	Sample (2) Eligible	(3) Not eligible
Unemployment rate	−0.295	−0.325	−0.164[a]
Net earnings	1.694	1.793	1.196
Eligible:			
Virtual non-labour income	1.307	1.297	n/a
SB guarantee level	−1.230	−1.297	n/a
Not eligible:			
Virtual non-labour income	−0.336	n/a	−0.524
SB guarantee level	0.190[a]	n/a	−1.190[a]

Note: Calculated at the respective sample means.
[a] Not significantly different from zero at levels below 0.20.

After the age of the youngest child, SB guarantee and other variables are held constant, the probability of employment is not affected by the number of other children among lone mothers eligible for SB.[14] This suggests that the increase in 'goods requirements' (X_c) with the number of children is offset by the increase in time requirements (L_c). There is, however, some indication that having more than one child *increases* the probability of employment among mothers not eligible for benefit.

Finally the probability of employment varies with the age of the mother.[15] Very similar estimates of all the other parameters were obtained when a set of dichotomous variables for five-year age groups replaced age and age squared.

Robustness and comparability of results

When the definitions of non-labour income and net wages ignore taxes and FIS, results that are generally similar to the findings from the models in table 6.1 are obtained (see table 6A.3). Most importantly, the impact of the SB guarantee on the probability of employment among women eligible for SB is only slightly smaller than in the model with taxes and FIS.

Furthermore, the estimate of the SB effect in table 6.1 is almost identical to Walker's (1990) estimate, obtained from different data, a series of *Family Expenditure Surveys* from 1979–84. The *Family Expenditure Survey* also provides information on housing costs, which helps identify the SB effect. In order to compare the two estimates, Walker's estimates are adjusted for the different price basis (1979) and the difference in coefficients between logit and probit models.[16] After these adjustments, his coefficient is −0.0582, compared with −0.0581 in the first column of table 6.1. While our estimate varies with different specifications of unemployment, regional and year dummy variables within the model with taxes and FIS, its range is fairly small. It is largest when the unemployment rate is excluded from the model (−0.078), and smallest in a model with both regional and year dummies and the unemployment rate (−0.056).[17]

It should be stressed that the identification of the effect of SB in our analysis crucially depends on the time series variation in the SB guarantee level. The 'true' number of degrees of freedom in identifying this effect is, therefore, far smaller than suggested by the size of the sample. Evidence that the time series variation in the SB guarantee is contributing information about the size of its effect is provided by declines in the size of coefficient of the SB guarantee and its t-value in a specification that includes year-by-year dummy variables, shown in table 6A.4. In that specification the coefficient of the SB guarantee and its t-value fall in size from −0.0581 and 3.43 to −0.0556 and 3.19 (column 1 model); for eligible women only, these fall from −0.0491 and 2.77 to −0.0469 and 2.56.

The welfare benefits' elasticity of −1.23 in table 6.2 may appear large relative to labour supply elasticity estimates reported in the American welfare benefits' literature (Blank, 1985, Hausman, 1980, Moffitt, 1983), but the latter are usually hours-of-work elasticities, while that in table 6.2 is the elasticity of employment participation. It is well known that the participation elasticity can differ substantially from the hours elasticity, particularly if there are large fixed costs of employment, and Mroz's (1987) thorough study of the sensitivity of a model of married women's hours of work to different economic and statistical assumptions concludes that 'the hours of work decisions made when the woman is in the labor force appear quite distinct from her labor force participation decision' (p.790). The non-convex budget constraints faced by lone parents make it likely that this conclusion also applies to lone parents' work decisions.

Moffitt (1983) reports an elasticity of welfare participation with respect to the AFDC (American Aid to Families with Dependent Children) guarantee of 0.6 (p.1032). We have argued that, because of the 100 per cent benefit reduction rate, welfare participation in Britain (that is, receipt of SB) is virtually the complement of employment participation, but this is not the case for AFDC in the years that Moffitt (1983) and Blank (1985) study: 25 and 42 per cent of AFDC recipients are employed in their respective samples. In their models, the elasticity of welfare participation is larger when the hours worked on welfare are smaller.[18] Thus, we would expect a larger elasticity of welfare participation with respect to the guarantee in the British case, because very few SB recipients work, and those who do work very few hours.

If we use Moffitt's (1983) parameter estimates, but calculate the elasticity of welfare participation with respect to the AFDC guarantee on the assumption that welfare recipients do not work, then the elasticity rises to unity. Similarly, if we use Blank's (1985) parameter estimates under this assumption, the welfare participation elasticity is about 1.6. The corresponding elasticities of *not* receiving AFDC with respect to the guarantee are −0.6 for Moffitt's and −1.24 for Blank's parameter estimates.

The estimate of the elasticity of employment participation with respect to the SB guarantee in table 6.2 is approximately the elasticity of *not* receiving SB. Thus, it is comparable to these last estimates, and its size is similar to the estimate derived from Blank's parameter estimates.

Hausman's (1980) analysis specifically examines the employment participation decision, but his paper does not provide sufficient information to calculate the elasticity of participation from his parameter estimates. A crude estimate of the elasticity of employment participation with respect to the guarantee can, however, be made from his simulations (in his table 4). The log change in the employment probability relative to the log change in the guarantee when moving from AFDC (tax rate = 0.67) to a high guarantee (tax rate = 0.6) at a wage of \$2 suggests an elasticity of about −1.3. A similar calculation using Blank's (1985, table 7) simulations of the probability of not working (for reference woman 1 in Mississippi and Wisconsin), suggests an elasticity of employment participation with respect to the AFDC guarantee of about −1.7. These elasticity estimates are in line with our estimate in table 6.2.

Returning to the comparisons of models with and without taxes and FIS, there are, however, a few differences in the coefficients for the sample of eligible mothers that are worth pointing out. Although not very precisely estimated, the coefficients of the number of other dependent children in the model without FIS and taxes suggest that the probability of employment may increase with the number of children. At the same time, the coefficient of non-labour income for eligible mothers (0.0187) is much smaller than in table 6.1. Recall that women deemed eligible for FIS if they take a job have the FIS entitlement included in their virtual non-labour income. Because FIS is directly related to the number of children, these results suggest that the positive effect of the number of children in a model that does not take FIS into account may be related to the FIS scheme.

The estimate of the impact of virtual non-labour income for eligible mothers in table 6.1 is very close to Walker's (1990) estimate, although he separates FIS entitlement from other non-labour income. After the adjustments described earlier, his estimate of the impact of non-labour income is 0.049, compared with our 0.0506. His estimate of the impact of FIS (and housing benefit) at 24 hours of work is only 0.013.[19]

One important way that our estimates differ from Walker's is in the measured impact of unemployment. Our estimate of the discouraging impact of unemployment is much larger (−0.088 as against −0.011). Furthermore, the estimated impact of the unemployment rate is even higher in the model not taking taxes and FIS into account (−0.121). As the size of the effect of unemployment is suspect, some different models were estimated. When the regional dummies are excluded, the unemployment coefficient falls to −0.045, but it is still statistically significant (t=2.83). When both regional and year dummies are included in the model it falls to −0.034, and, not surprisingly, it is no longer significant (t=0.5; see table 6A.4). But fortunately the coefficients of the other variables change very little across these specifications.[20]

The other way in which the estimates here differ from Walker's is in the estimated effect of a woman's potential earnings. The estimate in table 6.1 is much larger. This may reflect an ability to predict earnings better, because of access to information on a woman's most recent occupation. Furthermore, the estimate here is based on the predicted net marginal wage in a full-time job, while Walker uses the predicted gross wage. The impact of wages is slightly lower in the model ignoring taxes and FIS (see table 6A.3).

The estimates in table 6.1 assign an FIS entitlement to the top 30 per cent of the distribution of MHR (maximum hours for receipt of FIS). When women with an MHR in the top 50 per cent of the distribution are assumed to receive FIS if they take a job, the coefficients of the SB guarantee, non-labour income, potential wages and unemployment are smaller in absolute value than in table 6.1, but the conclusions are similar.

The data used in the estimation cover the period 1973–82. In late 1980, a tapered disregard of earnings between £4 and £20 per week was introduced. Thus, women with earnings in this range could receive SB and keep half of their marginal earnings. Whether this change had any significant effect on work incentives depends on the critical value of the benefit taper identified by Hanoch and Honig

(1978). They show that for each woman there is a critical benefit taper such that for values above it the tapered segment of the budget constraint is not effective, so that she would only work *and* receive SB on the first section of the budget constraint, where her earnings are less than or equal to the initial disregard (£4 in our case).[21] Thus, if this critical taper is less than 0.5 for most lone mothers, then introducing the tapered disregard described above would not have affected the decision whether to take a job or not for most lone mothers. As it was already noted that they are unlikely to take a job with earnings less than £4 per week, the choice would remain whether to take a job or receive SB.

This change in the benefit system suggests a potential structural break between the 1973–80 and 1981–2 periods. To explore this possibility the sample of lone mothers eligible for SB was divided into these two periods. The hypothesis that the parameters associated with net earnings, SB guarantee, virtual non-labour income and the constant are the same in the two periods cannot be rejected by a likelihood ratio test at significance levels of 0.05 or below ($\chi_4^2 = 9.44$ for the model in column 2 of table 6.1).[22] Thus, while there may be many reasons for this result, it is consistent with the introduction of the tapered disregard having had little effect on lone mothers' employment decisions, and with the study of Weale *et al.* (1984), which found no evidence that the tapered disregard encouraged more lone parents to work part-time. Moffitt's (1983) and Hausman's (1980) analyses also suggest very small changes in the probability of employment arising from changes in the implicit tax rate in the welfare benefit system, and this appears to be the general consensus (see Moffitt and Rangarajan, 1989). They also find that the guarantee level has a strong effect on lone mothers' employment, and this is confirmed for Britain in this study, and by Walker's (1990) recent study.

CONCLUSION

The parameter estimates shown in table 6.1 confirm the hypotheses about the effects of the benefit system on the employment behaviour of lone mothers suggested by the theoretical model. In particular, a higher SB guarantee reduces the probability of employment among lone mothers whose SB guarantee exceeds their non-labour income (the 'eligible' group). As expected, the SB guarantee has no significant effect on this probability among mothers whose non-labour income exceeds their SB guarantee (the 'ineligible' group). Furthermore, as predicted, higher non-labour income increases the likelihood of working among lone mothers eligible for SB, but among those women not eligible, higher non-labour income reduces the probability of working.

Policies that raise a lone mother's income while in employment, such as larger One Parent Benefit, better enforcement of father's maintenance, or child care subsidies, could both improve the low living standards experienced by a large proportion of one-parent families while also reducing their dependence on welfare benefits. The quantitative impact of such policies on the proportion of lone mothers in employment are explored in Chapter 9.

It also appears that the rise in the general level of unemployment played a large part in the fall in the percentage of British lone mothers in employment during the past decade. Between 1978–80 and 1984–6, the average unemployment rate rose about 6 percentage points. According to our model, this would reduce the percentage of lone mothers working by about 9 percentage points. The percentage of lone mothers employed actually fell 6 percentage points between these two sets of years. The rise in the real value of the SB guarantee over that period would have also reduced this percentage, while increases in women's real wages and in real non-labour income would have worked in the opposite direction. The estimate of the impact of unemployment in table 6.1 is probably too large. When the regional dummy variables are omitted, a 6 percentage point rise in the unemployment rate reduces the per cent of lone mothers in jobs by a more plausible 4 percentage points. Despite being unable to estimate the impact of unemployment very precisely, it still appears that the rise in unemployment is a major reason for the fall in the proportion of lone mothers in a job between the late 1970s and the mid-1980s, and this fall should have been partially reversed as labour market conditions have improved in the past three years.

APPENDIX

FIRST ORDER CONDITIONS (EQUATION 6.7)

The first order conditions are:

$$\pi = \lambda w + \mu - \mu_H - (\lambda + \mu_s)\gamma w, \tag{6.7a}$$

$$\pi h'(M) = \lambda p - \mu_M, \tag{6.7b}$$

$$g_L = \lambda w + \mu - (\lambda + \mu_s)\gamma w, \tag{6.7c}$$

$$g_X = \lambda, \tag{6.7d}$$

$$\mu(T-L-H) = 0, \text{ where } \mu = 0 \text{ when } T > L+H$$
$$\text{and } \mu > 0 \text{ when } T = L+H, \tag{6.7e}$$

$$\mu_H[H-k] = 0 \text{ where } u_H = 0 \text{ when } H > k \text{ and } \mu_H > 0$$
$$\text{when } H = k, \tag{6.7f}$$

$$\mu_M M = 0 \text{ where } \mu_M = 0 \text{ when } M > 0 \text{ and } \mu_M > 0 \text{ when } M = 0, \tag{6.7g}$$

$$\lambda[w(T-L-H) + Z - X_c - X - pM - \delta FC] = 0, \text{ where } \lambda > 0, \tag{6.7h}$$

$$\pi[H + h(M) - L_C], \text{ where } \pi > 0. \tag{6.7i}$$

$$\pi_s S = 0 \text{ where } \mu_s = 0 \text{ when } S > 0 \text{ and } \mu_s > 0 \text{ when } S = 0. \tag{6.7j}$$

Assume that $Z < B$ and $H > k$. If $S > 0$, then, from (6.7j), $\mu_s = 0$, and, from (6.7a) and (6.7c), $g_L = \pi = \lambda(1-\gamma)w + \mu$. In the British system, $\gamma = 1$, which implies that $g_L = \pi = \mu$. Since $g_L > 0$ and $\pi > 0$, μ must be greater than zero, and this entails that $E = T-L-H=0$ (from [6.7e]).

Table 6A.1 *Parameter estimates of full-time earnings equations, female lone parents, Great Britain,* 1973–82

Variable	Coefficient (t-ratio)	Mean (SD)
Education:[a]		
CSEs other	−0.0197 (0.39)	0.177
O-level(s)	−0.0342 (0.63)	0.161
A-level(s)	0.0535 (0.59)	0.036
Higher	0.161 (2.36)	0.172
Potential experience	0.00756 (0.80)	20.41 (8.39)
Potential experience^2/1000	−0.1095 (0.54)	0.48661 (0.3838)
Number of children:		
< Age 5	−0.0873 (1.11)	0.152 (0.41)
Age 6–10	−0.0498 (1.27)	0.578 (0.74)
Age 11–18	0.0231 (0.77)	0.800 (0.86)
Occupation class:		
Professional/managerial	0.248 (2.76)	0.082
Intermediate non-manual	0.213 (2.92)	0.225
Skilled manual	0.122 (1.64)	0.055
Clerical	0.0636 (1.26)	0.397
Unskilled manual	0.364 (2.74)	0.018
Unemployment rate	−0.0120 (0.62)	6.081 (3.17)
Region:		
North	−0.331 (2.64)	0.036
Yorkshire/Humberside	−0.169 (2.10)	0.077
North West	−0.238 (2.75)	0.127
East Midlands	−0.169 (2.13)	0.054
West Midlands	−0.161 (2.04)	0.082
East Anglia	0.134 (1.09)	0.020

Table 6A.1 (*cont.*)

Variable	Coefficient (*t*-ratio)	Mean (SD)
Region:		
South East	−0.160	0.186
	(3.10)	
South West	−0.146	0.075
	(1.82)	
Wales	−0.079	0.016
	(0.47)	
Scotland	−0.209	0.130
	(2.24)	
Year:		
1974	0.098	0.075
	(1.25)	
1975	0.135	0.116
	(1.79)	
1976	0.180	0.100
	(1.99)	
1977	0.079	0.095
	(0.83)	
1978	0.188	0.077
	(1.90)	
1979	0.210	0.095
	(2.29)	
1980	0.096	0.134
	(0.93)	
1981	0.221	0.127
	(1.38)	
1982	0.154	0.098
	(0.82)	
Constant	4.348	—
	(26.18)	
λ^b	−0.230	1.079
	(2.22)	(0.46)
R^2	0.384	—
F	7.22	—
S.E.	0.313	—
N (full-time)	441	441
Mean (ln)	—	4.400
	—	(0.40)
N	2,062	—

[a] The excluded categories for the binary variables are: no qualifications beyond basic school leaving; semi-skilled manual occupation; residing in Greater London; and the 1973 period. *t*-statistics in parentheses.

[b] Inverse of the Mill's ratio generated by an auxiliary (reduced-form) probit of the probability of being observed in full-time employment.

Table 6A.2 *Means (and standard deviations) of variables included in*
probability of being in employment models, female lone parents,
Great Britain, 1973–82

Variable	(1) All women	(2) Eligible	(3) Not eligible
Age	34.630 (8.94)	34.36 (9.05)	36.36 (7.98)
Age^2	1279.1 (663.9)	1262.6 (670.5)	1385.2 (610.0)
Youngest child:			
< Age 1	0.041	0.044	0.018
Age 1–2	0.131	0.136	0.105
Age 3–4	0.136	0.134	0.144
Age 5–10	0.403	0.393	0.473
Age 11–15	0.254	0.259	0.220
Age 16–18	0.035	0.034	0.040
Number of other children:			
None	0.447	0.465	0.331
One	0.336	0.319	0.448
Two	0.146	0.140	0.181
≥ Three	0.071	0.076	0.040
Unemployment rate	6.358 (3.41)	6.436 (3.44)	5.859 (3.18)
Net earnings	38.89 (22.62)	38.06 (23.62)	44.26 (13.45)
Virtual non-labour income	48.66 (30.78)	43.27 (22.04)	83.38 (50.38)
Benefit entitlement	39.82 (9.68)	39.79 (9.87)	40.04 (8.35)
Region:			
London	0.159	0.162	0.137
North	0.054	0.056	0.043
Yorkshire/Humberside	0.083	0.084	0.076
North West	0.125	0.125	0.126
East Midlands	0.063	0.064	0.058
West Midlands	0.091	0.095	0.065
East Anglia	0.034	0.031	0.054
South East	0.166	0.157	0.220
South West	0.073	0.072	0.076
Wales	0.048	0.046	0.058
Scotland	0.105	0.108	0.087
N	2,062	1,785	277

Source: *1973–82 General Household Survey Timeseries Database*

Table 6A.3 *Logit estimates of the probability of being in employment, female lone parents, Great Britain, 1973–82 (ignoring taxes and FIS)*

Variable	(1) All women	(2) Eligible	(3) Not eligible
Age[a]	0.0537	0.0635	−0.0756
	(1.03)	(1.12)	(0.48)
Age^2	−0.00096	−0.00107	0.000449
	(1.44)	(1.47)	(0.22)
Youngest child:			
< Age 1	−3.228	−3.205	
	(6.08)	(5.72)	−2.270[b]
Age 1–2	−1.968	−2.007	(3.98)
	(9.07)	(8.33)	
Age 3–4	−1.423	−1.353	−1.820
	(7.55)	(6.50)	(3.73)
Age 11–15	−0.246	−0.345	0.573
	(1.39)	(1.80)	(1.13)
Age 16–18	−0.163	−0.358	0.908
	(0.46)	(0.91)	(1.00)
Number of other children:			
One	0.409	0.246	1.131
	(1.97)	(1.09)	(1.93)
Two	0.381	0.366	0.720
	(1.04)	(0.93)	(0.69)
⩾ Three	1.030	0.792	1.015
	(1.71)	(1.22)	(0.55)
Unemployment rate	−0.1215	−0.1404	−0.0418
	(6.06)	(6.35)	(0.77)
Net earnings	0.0674	0.0760	0.0303
	(16.66)	(16.43)	(3.34)
Non-labour income	0.0187	0.0202	−0.0119
	(3.06)	(3.22)	(2.14)
SB guarantee level	−0.0525	−0.0447	−0.0572
	(3.11)	(2.48)	(1.16)
Not eligible• non-labour income	−0.0341	—	—
	(3.98)		
Not eligible• SB guarantee level	0.0351	—	—
	(3.40)		
Region:			
North	2.427	2.725	1.242
	(7.97)	(8.21)	(1.49)
Yorkshire/Humberside	1.502	1.605	0.974
	(6.10)	(5.93)	(1.46)
North West	1.590	1.730	0.812
	(6.82)	(6.76)	(1.31)
East Midlands	1.270	1.151	2.148
	(4.79)	(3.96)	(2.78)
West Midlands	1.183	1.315	0.709
	(4.86)	(4.96)	(1.03)

Table 6A.3 (*cont.*)

Variable	(1) All women	(2) Eligible	(3) Not eligible
Region:			
East Anglia	0.069	−0.060	0.661
	(0.22)	(0.16)	(0.92)
South East	1.315	1.404	1.055
	(6.48)	(6.24)	(2.07)
South West	1.150	1.152	1.417
	(4.54)	(4.10)	(2.11)
Wales	0.961	0.956	1.208
	(3.13)	(2.79)	(1.57)
Scotland	1.294	1.412	0.806
	(5.29)	(5.25)	(1.24)
Constant	−3.944	−4.952	1.956
	(3.60)	(4.16)	(0.59)
$-2.\ln L$	2,092.6	1,732.1	317.82
N	2,062	1,785	277
$\bar{P}$	0.469	0.465	0.491

[a]The reference categories for the binary variables are: youngest child age 5–10; no other dependent children; and residing in Greater London. Asymptotic '*t*-ratios' in parentheses.
[b]Youngest child less than age three.

Table 6A.4 *Logit estimates of the probability of being in employment, female lone parents, Great Britain, 1973–82 (with taxes and FIS and year-to-year dummy variables)*

Variable	(1) All women	(2) Eligible	(3) Not eligible
Age[a]	0.0587	0.0626	−0.0969
	(1.14)	(1.12)	(0.59)
Age^2	−0.00101	−0.00104	0.000792
	(1.52)	(1.44)	(0.38)
Youngest child:			
< Age 1	−2.921	−2.849	
	(5.73)	(5.40)	−2.369[b]
Age 1–2	−1.837	−1.857	(4.00)
	(8.68)	(7.99)	
Age 3–4	−1.407	−1.363	−1.910
	(7.53)	(6.63)	(3.77)
Age 11–15	−0.234	−0.272	0.577
	(1.31)	(1.40)	(1.10)
Age 16–18	−0.249	−0.433	0.623
	(0.70)	(1.10)	(0.65)
Number of other children:			
One	0.141	−0.077	1.126
	(0.69)	(0.35)	(1.83)
Two	−0.165	−0.260	0.598
	(0.45)	(0.67)	(0.55)
⩾ Three	0.241	−0.153	1.109
	(0.40)	(0.24)	(0.57)
Unemployment rate	−0.0337	−0.0751	0.2486
	(0.53)	(1.09)	(1.36)
Net earnings	0.0867	0.0929	0.0594
	(15.88)	(15.51)	(3.61)
Virtual non-labour income	0.0520	0.0578	−0.0139
	(8.37)	(8.57)	(2.39)
SB guarantee level	−0.0556	−0.0469	−0.0527
	(3.19)	(2.56)	(1.01)
Not eligible• non-labour income	−0.0661 (7.68)	—	—
Not eligible• SB guarantee level	0.0706 (5.23)	—	—
Region:			
North	1.701	1.917	0.178
	(4.32)	(4.49)	(0.15)
Yorkshire/Humberside	1.135	1.173	0.776
	(4.19)	(3.96)	(1.01)
North West	1.116	1.264	0.010
	(3.73)	(3.85)	(0.01)
East Midlands	0.959	0.770	2.149
	(3.56)	(2.61)	(2.69)

Table 6A.4 (*cont.*)

Variable	(1) All women	(2) Eligible	(3) Not eligible
Region:			
West Midlands	0.797	0.894	0.305
	(2.87)	(2.95)	(0.39)
East Anglia	−0.032	−0.136	0.520
	(0.10)	(0.38)	(0.70)
South East	1.129	1.106	1.219
	(5.69)	(5.05)	(2.27)
South West	0.760	0.671	1.007
	(2.77)	(2.22)	(1.36)
Wales	0.561	0.611	0.281
	(1.42)	(1.39)	(0.27)
Scotland	0.852	0.974	−0.014
	(2.63)	(2.75)	(0.02)
1974	−0.198	−0.217	−0.093
	(0.72)	(0.72)	(0.12)
1975	−0.430	−0.298	−1.030
	(1.55)	(0.98)	(1.35)
1976	−0.848	−0.743	−1.696
	(2.71)	(2.19)	(1.90)
1977	0.022	0.105	−0.466
	(0.07)	(0.31)	(0.46)
1978	−0.907	−0.730	−1.804
	(2.80)	(2.08)	(1.94)
1979	−0.936	−1.003	−1.051
	(3.06)	(3.01)	(1.18)
1980	−0.227	−0.112	−1.295
	(0.64)	(0.29)	(1.28)
1981	−0.911	−0.593	−3.182
	(1.67)	(1.00)	(1.97)
1982	−0.777	−0.450	−3.019
	(1.22)	(0.65)	(1.66)
Constant	−3.679	−4.382	2.096
	(3.29)	(3.64)	(0.60)
$-2.\ln L$	2,110.8	1,770.1	305.62
N	2,062	1,785	277
$\bar{P}$	0.469	0.465	0.491

[a] The reference categories for the binary variables are: youngest child age 5–10; no other dependent children; and residing in Greater London. Asymptotic '*t*-ratios' in parentheses.
[b] Youngest child less than age three.

7

EMPLOYMENT DYNAMICS AMONG
LONE PARENTS

As the previous chapter showed, lone parents not in employment are likely to be dependent on means-tested state benefits. Thus, movements in and out of employment are likely to approximate flows on and off welfare benefits. The empirical analysis of these movements in this chapter focusses on previously-married lone mothers, who constitute the major group of lone parents and whose greater number facilitate analysis of these employment transitions. As in Chapter 5, the *Women and Employment Survey* (WES) is the source of the statistical analysis. We first consider movements in and out of paid employment around the time that a mother becomes a lone parent and then develop and estimate a model of labour market turnover for lone parents.

EMPLOYMENT TRANSITIONS AROUND THE START OF LONE PARENTHOOD

In order to capture anticipatory behaviour, the start of the period of risk for a movement in or out of employment is taken to be six months before the end of the woman's first marriage (defining $t = $ month at the end of first marriage, the start of the period at risk for each woman is $t-6$). Initially, a period starting two years before the end of the first marriage was used, but not much out of the ordinary happened before $t-6$, and a large proportion of the sample of previously-married lone mothers made transitions before they became lone parents when $t-24$ was taken to be the starting time.

Chart 7.1 shows monthly transition rates from a woman's employment status at $t-6$ (full-time job, part-time job or no job) according to the time since the end of her first marriage. The calculation of these rates assumes that a woman is 'censored' when she remarries, or her child reaches the age of sixteen, or the survey occurs before she makes a transition from her employment state at $t-6$, or she makes another transition (for example, from no job to a full-time job when we are calculating the rate from no job to a part-time job).

There are some dramatic changes around the beginning of lone

Chart 7.1a *Transition from full-time to no job and from part-time to no job*

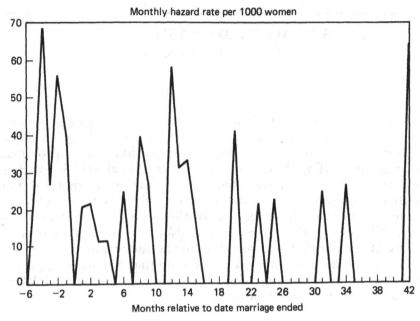

Months relative to date marriage ended

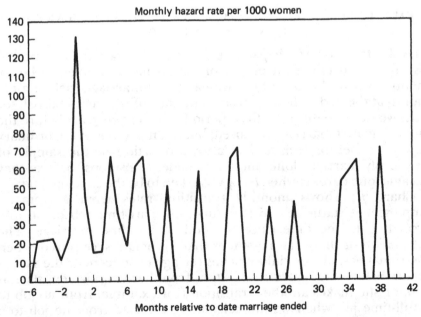

Months relative to date marriage ended

(a)

Source: Author's calculations from 1980 *Women and Employment Survey.*

Chart 7.1b *Transition from no job to full-time and from no job to part-time*

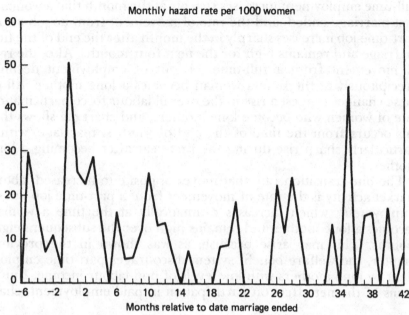

Monthly hazard rate per 1000 women

Months relative to date marriage ended

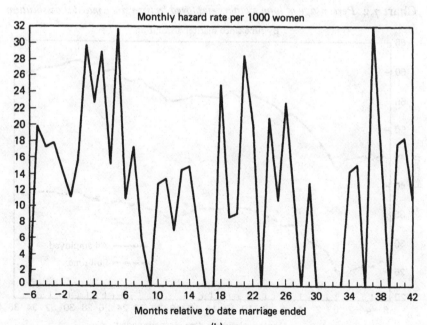

Monthly hazard rate per 1000 women

Months relative to date marriage ended

(b)

Source: As for chart 7.1a

parenthood. In particular, the rate of movement from no job into full-time employment increases sharply at the month that a woman's first marriage ended, and the rate of movement from no job into a part-time job increases sharply in the month after the end of the first marriage and remains high for the next four months. Also, the rate of movement from a full-time job out of employment declines precipitously at the time a woman becomes a lone mother. All of these changes suggest a rise in the overall labour force participation rate of women who become lone mothers, and chart 7.2 shows that this occurs from the time of the end of the first marriage, with a particularly sharp rise during the first year after becoming a lone mother.

The one transition rate that moves opposite to increased labour market activity is the rate of movement from a part-time job out of employment, which increases dramatically at the time a woman becomes a lone mother and remains high over the subsequent eight months. This may arise because, as was shown in the previous chapter, the welfare benefit system discourages part-time employment by lone mothers with low levels of non-labour income. But in terms of the net effect on participation in paid employment, chart

Chart 7.2 *Percentage of lone mothers employed by time since marital dissolution*

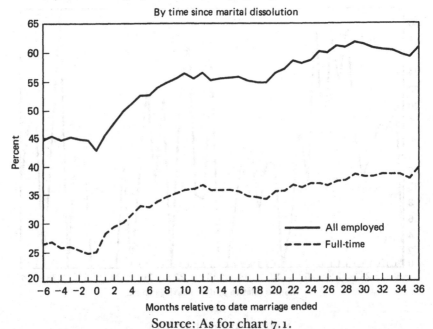

By time since marital dissolution

Months relative to date marriage ended

Source: As for chart 7.1.

Table 7.1 *Employment transitions of previously-married lone mothers (relative to time of marital dissolution)*

	Monthly hazard rate (per 1000 mothers) Duration segment:			
	6 months prior	First 6 months after	7–12 months after	13–36 months after
Full-time to no job	35.1	12.9	20.5	8.5
Part-time to no job	16.8	50.5	35.5	17.6
No job to full-time	11.5	24.2	12.6	7.3
No job to part-time	13.3	22.2	9.5	11.1

7.2 shows that it is dominated by the changes in the other transition rates, causing an upward trend in labour force participation rates of lone mothers over the three years subsequent to becoming one.

The graphs of the transition rates according to time since becoming a lone parent in chart 7.1 have a saw-toothed look because of sampling variation. Table 7.1 recalculates the transition rates for four periods of time; (1) the six months prior to the time a woman becomes a lone mother; (2) the first six months of lone motherhood; (3) seven to twelve months after becoming a lone mother; and (4) the next two years.

The respective peaks and troughs in these transition rates during the first six months of lone parenthood are now very clear. With the exception of movement from a part-time job out of employment, the transition rates return to more 'normal' levels after this first six months. It should be noted that there is a tendency for women's transition rates between these three employment statuses to fall with duration in the state (see Wright and Hinde, 1991), which helps explain the generally lower transition rates after $t+6$ than before the start of lone motherhood. As discussed below, this 'negative duration dependence' may reflect differences between women, such that the more mobile women (for whatever reason) change states more quickly. In the case of the movement from a part-time job out of employment, the transition rate remains relatively high in the second six months after becoming a lone parent, and then it returns to a level near that in the six months preceding lone parenthood.

MODEL OF LABOUR MARKET TURNOVER

The previous chapter developed a static model of lone parents' employment decisions. In that model, the parent maximises utility in a single period subject to known wage offers and non-labour incomes. In the model developed and estimated in this chapter, there is uncertainty about wage offers, and parents maximise expected lifetime utility. Hours of employment and leisure are assumed to be fixed, but parents receive utility when not in employment as well as utility from consumption goods purchased with their earnings from employment.

Suppose a lone mother maximises lifetime utility (over an infinite life span, for simplicity). When out of paid employment, she receives utility flow u (measured in terms of consumption goods, or 'income' for short) at each instant, and u depends on the productivity of her time in the home, which varies with the number and ages of her children.[1] Additions to income when not in paid employment arising from the welfare benefit system clearly increase u, as is the case in the model of the previous chapter. Other non-labour income is ignored, because it is the same whether a woman is in a job or not.

The wage rate when employed, w, changes from time to time. New wage offers arrive according to a Poisson process with parameters α_i, where $i=1$ indicates being in paid employment and $i=2$ indicates being out of paid employment. The probability of receiving a new wage offer in a small interval of time ε when state i is occupied is $\alpha_i \varepsilon + o(\varepsilon)$.[2] Thus, this probability may differ according to whether she is employed or not. New wage offers received are from a distribution characterised by the distribution function $F(w;X)$, where X is a vector of fixed characteristics of the woman. Finally, μ is the arrival rate of a layoff when employed. Burdett et al. (1985) allow μ to be a decreasing function of duration since last being unemployed, but we shall ignore this complication.

Let $V_2(X)$ be the expected discounted lifetime income when not in paid employment, $V_1(w,X)$ be the maximum expected discounted lifetime income when employed at wage w, and let

$$T(X) = \int_{-\infty}^{\infty} \max\{V_2(X), V_1(w,X)\}dF(w,X) \tag{7.1}$$

Burdett et al. show that there is a stopping rule that guarantees the existence of this maximum. Note that $T(X)$ is the discounted expected value of the best option, employment or not employment.

We can write $V_2(X)$ as

$$V_2(X) = [1/(1+r\varepsilon)][u\varepsilon + \alpha_2\varepsilon T(X) + (1-\alpha_2\varepsilon)V_2(X)] + o(\varepsilon) \tag{7.2$'$}$$

where r is the discount rate. The first term in the second set of brackets is the utility flow from being out of employment; the second term is the product of the probability of receiving a wage offer and the expected value of the best option if an offer is received; and the third term is the probability of not receiving an offer times the expected lifetime income if no offer is received. Dividing (7.2′) by ε and letting ε go to zero, we obtain

$$V_2(X) = [u + a_2 T(X)]/(r+a_2) \tag{7.2}$$

Similarly,

$$V_1(w,X) = [1/(1+r\varepsilon)][w\varepsilon + a_1\varepsilon\{\mu\varepsilon V_2(X) + (1-\mu\varepsilon)T(X)\}$$
$$+ (1-a_1\varepsilon)\{\mu\varepsilon V_2(X) + (1-\mu\varepsilon)V_1(w,X)\}] + o(\varepsilon^2) \tag{7.3′}$$

In the case of women in employment, the probabilities of a layoff ($\mu\varepsilon$) or not ($1-\mu\varepsilon$) must be taken into account along with the probabilities of receiving another wage offer or not ($a_1\varepsilon$ and $1-a_1\varepsilon$ respectively) and wages received when employed ($w\varepsilon$) in assessing expected lifetime income when employed. Again, dividing (7.3′) by ε and letting ε go to zero,

$$V_1(w,X) = [w + \mu V_2(X) + a_1 T(X)]/(\mu+a_1+r) \tag{7.3}$$

Burdett *et al.* show that a woman will choose to be employed if and only if $V_1(w,X) > V_2(X)$. Furthermore, $V_1(w,X)$ is strictly increasing in w.

In chart 7.3, the relationships between w and $V_1(w,X)$ and $V_2(X)$ are

Chart 7.3 *Determination of the reservation wage*

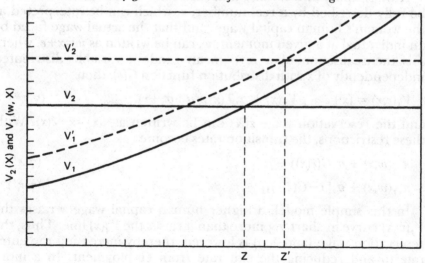

Wage offer, w

illustrated. It is clear from the graphical illustration that there is a 'reservation wage' above which $V_1(w,X) > V_2(X)$, so that a woman offered wages above it would be in employment. Burdett *et al.* demonstrate that the strategy that maximises the woman's expected discounted lifetime income can be characterised by a reservation wage function $z(X)$ such that she will choose to be employed if and only if $w > z(X)$, and $z(X)$ is a constant for given X (because of our assumption that the layoff rate μ does not vary with duration in employment).

It follows that a woman's labour market history can be described by a two-state Markov process with the following transition rates:

$$\pi_{12}(w,X) = \alpha_1 F(z(X),X) + \mu \qquad\qquad (7.4)$$

$$\pi_{21}(w,X) = \alpha_2 [1 - F(z(X),X)] \qquad\qquad (7.5)$$

where π_{12} is the exit rate from employment and π_{21} is the entry rate to paid employment.

From differentiation of expressions (7.1), (7.2) and (7.3) it can be shown that a higher utility flow received when out of employment (u), say because a woman has young children or many children, or because of higher welfare benefits, raises the $V_2(X)$ line in chart 7.3 more than it raises the $V_1(w,X)$ curve. As chart 7.3 illustrates, this raises the reservation wage $z(X)$. It follows from (7.4) and (7.5), that, through its effect on $z(X)$, a higher u raises the outflow rate, π_{12}, and lowers the rate of entry to employment, π_{21}.

If we simplify and assume that the vector of characteristics X can be fully described by a real number, x, which can be interpreted as the woman's human capital wage, and that the actual wage faced by an individual at a given moment, w, can be written as $w = x + e$, where e is the realisation of a zero mean random variable distributed independently of x with distribution function $G(e)$, then

$$V_1(e,x) = [x + e + \mu V_2(x) + \alpha_1 T(x)]/(\mu + \alpha_1 + r), \qquad (7.3^*)$$

and the reservation wage $z(X)$ can be written as $z(x) = x + \hat{e}(x)$. With these restrictions, the transition rates become

$$\pi_{12}(w,x) + \alpha_1 G(\hat{e}(x)) + \mu \qquad\qquad (7.4')$$

$$\pi_{21}(w,x) + \alpha_2 [1 - G(\hat{e}(x))] \qquad\qquad (7.5')$$

In this simple model, a higher human capital wage x raises the $V_1(w,x)$ curve in chart 7.3 more than it raises the $V_2(x)$ line. Thus, the reservation wage (and $\hat{e}(x)$) is lowered, thereby increasing the entry rate to and reducing the exit rate from employment. In a more complicated model with duration dependence in the layoff rate,

Burdett *et al.* also show that π_{12} decreases as x increases and π_{21} increases with x. That is, the transition rate out of employment falls as the human capital wage increases, while the transition rate into employment increases as the human capital wage increases. These predictions concerning the human capital wage and factors affecting the utility flow when out of employment, u, are tested below.

In a steady-state, the probability of a woman with characteristics X being in employment at a point in time is

$$p_e(w,X) = \pi_{21}(w,X)/[\pi_{12}(w,X) + \pi_{21}(w,X)] \tag{7.6}$$

This forges a link between the dynamic model of employment participation above and a static model of the state probability of participation, like that in the previous chapter. Note that it follows from (7.6) that

$$dp_e = (\pi_{12}d\pi_{21} - \pi_{21}d\pi_{12})/(\pi_{12} + \pi_{21})^2 \tag{7.7}$$

Thus, from the predictions derived above, a higher utility flow when out of employment (u) lowers p_e (because $d\pi_{21} < 0$ and $d\pi_{12} > 0$), while a higher human capital wage (x) raises p_e.

ESTIMATION OF THE MODEL'S REDUCED FORM

As in the analysis of Chapter 5, the statistical analysis employs the so-called *proportional hazards model*. Although the theoretical development implied a Markov model, the empirical analysis allows the transition rates π_{ij} to vary with duration t_i in state i, so that $\pi_{ij}(t_i, X_t)$ is given by

$$\pi_{ij}(t_i, X_t) = \lambda_i(t)\exp(X_t\beta_i), \quad i \neq j, \; i,j = 1,2. \tag{7.8}$$

where $\lambda_i(t)$ is some function of duration; X_t is a vector of characteristics of the mother and her family at duration t_i; and β_i is a vector of parameters to be estimated. Some of the elements of X (for example, welfare benefits) may vary over time. If all of the elements were fixed, the relationship between the transition rate $\pi_{ij}(t_i, X)$ and duration would be the same for everyone, but the rate would vary proportionally with a mother's characteristics X. The parameters of the model are estimated by maximum likelihood using methods described in Allison (1982).[3]

Duration is measured from the time of the last employment transition, but only those months of exposure in which a woman is a lone mother enter the analysis. If a woman's youngest child reaches the age of sixteen or she remarries, her duration is treated as 'censored' (as is also the case when the survey intervenes before another transition), because she is no longer a lone mother according to the definition used here.

In specifying $\lambda_i(t)$, a compromise between flexibility and the number of parameters to be estimated is struck by assuming that, given the values of the explanatory variables, the transition rate is constant within each of ten duration segments, but can vary between the segments. These segments are constructed so that each contributes about a tenth of the monthly 'exposures to risk'. More parsimonious parametric specifications for $\lambda_i(t)$ are also considered. In particular, the analysis explores whether a Weibull specification for duration dependence, essentially $\log[\lambda_i(t_i)] = (p-1)\log(t_i)$, or a quadratic one, $\log[\lambda_i(t_i)] = b_1 t_i + b_2 t_i^2$ provide an adequate representation of duration dependence.

There may appear to be a decline in the transition rate with duration because of persistent differences in transition rates between women that are not accounted for by measured variables in X (for example, the 'mover–stayer' dichotomy). In general, failure to account for such unobserved heterogeneity biases estimates of $\lambda_i(t_i)$ in the direction of negative duration dependence, and it also produces biased estimates of β_i, even if the unobserved characteristics of women are uncorrelated with the variables in X (for example, see Lancaster, 1979, and Lancaster and Nickell, 1980). In order to explore the sensitivity of our estimates to the presence of unobserved differences among women, we estimate a model that adds a woman-specific variable, ε_k, to (7.8):

$$\pi_{ij}(t_i, X_{tk}, \varepsilon_k) = \lambda_i(t_i) \exp(X_{tk}\beta_i + \varepsilon_k), \quad i \neq j, \; i,j = 1,2. \tag{7.8'}$$

We assume that ε_k is independent of t_i and of the explanatory variables in X, that ε_k follows a normal distribution with zero mean and standard deviation σ, and that $\lambda_i(t_i)$ takes the Weibull form.[4]

Non-stationarity

The model of labour market turnover outlined in the previous section is a stationary model; that is the exogenous variables, like real welfare benefits, the human capital wage, or the moments of the wage offer distribution $(F(w,X))$ are not expected to change over the spell of employment or non-employment. As a consequence, a woman's reservation wage is constant over the spell, and it determines the employment transition rates (from (7.4) and (7.5)).

Stationarity is not very realistic. For instance, women are likely to expect their real human capital wage and the mean and variance of their wage offer distribution to rise over time because of general increases in real wages. In a non-stationary model of job search,[5] van den Berg (1990) shows that, all else being equal, expectation of an increase in the mean and variance of the wage offer distribution produces a reservation wage that is higher than would be the case if they were constant, and one that increases over the spell of non-employment. This is because increases in the mean and variance of $F(w,X)$ increase the value of search. In other words, future trend increases in real wages are anticipated and incorporated in the present reservation wage and its pattern over the spell of non-employment.

This strongly suggests that secular increases in the real wage are likely to have little effect on a woman's transition rates, because they reflect anticipated developments. In particular, their effect would be much smaller than the effect of differences in the human capital wage between women. This hypothesis is tested below.

An estimate of the 'stationary component' (x) of the human capital wage is constructed for each employment and non-employment spell of a woman based on her education and work experience and the wage equation for women in full-time jobs estimated by Ermisch and Wright (1988). It is measured at the start of each spell of employment or non-employment (that is, at $t_i=0$), based on her work experience and education up to that time.

Welfare benefits

During our period of analysis, 1948–80, Supplementary Benefit (SB) was the main welfare benefit received by lone mothers.[6] The previous chapter showed that, because of the 100 per cent tax rate on income implicit in the supplementary benefit system, SB is usually received only by women not in employment. A measure of real SB benefits that would be received by a lone mother (based on the number of her children and calendar time) when out of employment with no other income was constructed in the way described in Chapter 5. It is not possible to measure mothers' other non-employment income (such as maintenance payments from her husband) at each point in time; thus we do not know how much (if any) extra income a woman receives when out of employment as a consequence of the benefit system. Thus, there may be omitted variable bias in our estimates.[7] While other non-employment income and SB entitlement may not be highly correlated across women, its real value is likely to be correlated with real SB entitlement over time.

Another potential difficulty is the high correlation between SB and Family Income Supplement (FIS) benefit scales (for example, a correlation of 0.999 during 1971–87 for lone mothers of one child aged 5–10).[8] The two scales are raised together in order to keep work incentives the same. The combination of SB and FIS reflected in the top budget constraint in chart 6.1 of the previous chapter could be viewed as one tax-transfer system, albeit one with a strange pattern of tax rates. Gottschalk's (1988) analysis of the effects of tax-transfer systems on the duration of time out of employment suggests that an equivalent increase in both scale rates need not raise the reservation wage (and lower the probability of entering employment) for lone mothers eligible for FIS. He shows that for lone mothers not in employment with a reservation wage less than the wage that would take them off FIS, a higher benefit scale reduces the reservation wage.[9]

If real welfare benefits were constant over a spell of employment or non-employment, the model outlined in the second section of the chapter would apply directly to lone mothers not eligible for FIS. For them, a higher SB benefit entitlement at zero income would increase the utility received when not employed and raise the reservation wage. Thus, the effects of SB entitlement for the entire population of lone mothers would depend on the proportion of them eligible for FIS.[10] Although FIS was not available during the entire period of analysis, two-thirds of the months of exposure to risk of exit from or entry to full-time employment have occurred since 1970.

Non-stationarity of welfare benefits over a spell can, however, confound the predictions of the effects of benefits derived from our stationary model. As chart 7.4 illustrates, real benefits have tended to increase over time; thus, it is reasonable to suppose that women anticipate increases in real benefits during their employment or non-employment spell. If so, then these trend increases are already incorporated in the present reservation wage and its pattern over the spell. For instance, in van den Berg's (1990) model of job search, expectation of increasing welfare benefits implies that the reservation wage would tend to increase over the spell and be higher than if real benefits remained constant during the spell.[11]

Because they are anticipated, the effects of trend increases in real welfare benefits on transition rates are likely to be small, and almost certainly smaller than the effects of differences in benefit entitlement between women. But differences in welfare benefits between lone mothers at a point in time primarily reflect differences in family composition; thus, the effects of these cannot easily be identified separately from the effects of the age and number of children.[12]

Other considerations

Labour market conditions may affect the rate at which offers arrive, α_i (for example, the 'thin market' externality suggested by Morten-

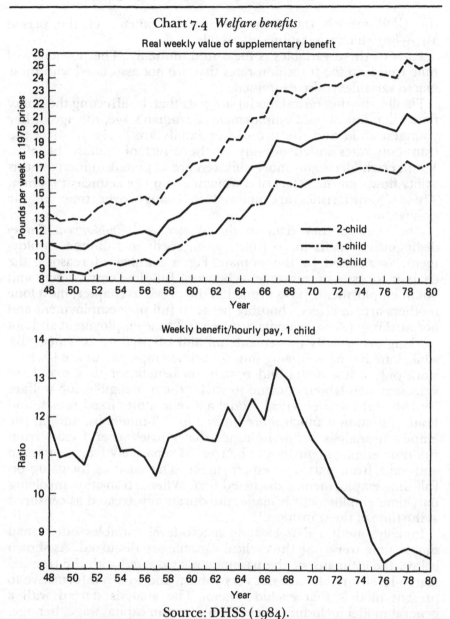

Chart 7.4 *Welfare benefits*

Real weekly value of supplementary benefit

Weekly benefit/hourly pay, 1 child

Source: DHSS (1984).

sen, 1982). Although this would be another source of non-stationarity, changes in α_i are unlikely to be anticipated. We explore, therefore, whether the unemployment rate in the economy or a variable measuring the position in the 'business cycle' affect the employment transition rates. The cyclical variable is the deviation of the GDP growth rate from its average value over the period 1948–80, which is a stationary variable.

Each of these variables is measured annually. The possibility of time trends in the transition rates that are not associated with these macro variables is also examined.

Finally, the theoretical model suggests that, by affecting the utility flow when out of paid employment, a woman's age, the age of her youngest child and the size of her family are likely to affect the transition rates independently of the effect of welfare benefits. Younger children and more children are expected to increase this utility flow, but the effect of a woman's own age is unclear *a priori*. These characteristics are allowed to change over time in our estimation.

The work history data in the *Women and Employment Survey* distinguishes spells in part-time from spells in full-time employment, as assessed by the woman. For a number of reasons, the chapter focusses on movements between full-time employment and out of employment: (1) as argued in the previous chapter, most lone mothers are, in effect, choosing between full-time employment and not working; (2) movements between full-time employment and not working are usually movements on and off welfare benefits (SB), while lone mothers moving into part-time employment are likely to work only a few hours and remain on benefit, or they may have sufficient non-labour income to make them ineligible for welfare benefits; (3) the theoretical model above assumes fixed hours, and hours variation is much more limited in full-time jobs; and (4) the empirical analysis below indicates that entries to and exits from full-time employment should be treated separately from entries to and exits from part-time employment. The analysis focussing on full-time employment is discussed first. When a transition involving part-time employment is made, the duration is treated as censored at the time of the transition.[13]

Initially, models that exclude macro-level variables other than simple time trends or the cyclical variable are discussed. As shown below, the estimates of the parameters associated with the trended macro-level variables are not very robust, and so it is informative to present models that exclude them. The analysis started with a general model including the woman's human capital wage, her age, the age of her youngest child, the number of children, the cyclical variable and a time trend. Other than the human capital wage and the cyclical variable, the other variables were specified in two ways: as a set of dichotomous variables and as a continuous variable. More parsimonious models, which eliminated particular variables and

Table 7.2 *Parameter estimates of model of entry to full-time employment by previously-married lone mothers*

Variable[a]	Without heterogeneity	With heterogeneity
Age of mother	−0.047 (0.0173)	−0.0824 (0.0274)
Age of youngest child	0.0471 (0.0292)	0.0981 (0.0421)
Number of other children: 3 or more	−0.964 (0.463)	−1.390 (0.532)
Log (potential wage)	2.176 (0.431)	2.460 (0.664)
Business cycle	8.218 (3.092)	7.451 (3.740)
Weibull parameter, $p–1$	−0.348 (0.059)	−0.131 (0.086)
Intercept	−2.545 (0.447)	−2.848 (0.708)
σ (Standard deviation)	n/a	1.409 (0.235)

[a] Standard errors in parentheses. The reference category is 1–2 children.

The means (and standard deviations) are as follows:

calendar year	71.7	(7.77)
age of mother	34.5	(8.14)
age of youngest child	6.8	(4.47)
logarithm of the potential wage	0.256	(0.172)
business cycle	0.0	(0.0275)
log (duration)	3.937	(1.283)

There are 12,597 months of exposure in the analysis and 144 entries to full-time employment from non-employment.

regrouped classes of categorical variables, were estimated, and when the specifications were nested, tests of whether these restrictions were statistically acceptable were performed using likelihood ratio tests. Table 7.2 shows the estimates of the parameters (β_i) and their standard errors for a statistically acceptable restricted version of the general model for entries to full-time employment (from non-employment), and Table 7.3 shows the same for exits from full-time employment (to out of employment).

Table 7.3 *Parameter estimates of model of exits from full-time employment
by previously-married lone mothers*

Variable[a]	Without heterogeneity	Without heterogeneity	With heterogeneity
Calendar year	0.0651 (0.0166)	0.0632 (0.0166)	0.0735 (0.0239)
Age of mother less than 25	0.801 (0.321)	0.766 (0.323)	0.923 (0.422)
Youngest child aged: less than 1	2.163 (0.533)	1.930 (0.583)	2.311 (0.629)
1–5	1.147 (0.306)	1.037 (0.326)	1.231 (0.384)
6–9	0.725 (0.317)	0.685 (0.319)	0.806 (0.340)
Number of other children:	0.241 (0.124)	0.225 (0.125)	0.240 (0.146)
Log (potential wage)	−1.359 (0.763)	−1.348 (0.759)	−1.924 (0.831)
Weibull parameter, p–1		−0.098 (0.102)	0.094 (0.114)
Intercept	−10.211 (1.234)	−9.682 (1.342)	−11.298 (1.743)
σ (Standard deviation)	n/a	n/a	0.962 (0.320)

[a] Standard errors in parentheses. The reference categories are: mother aged 25 or more and her youngest child aged 10–15. The means (and standard deviations) of calendar year, number of other children, and logarithm of the potential wage are 69.8 (7.5), 0.57 (0.77) and 0.176 (0.177) respectively. There are 11,533 months of exposure in the analysis, and 89 exits from full-time employment to out of employment.

PARAMETER ESTIMATES

Entry to employment

As the theoretical model predicts, a higher human capital wage raises the rate of entry to employment. The likelihood of entry to full-time employment increases with the age of the youngest child, but it is much lower for mothers with four or more children. These results are consistent with younger children and a large number of children making larger demands on their mother's time, which increases her productivity in the home and her utility when out of

Table 7.4a *Proportional hazard analysis of entry to part-time employment by previously-married lone mothers*

Variable[a]	Parameter	Standard error	Chi-square
Calendar year	0.0248	0.0126	3.86
Log (potential wage)	1.187	0.460	6.66
Weibull parameter, p–1	−0.166	0.062	7.16
Intercept	−6.024	0.991	36.92
Model Chi-square = 16.27 (3 d.f.)			

Note: The means (and standard deviations) are as in table 7.2. There are 12,597 months of exposure in the analysis, and 133 entries to part-time employment.

Table 7.4b *Proportional hazard analysis of exits from part-time employment by previously-married lone mothers*

Variable[a]	Parameter	Standard error	Chi-square
Calendar year	0.0654	0.0193	11.55
Age of mother	−0.0654	0.0141	21.36
Youngest child aged 6–9	−0.489	0.249	3.87
Number of other children	0.234	0.115	4.17
Log (potential wage)	0.266	0.660	0.16
Intercept	−6.868	1.506	20.81
Model Chi-square = 39.52 (5 d.f.)			

[a] The reference categories are the youngest child aged less than 6 or 10–15. The means (and standard deviations) of calendar year, age of mother, number of other children, and logarithm of the potential wage are 72.1 (6.5), 37.5 (7.66), 0.81 (0.91) and 0.087 (0.173) respectively. There are 7,138 months of exposure in the analysis, and 92 exits from part-time employment.

employment. All else being equal, older mothers are also less likely to enter full-time employment.

There is no evidence that a mother's age or that of her children, or the number of children, affects entry to part-time employment. While table 7.4 shows that a higher human capital wage raises the probability of entry to part-time employment, its impact is only half as large as its impact on entry to full-time employment.

The analysis also indicates that above-trend rates of GDP growth raise the rate of entry to full-time jobs, and this effect may be associated with better (or more) wage offers during favourable periods of the business cycle. No such cyclical effect is evident for the entry rate to part-time jobs, but there is evidence of an upward trend in the part-time entry rate (see table 7.4). This probably reflects the general trend toward more part-time employment by women (see Wright and Hinde, 1991). The coefficients of the other variables are almost the same when the cyclical and time trend variables are excluded.

Finally, after controlling for these observable characteristics of women and their environment, there appears to be negative duration dependence in the rates of entry to employment, with this being stronger in full-time employment. The parameters associated with the set of dichotomous duration variables show a downward trend. A Weibull specification for the duration dependence is a good representation, with only a small fall in the log-likelihood traded for a saving of eight parameters. Also, the coefficients of the other variables are little affected by substituting the Weibull for the set of duration parameters.

As expected, the parameter estimates allowing for unobserved differences between women in the entry rate to full-time employment (table 7.2) show a large reduction in the Weibull parameter, indicating much less negative duration dependence. Lancaster and Nickell, (1980) also show that, for many distributions of ε_k, the absolute value of the parameter estimates increases when residual unobserved heterogeneity is taken into account, and we indeed find that with the exception of the parameter associated with the business cycle variable, all the other estimates of the parameters in β_i are larger in size.

One potential source of 'true' duration dependence is the strong negative impact that time out of employment has on the human capital wage: about 1 per cent reduction per annum, according to estimates by Ermisch and Wright (1988).[14] Recall that the measure of the human capital wage is taken at the time of the last transition. Thus, while the human capital wage falls with time out of employment, the measure does not account for this. The appendix to this chapter shows that if duration out of employment only affects the entry rate through its impact on the potential wage, then the duration dependence parameter divided by the product of duration and the parameter in table 7.2 associated with the log of the human capital wage is equal to the impact of duration out of employment on the log wage. The estimates in table 7.2, taking account of unobserved heterogeneity, entail an estimate of this impact that is very close to that estimated directly by Ermisch and Wright (1988).

Exits from employment

In contrast, neither exits from full-time nor part-time employment show evidence of duration dependence. In the model without residual heterogeneity, the chi-square statistic for the joint statistical significance of the nine dichotomous duration variables is 16.53 for full-time employment and 14.47 for part-time employment, which are not significant at the 5 per cent level. While the former is significant at the 10 per cent level, the duration parameters show no pattern. When more parsimonious specifications of duration dependence for exits from full-time jobs are considered, the chi-square statistic for quadratic duration dependence is 2.66 (2 d.f.) and that for Weibull dependence is 0.93 (1 d.f.).

As table 7.3 shows, in the model allowing for unobserved differences between women, the estimated Weibull parameter indicates positive duration dependence, but it does not exceed its standard error. Thus, even though a likely decline in the layoff rate with duration and a positive impact of job tenure on the human capital wage (about 3 per cent per annum around the mean, according to the wage equation for women in full-time jobs estimated by Ermisch and Wright, 1988) both produce a tendency toward negative duration dependence in the exit rate, there is little evidence of it.

The coefficients of the other variables are little affected by whether duration dependence is specified or not. As expected, these coefficients increase in size when residual heterogeneity is taken into account.

Consistent with the theoretical model, a higher human capital wage lowers the exit rate from full-time employment, but the wage has no effect on the exit rate from part-time employment (table 7.4). Mothers with young children and a larger number of children have a higher exit rate from full-time employment. While the relationship between the age of the youngest child and the exit rate is monotonic for exits from full-time jobs, it is U-shaped for exits from part-time employment. Also, younger women appear more likely to leave employment.[15]

Finally, the estimates indicate an upward trend in exit rates of a similar magnitude for exits from full-time and part-time employment. This trend was explored further with a set of six five-year dummy variables, which show an upward trend from the mid-1950s for full-time employment and from the early 1950s for part-time. These sets are jointly statistically significant. Because months since 1955 contributed 95 per cent of the exposures for exits from full-time jobs, and 98 per cent for part-time jobs, it is not surprising

that a simple linear trend is a good parsimonious representation of
each trend. Exclusion of the trend from the exit equations reduces
the coefficient of the human capital wage for full-timers (it is now
only significant at the 0.2 level) and lowers the estimated effect of
the number of children among part-time workers, but in both cases
these coefficients are within one standard error of the estimates in
tables 7.3 and 7.4, and the impacts of the other variables are hardly
affected.

The trends in exit rates and in entry to part-time employment beg
the question of what lies behind these trends. Can changes in the
economy or the welfare benefit system account for these trends?

Real welfare benefits vary both over time, as benefit rules and rates
change, and over women because benefits vary with the age and
number of children. As chart 7.4 shows, welfare benefits generally
increased faster than women's wages until 1967, but during 1968–
80 they fell substantially relative to average women's hourly pay (by
about 35 per cent).

The analysis so far has used an estimate of each mother's human
capital wage in 1980 for all observed months of exposure. In the
simple version of the theoretical model above, in which $w=x+e$, each
woman's human capital wage and the mean of her wage offer
distribution would change over time with women's average real
hourly pay. If women did not anticipate the trend increases in real
wages and welfare benefits, and if the distribution function $G(e)$ did
not change, then the stationary theoretical model would be a good
approximation, and a reasonable estimate of a mother's human
capital wage in any particular month before 1980 could be obtained
by using an index of changes in average women's real hourly pay to
make pro rata adjustments to her 1980 human capital wage. This
index is based on the Department of Employment's measure of real
hourly earnings for full-timers in manual occupations from their
October Enquiry.

The estimates of the parameters of the indexed human capital
wage and real welfare benefits in this model are shown in the middle
panel of table 7.5 (constrained model 1) for entries to and exits from
full-time employment. The estimates are consistent with the theoretical model: higher benefits significantly reduce entry to full-time
employment and raise exit rates from it, while the human capital
wage has the opposite effects, although it is only statistically significant for entries in the model without residual heterogeneity.[16]

Table 7.5 *Coefficients of benefit and wage variables (standard errors in parentheses)*

	Entry		Exit	
	Without heterogeneity	With heterogeneity	Without heterogeneity	With heterogeneity
Unconstrained model: *Coefficient of logarithm of*:				
Potential wage (x), β_1	2.114^a (0.449)	2.277^a (0.689)	-1.332^a (0.760)	-1.843^a (0.832)
Average wage index (w), β_2	-0.244 (0.416)	-0.366 (0.642)	1.280 (0.800)	1.114 (1.061)
Real welfare benefit (B), β_3	0.018 (0.550)	-0.316 (0.786)	0.475 (1.440)	1.105 (1.780)
Test for exclusion of w and B: $\chi^2(2)$	0.73	1.95	15.92^a	14.01^a
Constrained Model 1: $\beta_1 = \beta_2$				
$\beta_1 (= \beta_2)$	0.811^a (0.313)	0.761 (0.477)	-0.147 (0.501)	-0.480 (0.707)
β_3	-1.305^a (0.436)	-1.627^a (0.663)	2.576^a (1.151)	3.380^a (1.429)
Test of restriction: $\chi^2(1)$	13.89^a	8.55^a	5.84^a	5.45^a
Constrained Model 2: $\beta_2 = -\beta_3$				
β_1	2.189^a (0.433)	2.476^a (0.662)	-1.147 (0.741)	-1.506^a (0.787)
$\beta_3 (= -\beta_2)$	0.243 (0.415)	0.307 (0.623)	-2.287^a (0.693)	-2.290^a (0.891)
Test of restriction: $\chi^2(1)$	0.39	1.66	5.02^a	6.13^a

^{a} Statistically significant at the 0.10 level or less.

The estimated impacts of the human capital wage in this model differ substantially from those in tables 7.2 and 7.3. In contrast, the coefficients associated with the characteristics of a woman and her family and with duration dependence (not shown) are not very different. The only exception to this is the coefficient on the number of children, which changes when welfare benefits are included. Because benefits are based on the number of children, this is to be expected.

The model in the middle panel of table 7.5 has constrained changes in average wages over time to have the same impact on transition rates as differences among women in the human capital wage at a point in time. As noted earlier, a non-stationary job search model suggests that this constraint is not valid, and we now test it.

Let Z be the appropriate set of variables from table 7.2 or 7.3, excluding the time trend and the log of the potential wage. Suppressing the subscript for the origin state i, we then re-write (7.8) as

$$\log[\pi_{ij}(k,s)] = Z\gamma + \beta_1\log(x_k) + \beta_2\log(w_s) + \beta_3\log(B_{ks}) \qquad (7.9)$$

where x_k is the human capital wage for the k–th woman in 1980 wages, w_s is the hourly wage index for year s ($w_{1980}=1$) and B_{ks} is the real welfare benefit per week paid to woman k in year s if she has no other income. Estimates of the β_js for this unconstrained specification are given in the top panel of table 7.5.

While the estimate of β_1 is well determined in both transitions and very similar to its corresponding estimate in tables 7.2 or 7.3, precise estimates of the parameters associated with w_s and B_{ks} are not obtained. Indeed for entries, we cannot reject the exclusion of these two variables from the specification. We can, however, for exits, but collinearity makes it difficult to estimate their parameters with any precision.[17]

When freely estimated, the estimates of the parameters associated with the characteristics of a woman and her family (other than number of children) and with duration dependence are hardly affected by which macro-variables are included. The discussion focusses, therefore, on the impacts of average women's real wages and real welfare benefits under different specifications.[18]

As noted above, the constrained model in the middle panel of table 7.5 assumes that $\beta_1=\beta_2$. Tests for the validity of the restriction in this specification soundly reject it.[19] This suggests that women take account of anticipated trend increases in the mean of their wage offer distribution, their human capital wage and real welfare benefits in their decisions.

The second constrained specification comes from the form of the welfare system in Britain, illustrated in chart 6.1 of the previous chapter. Letting W be a woman's wage, H her hours of paid employment, M her income not coming from employment nor the welfare system (for example, maintenance), and B her benefit entitlement at zero income, as above, the welfare payment is $B-WH-M$ (ignoring the £4 earnings disregard). As in the previous chapter, her 'breakeven hours' can be defined as the number of working hours that would yield the same earnings as her welfare payment if not employed; that is, her breakeven hours H_b are such that $B-M=WH_b$. If a woman places any value on home time, she will not work less than H_b hours, and for most preferences, the probability that she takes employment decreases as H_b increases.

Note that if M were o, then $H_b=B/W$. Thus, B_{ks}/w_s could be interpreted as an indicator of how breakeven hours for an 'average' woman with a given number of children change over time (it is shown for a one-child family at the bottom of chart 7.4), and this can be used to represent changes in the benefit system over time. Alternatively, B_{ks}/w_s could be interpreted as being proportional to an average 'replacement ratio', which relates benefits to the location of the wage offer distribution. Using this representation of the benefit system amounts to constraining $\beta_2=-\beta_3$. Because the probability that she takes employment decreases with higher breakeven hours ('replacement ratio'), we expect β_3 to be negative for entry rates and positive for exit rates. Estimates of the second constrained specification of (7.9) are in the last panel of table 7.5.

Breakeven hours do not appear to affect the entry rate significantly, but they appear to have a perverse negative effect on the exit rate. The restriction in this specification is, however, rejected.[20] In the light of the large decline in breakeven hours after 1967 (chart 7.4), the negative impact in the exit equations probably reflects the (unexplained) upward trend in the exit rates evident in table 7.3. Indeed, when we test for the exclusion of B_{ks} and w_s from the specification in the third column of table 7.3, which includes the trend variable, we can accept their exclusion ($\chi^2(2)=1.19$). Thus, the benefit and wage variables, B_{ks} and w_s, cannot account for the upward trend in lone mothers' exit rate from full-time employment.

Gottschalk's analysis of the effect of tax-transfer systems on the employment entry rate could conceivably account for the lack of a significant welfare benefit coefficient in the entire population of lone mothers, because of effects in different directions by some mothers eligible for FIS if they take a job and mothers not eligible. It appears unlikely, however, that the population of lone mothers with earnings low enough to be eligible for FIS and with a reservation wage less than the wage that would take them off FIS is large enough for this account to be plausible.

A more plausible explanation is that trend increases in welfare benefits are anticipated, and therefore have little additional effects on employment transition rates. It is noteworthy that in the models without average wage and welfare benefit variables (tables 7.2 and 7.3), the probability of exit from full-time employment increases with the number of children in the family, and the entry rate to full-time employment is lower for large families. Thus, the effect of benefit entitlement may be partly operating through the family size variable.

The inability to measure income other than that from employment or welfare benefits (for example, maintenance payments and asset income) in the WES data probably also plays an important role in accounting for these results. The lack of a significant benefit effect contrasts with the results of the previous chapter's analysis of lone mothers' (state) probability of employment using *General Household Survey* (GHS) data during 1973–82. When non-labour income, and the sample separation it allows, is ignored in the analysis of the GHS data, welfare benefits appear to have a much weaker impact on the probability of employment.[21]

TRANSITION RATES AND DURATIONS

The estimated effects of attributes of a lone mother and her environment on her employment can be expressed in more familiar terms if we use the estimated models to calculate transition rates for women with different characteristics. As the models without welfare benefits are statistically acceptable, these are used in the calculations. In particular, the estimates in the last columns of tables 7.2 and 7.3, which incorporate residual heterogeneity, are used, and the focus is on full-time employment.

But in contrast to the simple Markov models in the theoretical section, the estimated models do not yield single exit and entry rates. They vary with duration in or out of employment and with the age of the mother and her youngest child, which of course also vary predictably with duration. Furthermore, lone mothers face competing risks of entry to or exit from full-time employment. For example, women out of employment could enter part-time employment.

These considerations are taken into account in some simple summary measures of transition rates. The first is a 'Markov-type' transition rate calculated over the first 100 months in or out of full-time employment. The estimated models are used to predict the level and duration pattern of each transition rate (including the pattern produced by the ageing of the mother and her youngest child). These are used to calculate the 'average' transition rate over the first 100 months as the ratio of total transitions to full-time employment to total months of exposure to risk of a transition. The latter takes into account the competing risk of moving to part-time employment, using estimates of part-time transition rate models in table 7.4.[22] The reference, or 'typical', lone mother is aged 35 with two children, aged seven and nine, at the start of the spell of non-employment or full-time employment; she can earn the mean human capital wage, and the year is 1980. Estimates of these 'average' transition rates are shown in the first two columns of table 7.6.

Table 7.6 *Illustrative transition rates and durations*

Case	'Average' transition rates		Probability of employment
	Entry	Exit	(p_e)
Reference[a]	0.008	0.007	0.53
Wage 1 S.D. higher	0.012	0.005	0.71
Wage 1 S.D. lower	0.005	0.010	0.33
GDP growth rate 1 S.D. higher	0.010	0.007	0.58
1970 environment	0.008	0.003	0.70
Third child aged 10[b]	0.008	0.009	0.48
Youngest child aged 3[b]	0.005	0.014	0.28

Duration: (months)	Out of employment		In full-time employment	
	Median	Lower Quartile	Median	Lower Quartile
Reference[a]	30	11	82	23
Wage 1 S.D. higher	22	8	>100	39
Wage 1 S.D. lower	41	15	53	17
GDP growth rate 1 S.D. higher	28	10	82	23
1970 environment	36	13	>100	68
Third child aged 10[b]	30	11	60	18
Youngest child aged 3[b]	35	13	35	16

[a] The reference mother is aged 35 with two children, aged seven and nine at the start of the spell of non-employment or full-time employment; she has the mean human capital wage and the year is 1980.
[b] At the start of spell, keeping other children at the same age as reference mother's.

In the simple Markov model, the steady-state probability of employment is easily calculated (equation (7.6) above). This equation does not apply to the estimated models, and the concept of a steady-state probability is less meaningful when the age of a mother and her children affect the transition rates. Nevertheless, equation (7.6) has been used to calculate a probability of employment on the assumption that the 'average' transition rates are Markov rates, and it is shown in table 7.6. While the competing risk of part-time employment is taken into account in these calculations, the estimated 'average' transition rates and probability of employment are very similar when the competing risk is ignored. The estimates of lower quartile and median durations out of employment in table 7.6 are, however, sensitive to assumptions about competing risks.

The transition rates and durations are affected most by differences in a mother's human capital wage. A wage one standard deviation higher raises the monthly 'average' entry rate of our 'typical' lone mother from 0.008 to 0.012, and lowers the exit rate from 0.007 to 0.005, thereby increasing the steady-state probability of employment from 0.53 to 0.71. Among a group of our typical lone mothers who had just left employment, a quarter would remain out of employment for less than eleven months, and half would enter employment within 30 months. If these women had a wage one standard deviation higher, the corresponding figures would be eight months and 22 months respectively. Similarly, among a group of typical mothers who just entered full-time employment, 25 per cent would leave within 23 months and half would leave within 82 months. If their human capital wage were a standard deviation higher, it would take 39 months for a quarter to leave, and over a half would still be working when their lone parenthood ended.

Annual GDP growth one standard deviation higher than average raises the entry rate to 0.01 and reduces the median duration out of employment by two months.[23] The model estimates that the average exit rate of our typical woman increased from 0.003 in 1970 to 0.007 in 1980, thereby reducing the lower quartile duration in full-time employment by 45 months. The age of the youngest child at the start of the spell also has dramatic effects: if he/she were aged three rather than seven, then the entry rate would fall to 0.005, and the exit rate would double, lowering the probability of employment to 0.28.

CONCLUSION

In most respects, the dynamic analysis in this chapter confirms the predictions of a (stationary) theoretical model of labour market turnover, and the results of the analysis in the previous chapter. The dynamic analysis has the advantage of providing more information about how differences in the probability of being employed associated with characteristics of a woman and her family come about, through their effects on flows into and out of employment. In particular, a higher potential wage raises the rate of entry to employment, with the effect on the rate of entry to full-time employment being roughly twice as strong as on the rate of entry to part-time employment. A higher human capital wage also lowers the exit rate from full-time employment, but the wage has no effect on the exit rate from part-time employment.

The likelihood of entry to full-time employment increases with the age of the youngest child, but it is much lower for mothers with four or more children. We also find a higher exit rate for women with young children and a larger number of children. These results are consistent with younger children and a large number of children making more demands on their mother's time, which increases her productivity in the home and her utility when out of employment. All else being equal, older mothers are less likely to enter full-time employment, and less likely to leave either form of employment. There is no evidence that a mother's age or that of her children, or the number of children, affects entry to part-time employment.

Above-trend rates of GDP growth raise the rate of entry to full-time jobs, and this effect may be associated with better (or more) wage offers during favourable periods of the business cycle. No such cyclical effect is evident for the entry rate to part-time jobs, but there is evidence of an upward trend in the part-time entry rate.

There is also evidence of a strong upward trend in lone mothers' exit rate from employment, which dates back to the mid-1950s and which cannot be accounted for by our measures of changes in welfare benefits, women's real wages or unemployment. The reasons for this trend clearly require further study, but the trend certainly indicates a decreasing reliance on earnings as a source of support for lone mothers.

While there is some evidence that higher welfare benefits increase exits from and reduce entries into full-time employment, the parameter restrictions entailed by that specification of the model are rejected by the data. The unconstrained empirical results suggest that women may take account of anticipated trend increases in real welfare benefits, the mean of their wage offer distribution and their human capital wage in their employment decisions, as a non-stationary model would suggest, but they may also reflect our inability to measure lone mothers' other non-labour income.

WITH WEIBULL DURATION DEPENDENCE, WE CAN RE-WRITE EQUATION
(7.8) AS

$$\log(\pi_{21}) = (p-1)\log(t_2) + \gamma\log(w_s) + \dots \qquad (7A.1)$$

where t_2 is the duration out of employment and w_s is the potential
wage when the woman left employment. The wage t_2 months after
leaving employment is given by

$$\log(w) = \alpha t_2 + \log(w_s) \qquad (7A.2)$$

Note that $\delta\log(\pi_{21})/\delta\log(w) = \delta\log(\pi_{21})/\delta\log(w_s) = \gamma$

If duration (t_2) only affects π_{21} through its influence on w, then
$\delta\log(\pi_{21})/\delta t_2 = [\delta\log(\pi_{21})/\delta\log(w)][\delta\log w/\delta t_2] = \gamma\alpha$. Because, from
(7A.1) $\delta\log(\pi_{21})/\delta t_2 = (p-1)/t_2$, it follows that

$$(p-1)/t_2 = \gamma\alpha, \text{ or} \qquad (7A.3)$$

$$\alpha = (p-1)/\gamma t_2$$

The estimates of γ and $(p-1)$ in table 7.2, and a (geometric) mean
duration of 51 months, imply an estimate of α of about -0.0031 for
full-time employment (-0.0027 for part-time employment from
table 7.4) when residual heterogeneity is not taken into account, and
-0.001 when it is. The latter estimate is close to Ermisch and
Wright's (1988) direct estimate of α of -0.0009 for women in
full-time jobs; their estimate for those in part-time jobs is -0.0004.

Table 7A.1 *Coefficients of benefit and wage variables (standard errors in parentheses)*

	Entry Part-time	Exit Part-time
Unconstrained model: *Coefficient of logarithm of:*		
Potential wage (x), β_1	1.218^a (0.469)	0.201 (0.658)
Average wage index (w), β_2	0.388 (0.360)	2.325^a (0.887)
Real welfare benefit (B), β_3	0.248 (0.423)	-1.747 (1.725)
Test for exclusion of w and B: $\chi^2(2)$	3.08	14.68^a
Constrained Model 1: $\beta_1 = \beta_2$		
$\beta_1(=\beta_2)$	0.687^a (0.296)	0.952^a (0.480)
β_3	-0.033 (0.380)	0.630 (1.221)
Test of restriction: $\chi^2(1)$	1.96	3.71^a
Constrained Model 2: $\beta_2 = -\beta_3$		
β_1	1.028^a (0.459)	0.184 (0.656)
$\beta_3 (= -\beta_2)$	-0.185 (0.339)	-2.630^a (0.715)
Test of restriction: $\chi^2(1)$	2.78	0.32

^{a} Statistically significant at the 0.10 level or less.

THE DURATION OF LONE PARENTHOOD

The outflow from lone motherhood occurs through (re)marriage or the youngest child reaching adulthood (sixteen years of age). As noted in Chapter 5, the start of lone motherhood for a never-married mother is the date of her first birth, and it is the date of the marital dissolution for a previously-married mother. The proportions of previously-married and never-married lone mothers remaining lone mothers at yearly intervals since the start of lone parenthood, computed from the WES data by lifetable methods (the Kaplan–Meier estimator), are shown in chart 8.1. These estimates indicate a median duration of lone motherhood of 59 months for previously married lone mothers. In contrast, single mothers leave lone parenthood much quicker, exhibiting a median duration of 34 months. Thus, one of the reasons that single mothers represent a relatively small proportion of lone mothers is their much shorter average duration as lone parents.

Chart 8.1 *Survival as lone mother: never and previously-married women*

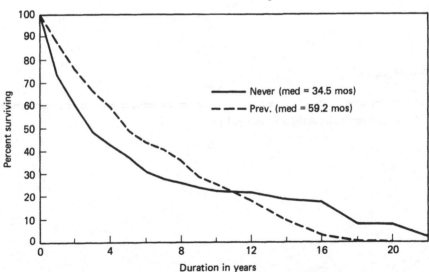

Duration in years

Source: Author's calculations from 1980 *Women and Employment Survey.*

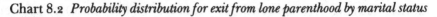

Chart 8.2 *Probability distribution for exit from lone parenthood by marital status*

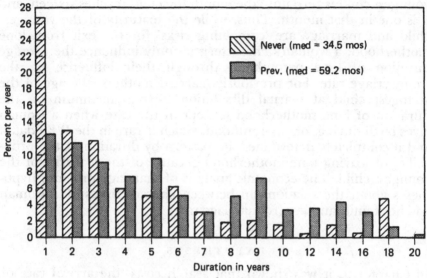

Source: As for chart 8.1.

Chart 8.2 shows that the distribution of durations for each type of lone mother is not concentrated around a modal duration, but is somewhat like a gentle ski-slope (steeper for never-married mothers). Many leave lone parenthood very quickly, but a substantial proportion also remain lone parents for a relatively long time. Because of this skewness in the distribution, the mean, or expected duration of lone motherhood exceeds the median duration.

While clearly of interest, the empirical distribution of the duration of lone parenthood among previously-married lone mothers reflects the distribution of the age of the youngest child at marital dissolution in the sample, because it determines the length of time before the youngest child reaches adulthood. This is why the rate of outflow among previously-married lone mothers remains relatively high beyond seven years duration. If characteristics of a woman or her family influence the chances that she marries, then the distributions of the duration of lone parenthood in chart 8.2 also reflect the distributions of these characteristics in the two samples. In other words, the expected duration of lone parenthood may vary with particular characteristics of a woman and her family. This chapter investigates whether this is the case.

In order to do so, we only need to study how a woman's characteristics affect her (re)marriage chances. The probability of a mother leaving lone parenthood because of the maturity of her youngest child is zero until the month the child reaches sixteen, and it is one in that month. Thus, while the maturity of the youngest child and marriage are 'competing risks' for the exit from lone motherhood, a woman's characteristics only influence the average duration of lone parenthood through their influence on the (re)marriage rate. For previously-married mothers, the age of the youngest child at marital dissolution puts a maximum on the duration of lone motherhood (except in the case when a woman gives birth during lone parenthood, which is rare in the WES data), and it completely determines the pattern by duration of the probability of leaving lone motherhood because of the maturity of the youngest child. The economic analysis of marriage provides hypotheses about the relationship between characteristics of a woman and her family and her (re)marriage rate.

HYPOTHESES

In Chapter 4, it was shown that search costs, the arrival rate of marriage offers, wealth outside marriage, and the gain from marriage in an optimal sorting of mates, affect the likelihood of searching for a(nother) mate and the probability of receiving an acceptable marriage offer in any given time interval. A woman will only search for a(nother) mate if the minimum acceptable marriage offer that can be expected exceeds the expected wealth if she remains unmarried ('single wealth'). It was shown that the probability of that occurring is higher the lower is single wealth, the lower are her search costs, the higher is the arrival rate of marriage offers and the higher is the woman's gain from marriage in the optimal sorting of mates. Characteristics of the woman which affect these variables influence the probability of searching for another mate.

Given that a woman is searching, the likelihood of remarrying in any given interval of time depends on the probability of receiving an acceptable offer in that interval. The latter probability is higher for women with higher search costs and lower wealth if remaining unmarried. The arrival rate of marriage offers and a woman's gain from marriage in the optimal sort have ambiguous effects on this probability, the effects depending on the distribution of offers. For instance, if offers followed a uniform distribution, a higher gain from marriage would increase the probability of receiving an acceptable offer in the interval, and a higher arrival rate of marriage offers would also increase this probability if the arrival rate is large or offers follow particular distributions (see Chapter 4).

Observable characteristics of a woman can be related to the concepts of search costs, single wealth, rate of receipt of marriage offers and the expected gain from marriage in the optimal sort, thereby making it possible to derive some predictions concerning how these characteristics may influence the probability of (re)marrying within any given number of years since becoming a lone parent.

There tends to be a poorer marriage market for older women, but particularly for previously-married women, because of the steep decline with age in the ratio of unmarried men to women. Older women tend to have lower childbearing capacity. 'Youth' may also be an important element in the physical attractiveness of women, and because attractiveness is a trait that is positively sorted, older women would tend to gain less from remarriage. All of these considerations suggest a lower expected gain from marriage for older women, and the 'thinness' of their marriage market may also entail higher search costs and the arrival of fewer offers.

In these circumstances, it is less likely that older women will search at all, but if they do search, they may be more likely to accept an offer within a given time, although strictly speaking the impact on their probability of receiving an acceptable offer is ambiguous. There is not, therefore, a clear prediction of the effect of *age at the start of lone parenthood* on the probability of (re)marrying.

Note that the suggested channels through which age may affect this probability apply particularly to women. In analysis of American data, Becker et al. (1977) found a significant negative effect of age at divorce on the probability of remarriage among women, but no significant effect of age at divorce among men, which is consistent with the hypotheses advanced above.

Children from another father would be valued less by a new husband than by their own parents, and they may cause friction in the new marriage. Thus, a larger number may lower marriage offers and the expected gain from marriage. Furthermore, more children may raise the cost of searching for a husband because they increase the value of their mother's time, may involve direct costs of care (baby-sitters when the mother is out on dates), and may inhibit search in other ways, so that mothers of more children have fewer opportunities to receive a marriage offer.

As was the case with age, the net effect of these considerations on the probability of remarriage is ambiguous. They reduce the likelihood of searching for a mate, but if the woman searches the net impact of her higher costs of search and her lower expected gain from remarriage on the probability of receiving an acceptable offer is unclear.

The easier grounds for divorce after the Divorce Reform Act came into effect in 1971 may have shortened the time between marital breakdown and divorce, thereby tending to shorten the interval between breakdown and remarriage. Perhaps more importantly, divorce increased dramatically during the 1970s, at least in part because of the Act.

More divorces provide a better marriage market (better chances of a 'good sorting of mates'), which entails more and better marriage offers, some of which may have been made before the end of the first marriage. Thus, a larger number of divorces in the population would tend to be associated with a higher probability of remarriage and speedier remarriage.

Women with larger expected gains from marriage, for whatever reason, would tend to have been married longer than other women whose first marriage had ended because more time is required to accumulate a sufficient amount of adverse information to offset a larger expected gain from marriage. Thus, duration of first marriage could be a proxy for unobserved traits of a woman associated with a larger expected gain from marriage. A large expected gain would increase the likelihood of searching for another mate, but, as noted before, it has an ambiguous impact on the probability of receiving an acceptable offer if the woman is searching.

More work experience is associated with higher earning capacity for the woman, which, as Chapter 4 showed, has an ambiguous effect on the expected gain from remarriage. Higher earning capacity also may be associated with higher costs of search. Thus, the predicted net effect on the probability of remarrying in a given time interval is ambiguous.

More work experience during a first marriage, may, however, also be associated with better search opportunities for a new mate within the first marriage. These would make it more likely that a better marriage offer is received, thereby precipitating divorce and early remarriage.

Current participation in paid employment is likely to provide better search opportunities, which lead to more marriage offers and a lower cost of search for a husband. While these make it more likely that a woman will search, they also increase the value of further search, which makes it less likely that an offer is accepted. There is, therefore, no clear prediction of the direction of the influence of being in paid employment on the probability of marrying.

As noted earlier, higher education tends to increase the gain from marriage given the marital division of labour, but it also increases earning capacity and labour force participation, which reduce the benefit of the traditional marital division of labour. Through its effect on earning capacity, it may also affect search costs.

As in earlier chapters, a woman's economic environment may affect her (re)marriage rate. The ratio of average women's to men's hourly wages is taken as an indicator of changes over time in the gains from the division of labour within marriage. As women, on average, receive lower pay than men, when this ratio is higher the benefits from the conventional marital division of labour is lower, thereby tending to reduce the remarriage rate. Ermisch (1981) found that this ratio had a negative influence on first marriage rates in Britain.

Women's average real hourly wage and weekly real state welfare benefits which would be received by a lone mother (based on her number of children) if she is not employed are indicators of sources of income outside of marriage. The hypothesis is that the larger are these alternative sources, the lower the probability of searching for a husband, and the higher the 'reservation marriage offer' if the woman is searching (see Chapter 4). The higher the reservation offer, the lower the (re)marriage rate and the longer the expected search time. Thus, we expect these variables to be negatively related to the (re)marriage hazard.

Finally, the unemployment rate in the economy is included in the analysis. A higher rate may indicate poorer alternative sources of income for a woman, but it may also be associated with poorer and fewer marriage offers. Thus, its effect on the (re)marriage rate is not clear.

EMPIRICAL ANALYSIS

In keeping with our definition of lone parenthood, the analysis is confined to mothers whose youngest child is aged under sixteen at the beginning of her lone parenthood. The (re)marriage analysis again employs the *proportional hazards model*. The date of (re)marriage is the legal date, which may be after the date when a new union is formed. If a woman's youngest child reaches the age of sixteen, her duration is treated as 'censored' (as is also the case when the survey intervenes before (re)marriage), because she is no longer a lone mother according to the definition used here. In line with the analysis of inflows to lone parenthood, the sample is restricted to marriages ending in 1960 or later. In the light of the importance of previously-married mothers among one-parent families, remarriages are considered first.

RESULTS: PREVIOUSLY-MARRIED MOTHERS

The discussion of hypotheses above suggests a number of character-istics of a woman and her family that may affect her remarriage rate. Descriptive statistics (from the WES) for those attributes measured at or before the end of the first marriage are shown in table 8.1. In addition, we consider characteristics that change over time, includ-ing whether the woman is employed or not, work experience and age of the youngest child (in categories). In addition to the real value of welfare benefits, the discussion of hypotheses suggests that some other variables that do not refer to the woman but to her economic environment should also be included in the analysis.[1] These latter variables are the ratio of average women's to men's hourly wages (for adults of each sex working full-time in manual occupations),

Table 8.1 *Variables used in analysis of remarriage*

Variable		Mean	SD
Occupation in last job before first birth:	Manual	0.459[a]	
	Non-manual	0.541	
Children at time of marital dissolution:	1	0.261	
	2	0.372	
	3	0.205	
	4 or more	0.162	
Age of youngest child at marital dissolution:	under 5	0.498	
	aged 5–9	0.293	
	aged 10–15	0.209	
Period of marital dissolution:	1971 or later[b]	0.641	
	before 1971	0.359	
Age at time of marital dissolution:		32.50	7.91
Duration of first marriage (years):		11.58	6.79
Work experience at end of first marriage (years):		9.08	5.87
Employed sometime in 12 months prior to marital dissolution:	Yes	0.553	
	No	0.447	
Highest educational qualifications:	A-level or above	0.115	
	O-level	0.128	
	Other	0.155	
	None	0.594	

Note: Number of previously-married lone mothers = 468.
[a] Includes 2 per cent of mothers who never had a job.
[b] After the Divorce Reform Act came into effect.

Table 8.2 *Proportional hazard rate analysis of remarriage*

Variable[a,b]	All	Manual	Non-manual
Employed sometime during 12 months prior to dissolution	0.355** (0.158)	0.324 (0.236)	0.387** (0.216)
Current employment status	−0.166 (0.164)	0.068 (0.239)	−0.360* (0.223)
Marriage ended after 1971	0.704*** (0.177)	0.432** (0.256)	0.948*** (0.258)
4 or more children	−0.806*** (0.286)	−0.607* (0.370)	−0.961** (0.459)
Duration of first marriage	0.094*** (0.036)	0.193*** (0.059)	0.039 (0.046)
Age at dissolution	−0.133*** (0.031)	−0.247*** (0.053)	−0.073** (0.037)
log (Welfare benefit ÷ average woman's wage)	1.001*** (0.386)	0.304 (0.520)	1.749*** (0.571)
Manual occupation	−0.361** (0.152)	—	—
Constant	−4.287** (1.214)	−0.538 (1.80)	−7.416*** (1.70)
Model χ² (d.f.)	86.21 (8)	51.40 (7)	41.24 (7)
N of women	468	215	253
N of events	189	85	104

[a] The reference categories for the dichotomous variables are: not employed in the 12 months prior to marital dissolution, nor after; non-manual occupation before first birth; marriage ended before 1971; and 1–3 children.
[b] Standard errors in parentheses: *significant at the 0.10 level; **significant at the 0.05 level; and ***significant at the 0.01 level.

women's average real hourly wage (for full-timers in manual occupations), and the unemployment rate in the economy.

As in Chapters 5 and 7, the analysis started with a general model including all of the variables in table 8.1 plus variables indicating a woman's current employment status or work experience to date and the 'macro' environmental variables. Then more parsimonious models, which eliminated particular variables and regrouped categories of categorical variables, were estimated. Table 8.2 shows the estimates of the parameters (β) and their standard errors for a statistically acceptable restricted version of the general model.

In a model including all of the macro variables, in addition to the characteristics of a woman and her family in table 8.2, only women's real wages and real welfare benefits approach statistical significance, and estimates of the parameters associated with the unemployment rate and the ratio of women's to men's hourly wages never exceed their standard error in any specification. Of the macro variables, we therefore concentrate on the effects of women's real wages and welfare benefits.

As in Chapters 5 and 7, welfare benefits are defined as the real value of *Supplementary Benefit* (deflated by the Retail Price Index) that would be received by a lone mother if she is not employed. They vary both over time, as benefit rules and rates change, and over women because benefits vary with the number of children. Welfare benefits generally increased faster than women's wages until 1967, but during 1968–80 they fell substantially relative to average women's hourly pay (by about 35 per cent, as chart 7.4 illustrates).

Direct effect of welfare benefits

Welfare benefits can have both direct and indirect effects on marriage by lone mothers. As a source of income outside marriage, we expect that higher welfare benefits would discourage (re)marriage. Chapter 6 showed that higher welfare benefits also discourage employment. If women in jobs have a different marriage rate from women not employed, then welfare benefits could affect marriage chances indirectly by affecting the proportion of lone mothers in jobs.

When the logarithm of real benefits is the only macro variable included, its impact on the remarriage rate is positive, but statistically insignificant ($\chi^2=1.16$), and when the log of the real wage is the only macro variable, it has a negative effect which is insignificant ($\chi^2=1.25$). When both of these variables are in the model, their estimated parameters are statistically significant with opposite signs, but of the same size. As this suggests, a statistically acceptable simplification is to include the logarithm of the ratio of benefits to women's hourly wages as the only macro variable, and this is the estimated model shown in table 8.2. This ratio measures benefits deflated by women's wages rather than prices, and it could be interpreted as being proportional to an average benefit 'replacement ratio'.

These results suggest that when women are able to earn more in a job, they are less likely to remarry, and they remain lone parents longer. This is consistent with the negative impact of a woman's own employment on remarriage discussed below. The estimated tendency for higher real welfare benefits to encourage remarriage is, however, surprising and difficult to explain.

Because the size and significance of the benefits' parameter depends so much on the inclusion of women's real wages in the model, and *vice versa*, some other specifications were estimated to examine the robustness of the effects of these variables. As benefits are paid to lone mothers out of employment and the average wage level is more immediately relevant to women in employment, the benefit and wage variables are interacted with the woman's current employment status. While this analysis suggests that the effect of the average wage on remarriage is smaller (that is, 'less negative') for employed women, the qualitative conclusions about the effects of the macro variables are not different from the model in table 8.2.

If increases in average real wages discourage remarriage, we may expect that women with higher earning power are also less likely to remarry. A predicted wage at the time of becoming a lone parent was constructed for each woman on the basis of estimates of a relationship between a woman's hourly pay and her education and work history (Ermisch and Wright, 1988) in the same way as in Chapters 5 and 7. When it is included with the other variables in table 8.2, its coefficient is virtually zero, and it remains insignificant ($\chi^2=0.11$) when employment status is dropped from the model. As in the previous chapter, the impact of a woman's predicted wage can be constrained to be the same as that of average real women's wages. This restriction just escapes being rejected at the 0.05 level ($\chi^2=3.49$) and the estimated negative wage impact is not statistically significant ($\chi^2=1.99$). Benefits continue to have a positive effect in this specification. American studies also fail to find a significant impact of a woman's wage on her probability of remarriage (Hoffman and Duncan, 1988a; Hannan *et al.*, 1977). These results induce scepticism about the estimated impact of average real wages on remarriage.

The growth in women's real wages accelerated in the first half of the 1970s, thereby contributing to the decline in the ratio of welfare benefits to wages. The dummy variable for the post-Divorce Reform Act period is unity after 1971. When this dummy variable is omitted from the model, the impact of average wages is virtually zero, but real benefits retain a positive and statistically significant coefficient.

The sample is split between women who had been in manual occupations before motherhood and those who had been in non-manual jobs. The difference between the two groups in the coefficient of the ratio of benefits to women's wages suggests that the

significant positive impact of this ratio on the hazard of remarriage
mainly comes from the behaviour of women who had non-manual
jobs before motherhood (see table 8.2).

While there must be concern that the impacts of the women's real
wages and real welfare benefits are spurious, there is certainly no
evidence that higher benefits discourage remarriage, which we
would expect from conventional economic reasoning. This result is
consistent with the evidence, from Hoffman and Duncan (1988a),
that American Aid to Families with Dependent Children benefits
(AFDC) to lone mothers do not discourage remarriage, and with the
finding, by Hannan *et al.* (1977), that different levels of income
maintenance in American negative income tax experiments have no
discernible impact on the remarriage rate of blacks and whites.

In the light of concern about the measured effect of the benefit–
wage ratio, it is noteworthy that the estimated impacts of the
characteristics of a woman and her family on her remarriage rate in
a model that excludes it are generally very similar to those in the
model of table 8.2. The exceptions are the parameters associated
with the dichotomous variables indicating whether a woman's first
marriage ended in 1971 or after and whether she has four or more
children, which are smaller (falling to 0.481 and −0.582 respectively) when the benefit–wage ratio is excluded (see table 8A.1 at the
end of this chapter). It is not surprising that these would be affected
by the inclusion of a variable that varies over time and over family
size.

Indirect effect of welfare benefits

Current employment status is a dichotomous variable indicating
whether a woman is employed or not in each month. Being in a job
is estimated to reduce the remarriage rate by 15 per cent, but the
coefficient is only the same size as its standard error. Thus, if
different at all, previously-married lone mothers dependent on
welfare benefits appear to be *more* likely to remarry, and if this is a
true 'structural effect', higher welfare benefits would encourage
remarriage by discouraging women from working (see Chapter 6).
In line with the differential impact of the benefit–wage ratio
discussed above, the negative impact of being in a job comes solely
from the behaviour of women who had non-manual jobs before
motherhood; it is virtually zero in the manual group (table 8.2).

One interpretation of the negative impact of employment is that
mothers with better earning opportunities find marriage less attractive. But it also may be the case that women who are not very
interested in remarrying look to the labour market for their present

and future livelihood. In other words, there may be an unobservable trait, call it 'taste for marriage', which is negatively correlated with participation in paid employment, so that the coefficient on employment status is at least partly reflecting this unobserved trait.

Some evidence favouring a role for unobserved heterogeneity in the measured association between work status and the remarriage rate comes from estimation of the model on different samples. The size of the coefficient of work status doubles (and becomes statistically significant) when the estimation is expanded to the period since 1948. When the sample is confined to women whose marriages ended after 1970, the coefficient of work status is virtually zero. Women's employment was more common in the post-1960 period than in the 1950s, and even more common in the 1970s, which would tend to make work status a less reliable indicator of tastes over time. Consistent with this interpretation is a decline in the coefficient of whether a woman worked in the year prior to dissolution (see table 8.2) as we use more recent samples.[2]

Thus, there may be no 'structural effect' of employment on the remarriage rate. To address this issue, we would need to model remarriage and participation in paid employment jointly, allowing for unobserved heterogeneity. But this is a much more formidable estimation task, which is beyond the scope of this book. It is, however, reassuring that the estimated effects of the other variables in table 8.2 are very similar to those in a model without the time-varying employment status variable.

Effects of characteristics of a woman and her family

One of the strongest influences on the remarriage rate is the age of the woman at marital dissolution. As earlier studies suggest, older women are less likely to remarry; thus they can expect a longer duration of lone parenthood.

For the reasons suggested above, the remarriage rate is likely to be higher after the Divorce Reform Act took effect in 1971. The estimates indeed show that women whose first marriage ended in 1971 or later are much more likely to remarry and have a shorter duration of lone parenthood, all else being equal.

As noted earlier, women with unobservable characteristics favourable to marriage would tend to have been married longer than other women whose first marriage ended. The duration of the first marriage could, therefore, be a proxy for these unobserved traits favouring marriage, and the results indicate that women whose first marriage lasted longer are, *ceteris paribus*, more likely to remarry. This variable primarily plays the role of a control for unobservable traits, so that better estimates of the influences of the other variables can be obtained.

Earlier analysis of remarriage (Ermisch, 1986) suggested that more experience in paid employment up to the end of the first marriage increases the likelihood of a woman's remarriage. But that analysis did not consider employment around the time of marital dissolution as a possible influence, nor the impact of current employment status on remarriage. When a dummy variable indicating whether a woman was employed or not sometime in the year before dissolution is included in the model, experience in paid employment before dissolution does not even approach having a statistically significant effect on remarriage. Further tests of the impact of work experience on remarriage were carried out using work experience measures (in months) that vary over time. Neither total work experience, not work experience since dissolution are statistically significant, even in the absence of the variable indicating whether the woman worked in the year prior to dissolution. When this variable is also included in the equation, the impacts of these work experience variables are virtually zero.

A number of alternatives to the recent employment indicator variable were considered, such as whether the woman worked in a full-time or a part-time job six months prior to divorce, or sometime in the two years prior to divorce, or months worked in the two previous years, and they all tell the same story as the variable reported in table 8.2. Whether a woman worked in the year prior to divorce appears to summarise this recent work experience best, and it has a strong effect.

Women in jobs in the year prior to the dissolution of their marriage are much more likely to remarry than those not employed. These effects may arise because participation in paid employment provides better opportunities for finding a new partner, and in some cases these opportunities may result in a woman finding another partner during the first marriage, thereby precipitating both divorce and early remarriage. The measured impact of employment status may also reflect traits of a woman which make her more attractive in both the job market and the marriage market.

The analysis also indicates that, all else being equal, women in manual occupations in their last job before their first birth have lower remarriage rates. It is possible that the marriage market for women who worked in manual occupations is different from that for women from non-manual occupations. While, as noted above, coefficients differ between the two groups (see table 8.2), these differences are only statistically significant at the 0.10 level: a likelihood ratio test could not reject the hypothesis that the hazard function parameters (other than the intercept) are the same for the two groups at the 0.05 level ($\chi_7^2 = 13.11$).

An earlier husband's children are often a source of friction in a second marriage. Thus, a large, ready-made family may make a woman less attractive in the marriage market, and a large family also reduces the opportunities for finding a new partner. The analysis shows that women with very large families (four or more children) are much less likely to remarry. There is no evidence, however, that different family sizes lower than four affect remarriage prospects. Thus, it is only very large one-parent families that are likely to remain one-parent families for a longer time.

Women with older children may also be less likely to remarry than women with younger children, because potential husbands perceive difficulties in fitting into a family with older children. While there is some evidence of this when the age of the youngest child (categorised as in table 8.1) is allowed to vary over time, it does not have a statistically significant impact on remarriage chances. For instance, although women with a dependent child aged five or more were estimated to have a remarriage rate about 20 per cent lower, the chi-square value associated with this parameter was only 0.36.

The analysis also explored whether the birth of another child affects the mother's chances of remarriage. This was done by including a dichotomous variable equal to one each month after the birth and zero otherwise. The coefficient of this variable is virtually zero. Its insignificance probably reflects the rarity of the event (only 6 per cent of the months of exposure occurred after another birth).

The parameters associated with ten duration segments (as in the previous chapter) are insignificantly different from zero; thus the duration segments were excluded from the model in table 8.2. It appears, therefore, that it is reasonable to assume that, conditional on the explanatory variables, the remarriage hazard rate does not vary with the length of time that has elapsed since the dissolution of the first marriage.

RESULTS: NEVER-MARRIED MOTHERS

In addition to the macro variables considered above, the analysis considered a large number of characteristics of a never-married mother that might affect her marriage rate. These include her last occupation before having a child, including whether she had a job before becoming a mother, the year in which she gave birth, her own birth cohort, her educational qualifications, her age at becoming a lone mother, her work experience before her motherhood,

Table 8.3 *Model of marriage of never-married mothers*

Variable[a]	Estimates
Age at giving birth	−0.082** (0.043)
In employment	0.380* (0.209)
Weibull duration parameter $(\gamma - 1)$	−0.403*** (0.081)
Constant	−1.339 (0.869)
Model χ^2 (d.f.)	29.88 (3)
N of women N of events	156 102

[a] Standard errors in parentheses: *significant at the 0.10 level; **significant at the 0.05 level; and ***significant at the 0.01 level.

and whether she was currently in a job or not. Of these many variables, only a mother's age at childbirth and her current employment status had a significant impact on her marriage rate, and these estimated impacts are shown in table 8.3.

There is no evidence that welfare benefits have a direct effect on marriage by never-married mothers. But never-married mothers in employment are about 45 per cent more likely to marry than other single mothers. This probably reflects in part better opportunities to find a husband and lower search costs for women who have jobs. This finding implies that never-married mothers dependent on welfare benefits are less likely to marry, which is what Hutchens (1979) found for previously-married American mothers receiving AFDC. Thus, by discouraging employment, higher welfare benefits may indirectly prolong single parenthood.

The positive association between employment and marriage could, however, also reflect some unobserved differences between women. Never-married mothers with the ability and motivation to be in employment may also be more attractive in the marriage market.

The older are women when they become single mothers the less likely they are to marry. Each additional year reduces their marriage chances by about 8 per cent. This could reflect a poorer marriage market for older women, or perhaps women who become a single mother at older ages do so with little intention to marry.

Duration dependence in the marriage hazard appears to be adequately captured by a simple 'Weibull' specification (that is, $\log[\lambda(t)]=(\gamma-1)\log(t)$) in equation (5.1) of Chapter 5). As the mother is getting progressively older as time goes by, the decline in the first marriage rate with duration is consistent with the lower marriage chances of older women discussed above. This negative duration dependence probably also reflects unobserved differences between women in their attractiveness in the marriage market or their inclination toward marriage: the population of never-married lone mothers is increasingly dominated by those less likely to marry. The next section provides evidence supporting this interpretation.

ESTIMATES CONTROLLING FOR UNOBSERVED HETEROGENEITY

In order to explore the sensitivity of our estimates to the presence of unobserved differences among women, we add a woman-specific variable, ε_i, to the hazard rate equation, as in equation (7.8') of the previous chapter. It is assumed that ε_i is independent of the explanatory variables in X and that ε_i follows a normal distribution.[3] For the sample of previously-married mothers, the parameter (β) estimates (including that associated with employment status) change little after the addition of this form of residual heterogeneity, and the estimated variance of the distribution of this residual is small and never larger than its standard error. This suggests, somewhat surprisingly, that the differences in the observed characteristics in our model capture almost all of the differences between women that matter for remarriage.[4]

In the sample of never-married mothers, the allowance for residual heterogeneity in the model has a larger effect on the parameter estimates. The impact of age at birth increases in size while duration dependence, as captured in the Weibull parameter, disappears. The latter finding is not surprising, as it is well known that failure to control for unobserved heterogeneity biases estimated hazards toward negative duration dependence (Lancaster, 1979). The coefficient of employment status changes little, but its standard error increases. Indeed, neither it nor the coefficient of age at becoming a lone mother is much larger than its standard error in the model including residual heterogeneity. Thus, the parameter estimates are less robust for the first marriage of never-married mothers than for remarriage, but other than duration dependence the qualitative conclusions remain the same as those derived from table 8.3.

SELECTION AND ECONOMIC CIRCUMSTANCES
OF LONE PARENTS

Women who experience longer durations of lone parenthood are
strongly represented in the population of lone mothers at a given
time. Thus, the characteristics of women associated with a longer
duration tend to be more common among the population of lone
mothers. From the parameters of the models in tables 8.2 and 8.3,
the expected (mean), median and first quartile durations of lone
parenthood for lone mothers with different attributes can be easily
calculated. These are shown for some selective cases in table 8.4.
The reference woman has the mean attributes for continuous ones
(like age) and the modal attribute for categorical ones (see table 8.1),
and the year is taken as 1980. Because dependency is defined to end
when a child reaches the age of sixteen, the age of a woman's
youngest child places a maximum on the duration of lone parenthood. A youngest child aged two is assumed in the calculations.

The previously-married reference woman can expect to remain a
lone parent for 7.7 years on average, but because of the skewness of
the duration distribution, half of women with her characteristics
would remain so for 5.3 years or less, and a quarter remain lone
parents for 2.2 years or less. This compares with the Kaplan–Meier
estimate above of a median duration for all previously-married lone
mothers of 4.9 years (see chart 8.1). If, however, she were employed
in the year prior to her marital dissolution, her expected duration is
reduced by about two years.

Women who had worked in manual occupations before
motherhood can expect to be lone parents about three years longer
than the reference woman. Being older or having a very large family
have the largest lengthening impacts on the duration of lone
parenthood. A woman aged 25 (seven years, or about one standard
deviation, younger than the reference woman) remains a lone
parent for, on average, about 4.5 years less than an otherwise
identical woman aged 32 at the end of her first marriage. Mothers of
four or more children have an average duration over five years
longer than mothers of two children.[5]

The average duration of lone parenthood among previously-
married mothers shortened by about four years after the Divorce
Reform Act came into operation in 1971. If the ratio of welfare
benefits to women's real wages returned to its higher level in 1968
(about a 55 per cent increase in benefits relative to wages), then the
median duration would be two years shorter. But, as noted earlier,

Table 8.4 *Expected durations of single parenthood for mothers with selected socioeconomic characteristics*

Characteristics	Duration (years)		
	Mean	Median	1st Quartile
Previously-married mothers:			
(1) Reference woman[a]	7.7	5.3	2.2
(2) Employed in year preceding marital dissolution	5.4	3.8	1.6
(3) Manual occupation in last job before motherhood	11.0	7.6	3.2
(4) Aged 25 at marital dissolution	3.1	2.1	0.9
(5) Ratio of welfare benefits[b] to women's wages increases from its level in 1980 to its level in 1968	4.9	3.4	1.4
(6) Four or more children	13.2	9.1	3.8
(7) Marriage ended before 1971	11.9	8.3	3.4
Never-married mothers:	Duration (months)		
(1) Reference woman[c]		33.4	7.7
(2) In employment		17.7	4.1
(3) Aged 22 at birth		44.0	10.1

[a] The Reference Woman is aged 32 when her marriage of eleven years dissolves; at this time, she has two children, the youngest of which is aged two, she was not employed in the year prior to the dissolution, and she does not have a paid job while a lone mother; her last job before motherhood was in a non-manual occupation; her marriage ended in 1971 or later, and she is assumed to face the ratio of benefits to wages prevailing in 1980. Estimates of the mean, median and 1st quartile durations in lines (1)–(5) are based on the parameter estimates in table 8.2, and lines (6) and (7) on the model excluding the benefit–wage ratio in table 8A.1.

[b] An increase in this ratio to the 1968 level represents a 55 per cent increase.

[c] The reference woman is age twenty at time of illegitimate birth and is not in employment.

we should be sceptical about the measured effect of this ratio on remarriage.

The implication of these associations between duration and women's characteristics is that older mothers, women with very large families, mothers who did not have jobs immediately before becoming a lone parent, and women who had worked in manual occupations would be strongly represented among previously-married lone mothers.[6] Setting age aside, these characteristics tend to be associated with poor economic circumstances. Large families are a larger financial burden, and women who did not have jobs just before becoming a lone parent, probably have lower than average earning capacity, and being from a manual occupation is usually associated with lower earning power. Richards *et al.* (1987) also find that lower income lone parents are more likely to remain lone parents longer.

The median and first quartile durations for never-married lone mothers with different characteristics are also shown in table 8.4. The reference woman becomes a lone mother at age twenty (the mean age) and is not in a job. The median duration for such a woman is about 33 months (comparable to the non-parametric Kaplan–Meier estimate above of 34 months for all lone mothers). A lone mother who is always in a job would remain one for about sixteen months less time, all else being equal. In contrast, a woman who becomes a lone mother when aged 22 would have a median duration almost a year longer than the reference woman aged twenty.

These results imply that never-married mothers without jobs, and therefore probably in receipt of welfare benefits, would tend to be more strongly represented among the population of lone mothers. Such mothers would tend to be worse off economically. The tendency for older mothers to have longer durations raises the average age of lone mothers above what it would otherwise be.

CONCLUSIONS

The analysis indicates that there are a number of characteristics of a woman and her family which are associated with the length of time that she remains a lone parent. Strongest of these is the age of the woman, but, for previously-married mothers, the type of job she had before becoming a mother and whether she had a job in the year prior to the dissolution of her marriage are also strongly associated with her duration of lone parenthood. Other than women with very large families (four or more children), there is no evidence that the age or the number of children affect a woman's remarriage chances. Taken together, for mothers of a given age, the results suggest that lone mothers in poorer economic circumstances remain lone parents longer. Previously-married mothers' duration of lone parenthood appears to have shortened after the implementation of the Divorce Reform Act, which increased the number of people re-entering the marriage market.

For the largest group of lone parents, previously-married mothers, there is no evidence that higher welfare benefits prolong the length of lone parenthood, either directly or indirectly. Among never-married mothers, there is evidence that welfare benefits may prolong single parenthood indirectly by reducing the probability that the mother works. The association of employment with a shorter duration may not, however, be a structural effect of having earning (and marital search) opportunities, but rather a reflection of unmeasured attributes of a woman that favour both employment and marriage. The lack of evidence that higher welfare benefits prolong lone parenthood probably reflects the low level of welfare benefits relative to the share of income in marriage going to a mother and her children.

APPENDIX

Table 8A.1 *Proportional hazard rate analysis of remarriage*

Variable[a,b]	All
Employed sometime during 12 months prior to dissolution	0.337**
	(0.157)
Current employment status	−0.203*
	(0.163)
Marriage ended after 1971	0.481***
	(0.177)
4 or more children	−0.582**
	(0.274)
Duration of first marriage	0.096***
	(0.036)
Age at dissolution	−0.137***
	(0.031)
Manual occupation	−0.345**
	(0.152)
Constant	−1.635**
	(0.646)
Model χ^2	79.42
(d.f.)	(7)
N of women	468
N of events	189

[a] The reference categories for the dichotomous variables are: not employed in the twelve months prior to marital dissolution, nor after; non-manual occupation before 1st birth; marriage ended before 1971; and 1–3 children.

[b] Standard errors in parentheses: *significant at the 0.10 level; **significant at the 0.05 level; and ***significant at the 0.01 level.

PROSPECTS AND POLICIES

PROSPECTIVE NUMBERS OF ONE-PARENT FAMILIES

It was shown in Chapters 2 and 3 that rising divorce has been primarily responsible for the creation of more one-parent families in Britain and elsewhere. Thus, the prospects for divorce in Britain are very important in assessing whether one-parent families will continue to grow in number relative to two-parent families.

It appears that the divorce rate stabilised during the 1980s, after its rapid increase during the 1970s. As chart 9.1 shows, the divorce rate was flat during the first half of the 1980s. It increased in 1985 as a consequence of the Matrimonial and Family Proceedings Act, which came into effect in October, 1984. The Act allowed petition for divorce to be filed after one year of marriage instead of three. Thus, it would tend to have a once-and-for-all effect of bringing petitions for divorce forward in time, and this appears to have happened in 1985. After this one-off increase, divorce rates have fallen back, although to a level above the rate experienced in 1980–84 (see chart 9.1). It appears, therefore, that divorce rates may be levelling out, or are increasing at a much slower rate than in the 1970s.

The analysis of Chapter 5 suggests that an important development operating to reduce divorce is the increase in the age at first marriage that has occurred in Britain since the early 1970s. Between 1971 and 1988, women's mean age at first marriage has increased from 22.6 to 24.6. It was argued in Chapter 2 that while this rise reflects the increase in cohabitation before marriage, much of it is due to later entry into a union with a man. According to the parameter estimates in table 5.4 (Model 3), this increase of two years in the age at marriage would reduce the risk of marital dissolution by 13 per cent. Although women who conceive their first child outside marriage and mothers in jobs are more likely to dissolve their marriage (table 5.4), there has been no trend in either the proportion of married mothers working (see chart 2.6), nor in the percentage of first births within marriage that are pre-maritally conceived (fluctuating between 15 and 16 per cent).

Chart 9.1 *Divorce decrees per 1,000 married women*

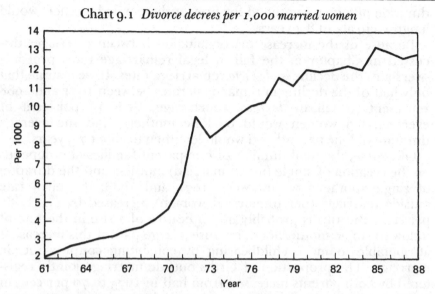

Sources: *Marriage and Divorce Statistics*, London, HMSO, various years and
Population Trends, London, HMSO, various issues.

Thus, neither the trends observed during the 1980s (chart 9.1)
nor other indicators suggest further dramatic increase in divorce.
This suggests that an upsurge in the creation of one-parent families
headed by previously-married mothers is unlikely.[1]

The number of previously-married lone mothers also depends
upon how quickly divorced mothers form a new union. We have
seen that remarriage rates have fallen dramatically in Britain (chart
2.3). The analysis of Chapter 8 (table 8.2) suggests that a small
decline in the average age at divorce (from 36.8 in 1971 to 35.7 in
1988) and a declining proportion of women in manual occupations
(to under a quarter of full-time workers in 1989) should have
moderated the fall in remarriage rates. While the fall partly reflects
more cohabitation between marriages, it suggests longer durations
of lone parenthood.

Using the simple Markov model of Chapter 3, it is possible to
estimate the proportion of ever-married women of childbearing age
(aged 16–44) who would be lone mothers if divorce and remarriage
rates remained at their 1988 values while other transition rates were
as estimated in Chapter 3 (table 3.1b).[2] With these assumptions, 15.5
per cent of ever-married women of childbearing age would be lone
mothers, compared with about 7 per cent in the early 1970s. The
assumed change in the remarriage rate implies that the average

duration of lone parenthood for previously-married mothers would lengthen to about 8.4 years.

Because of the increase in cohabitation between marriages discussed in Chapter 2, the fall in legal remarriage rates probably overstates the decline in *de facto* remarriage rates. If we assume that only half of the decline in remarriage rates between 1971 and 1988 represents a fall in *de facto* remarriage, then 14 per cent of ever-married women would be lone mothers, and the average duration of lone parenthood would lengthen to about 7.5 years.

Of course, the total number of one-parent families also depends on the creation of single (never-married) mothers and the duration of single motherhood. Between 1971 and 1988, the birth rate outside marriage (per unmarried woman) increased by nearly 60 per cent. But this is probably not indicative of a rise in the rate of inflow to single motherhood, because a large part of this increase is attributable to more childbearing by cohabiting couples outside marriage. The proportion of births outside marriage jointly registered by both parents increased from half in 1975 to 70 per cent in 1988. An increasing proportion of the joint registrations (71 per cent in 1988) show the same address for both parents, suggesting that these births are to cohabiting parents. Births outside marriage and registered solely by the mother have, therefore, increased relatively little.

If a solely registered illegitimate birth rate is calculated (that is, solely registered births outside marriage relative to the number of unmarried women), this birth rate has shown no trend between 1971 and 1988. Thus, in the calculation of the proportion of single women who are single mothers, using the analysis in Chapter 3, it will be assumed that the first birth rate outside *de facto* marriage is constant.

The first marriage rate fell by 44 per cent between 1971 and 1988, but it was shown in Chapter 2 that about half of this decline probably reflects more cohabitation without legal marriage. It is assumed, therefore, that the *de facto* first marriage rate of both childless women and single mothers fell by 22 per cent. According to the analysis of Chapter 8 (table 8.3), a small rise in the average age at giving birth outside marriage (from about 23.5 during most of the 1970s to 24.1 in 1988) contributed to a decline in first marriage rates among single mothers, which increases the average duration of single motherhood. Under these assumptions, about 5 per cent of single women would be single mothers, and once they became a single mother, their average duration of single motherhood would be 7.5 years.

Using equation (3.5) in Chapter 3, these estimates of the changes in transition rates, based on changes in conventional marriage, birth and divorce rates, suggest that about 19 per cent of families with dependent children would be headed by a lone parent if these transition rates were maintained. Estimates from the 1989 *General Household Survey* indicate that 17 per cent of families with dependent children were one-parent families. Thus, present demographic rates suggest a further increase in the relative number of one-parent families, but nothing like the doubling in this percentage that took place between 1971 and 1988.

POLICY OBJECTIVES

The primary social problem associated with one-parent families is their low incomes. The poor living standards of a large proportion of one-parent families were noted in Chapter 2. These are mainly attributable to the absence of a spouse's income to help support the children or any other source of income other than state benefits, and Chapters 5 and 8 argued that selective inflows to and outflows from lone parenthood contributed to the poverty of lone parents.

There is also concern about the possible adverse effects on the development of children. For instance, Wadsworth and Maclean (1986) show that, in Britain, there is evidence of lower educational attainment for both sexes and lower socio-economic achievements in males in their mid-twenties following experience of parental divorce or separation before the age of fourteen, and those children who experienced living in a one-parent family before the age of five continued to be more than usually vulnerable to certain kinds of criminal offending and to hospital treatment for psychosomatic and emotional disorders, as well as having a higher risk of an illegitimate pregnancy (Wadsworth, 1979). Part of these consequences may be able to be traced to the experience of growing up at the low standards of living of most one-parent families, but United States evidence suggests tht this is not the entire story (McLanahan 1988, and McLanahan and Bumpass, 1988). Kiernan (1986) shows that a marital breakdown in the family of origin increased the likelihood that teenage brides (who already have a high risk of marital dissolution) experienced a marital dissolution by their early 30s.[3]

The issue of poverty and its primary source, the lack of a father's income, and the possible intergenerational effects of spending part of childhood in a one-parent family both point to a need for policies that reduce the number of one-parent families. But such policies may either be ineffective or infringe on basic liberties in British society. Even if they can be effective, they will not eliminate one-parent families.

Thus, policies that improve the living standards of one-parent families are also needed. As it is generally not in the interest of either the lone parent or taxpayers for lone parents to be primarily dependent on means-tested benefits, policies that improve living standards while reducing welfare dependence are particularly desirable. The next section discusses policies affecting the number of one-parent families, and is followed by a discussion of policies aimed at raising the living standards of one-parent families, particularly by raising their employment. There are, of course, a large number of potential policies that could be discussed, but the focus here is on those policies upon which the research in this book could shed light.

EFFECTS OF POLICY ON THE NUMBER OF LONE PARENTS

The analyses in Chapters 5 and 8 indicated that welfare benefit policies have only increased the number of one-parent families through the influence of welfare benefits on the creation of single (never-married) mothers.[4] The parameter estimates in tables 5.6 and 5.7 indicate that a 10 per cent increase in real welfare benefits to single mothers would raise the first birth rate outside marriage by 13–38 per cent, depending on the specification of the model. Assuming again that *de facto* first marriage rates are 22 per cent lower than the estimates in table 3.1b, the analysis of Chapter 3 indicates that this 10 per cent increase in welfare benefits would raise the percentage of single women who are mothers to between 5.8 and 7 per cent, from 5.2 per cent. This, in turn, would raise the percentage of one-parent families among families with dependent children by 0.3–0.8 percentage points.

The favoured point estimate of the impact of welfare benefits on the pre-marital birth hazard comes from the model in Chapter 5 that treats young women's educational participation and employment as endogenous (model 3A in table 5.7). According to this estimate, 10 per cent higher benefits raise the pre-marital birth rate by 27 per cent, thereby increasing the percentage of families with dependent children headed by one parent by 0.6 percentage points, and the percentage of single women who are single mothers by 1.3 percentage points. Thus, the effect of higher welfare benefits on the relative number of one-parent families is not large. This is consistent with the American evidence. In his survey of incentive effects of the United States welfare system, Moffitt (1990, p.71) concludes that 'the welfare system does not appear to be capable of explaining most of the long-term trend or any of the recent trend of increasing number of female-headed families in the United States'.

Changes to the divorce law have, however, had a much larger impact on the relative number of one-parent families than changes in welfare benefits. If the Divorce Reform Act is largely responsible for the increase in the divorce rate during the 1970s and the duration of lone parenthood was not affected, then it would have increased the percentage of families with dependent children headed by one parent by as much as 6 percentage points (see table 3.2c), an increase of about 70 per cent.

The analysis in Chapter 8 (tables 8.2 and 8.4) suggested, however, that the Divorce Reform Act may also have raised the remarriage rate above the level it would have been by as much as 60 per cent,[5] by increasing the number of potential partners in the marriage market, and this would have reduced the average duration of lone parenthood proportionately. If both effects of the Act were operating at their maximum strength, the net impact of the Act on the percentage of families with dependent children headed by one parent would have been to increase it by about 4 percentage points, or about 50 per cent.

Policies that make marital dissolution more difficult or significantly less attractive probably have much more scope to affect the relative number of one-parent families than changing single mothers' welfare benefits. Making divorce more difficult is likely to have undesirable effects (for example, 'trapping people in unhappy marriages') which would contradict policy goals in this area in the last twenty years. Efforts to increase parental responsibility for child support after divorce could affect the attractiveness of divorce.

The net impact of better child support from the absent parent on the divorce rate is not, however, clear because it increases the incentive for divorce for the custodial parent (usually the mother), but reduces it for the absent parent. According to Becker's (1981) analysis of marriage, mandated changes in child support by the absent parent would be offset by redistribution between spouses, with no effect on the divorce rate. Furthermore, the prospects for remarriage of the absent parent (poorer prospects) and the custodial parent (better prospects) could be affected. Thus, the net effect on the percentage of families with dependent children headed by a lone parent is unclear, and it is not possible to quantify it. But this policy has other advantages, which are discussed in the next section.

EFFECTS OF POLICY ON LONE MOTHERS' INCOMES AND EMPLOYMENT

Despite the fact that poverty could be reduced most effectively by discouraging the formation of one-parent families and diminishing the duration of lone parenthood, it is difficult to devise policy changes that significantly reduce the number of one-parent families without having other effects that are undesirable. With little influence over their number, policies need to be directed at improving the living standards of one-parent families. A key policy issue is how this can be done while also reducing their dependence on means-tested state benefits.

The evidence presented in Chapter 6, that the United Kingdom benefit system affects significantly a lone parent's decision to take a job, not only supports the predictions of the theoretical model presented there, but allows us to quantify its effects. The model estimated there is used to predict changes in the percentage of lone parents in employment resulting from simulated changes in wages, benefit entitlements and non-labour income which approximate policy changes. The simulations are restricted to mothers eligible for SB using the model which incorporates taxes and FIS (that is, column 2, table 6.1).

As table 9.1 shows, if the Supplementary Benefit (SB) guarantee were increased by 10 per cent (about £5 per week), holding the Family Income Supplement (FIS) scales constant, then the percentage of lone mothers in jobs would fall from 46.5 to 42.4 per cent. But FIS scales are usually increased proportionately with increases in the SB guarantee. In that case, the percentage of lone mothers in employment only falls to 43.6 per cent.[6]

There are a number of policies that could alter lone parents' non-labour income other than FIS. For instance, One Parent Benefit could be increased, or a tax rebate (or a cash grant) could be paid to

Table 9.1 *Policy simulations: predicted percentages employed*

Baseline case	46.5
10% increase in SB guarantee	42.4
10% increase in SB guarantee and in FIS scale	43.6
£10 p.w. increase in One Parent Benefit	53.8
£10 p.w. increase in Child Support from father	52.7
£0.45 per hour subsidy for child care	61.3

Notes: Based on model in column 2 of table 6.1. Predicted percentage in employment is the mean predicted probability of employment among the 1,785 eligible lone mothers.

working lone mothers for child care expenses. Table 9.1 shows that an increase of £10 (1988 prices) per week in either of these would raise the percentage of lone mothers in employment by about 7 points. Rough calculations taking into account changes in SB payments and in tax collections suggest that the net Exchequer cost of this policy is about 65 per cent of the net cost of raising SB scales by £5 per week.[7] Higher Child Benefit has a similar effect, although it would clearly be larger for women with more children. Thus, 'targeting' benefits on the poorest through higher SB would increase lone mothers' dependency on SB, while higher 'universal' benefits would transfer money to less poor lone parents, but it would reduce welfare dependency.

Child support payments from fathers could be raised through better enforcement of existing child support orders and establishing more orders (see Robins, 1986), raising the size of court orders or guaranteeing them by the state. These changes have effects similar to those measures in the preceding paragraph, except that higher maintenance payments reduce FIS entitlements for women who would receive FIS if they took a job. Taking this into account, an increase of £10 per week in maintenance would raise the percentage of lone mothers working by about 6 percentage points.

Robins' (1986) analysis suggests that better enforcement and collection of existing child support orders may be an effective means for reducing government welfare expenditure, but it is unlikely to have a dramatic effect on reducing either welfare dependency or improving the living standards of one-parent families.[8] He finds that even if child support awards were established for all lone parents and fully collected, the proportion of families headed by a lone mother dependent on the main United States welfare programme, Aid to Families with Dependent Children (AFDC), would only fall by 0.02 relative to a situation of no child support at all,[9] and the proportion living below the poverty level by 0.06 (Robins, table 6). Thus, even in the best conditions, the child support system in the United States has little impact on welfare dependency and poverty, and we can expect a similarly small impact of better child support enforcement in Britain.

An important reason for such a small impact is the low child support awards. Robins estimated that amounts awarded to AFDC recipients are only about 60 per cent of AFDC payments on average, which is not large enough to have a significant impact on welfare dependency, even if fully paid.

Recent analysis by Garfinkel *et al.* (1990) of the impacts of different levels of child support for one-parent families in Wisconsin suggests that even substantially higher awards have a limited effect on AFDC dependency. Low levels of absent father's income limit the amount that awards can be increased, but their analysis suggests that even if the government guarantees a minimum amount of child support ($3,000 a year in their simulation), the reduction in welfare dependency is small. It should also be noted that the effect on total labour supply (in hours) is small. While the additional child support raises the labour supply of original AFDC recipients, it reduces the labour supply of non-recipients. Furthermore, as child support awards are set as a percentage of the absent father's income, they represent a tax on the father's income, which may reduce his labour supply and hence the amount of child support paid.

Thus, while enforcing the absent parent's child support responsibilities may be desirable for other reasons (for example, reducing government welfare expenditure), it is unlikely to reduce lone mothers' dependency on welfare benefits by very much because of limits on how much child support awards can be increased. Policies which help lone mothers combine employment and responsibilities to their children are probably more effective in reducing welfare dependency and improving living standards of one-parent families.

Child care subsidies are an obvious such policy. We have discussed a flat rate subsidy above. An hourly subsidy for child care paid to working lone mothers is equivalent to an increase in their net hourly wage. A supplement of about 45 pence per hour (1988 prices) would cover a quarter of the average hourly cost of a child minder.[10] This would raise the percentage working by an outstanding 15 percentage points, and its net cost is only a quarter of its gross cost and less than half of the net cost of raising SB scales by £5 per week. This subsidy could be targeted on lone mothers with low hourly pay, thereby reducing the deadweight loss of the subsidy while substantially discouraging dependence on SB. Some may object that targeting such child care subsidies on lone mothers may encourage more women to become lone mothers and remain so longer, but the analyses in Chapter 5 and 8 have shown little evidence that financial factors affect the entry to lone parenthood or (re)marriage by lone parents.

Another set of policies which operate through the effect of earning capacity on the probability of employment are education, training and job placement. A number of such programmes have been tested in the United States. For instance, a Minnesota experiment in the late 1970s provided education, training and temporary job placement to AFDC recipients in an attempt to improve their labour market position in the longer term. Steinberg's (1989) evaluation of the programme provides imprecise evidence that the programme increased the probability of post-programme employment participation and that there is a high labour market return to work experience. A diversity of programmes have been introduced and evaluated, and the details of each programme are likely to affect its impact. Despite the diversity, there is a clear indication that the American programmes of this sort do increase future earning potential (for a summary, see Moffitt, 1990, table 12). Because higher earning capacity was found in Chapter 6 to increase substantially the likelihood that a lone mother takes a job, such training programmes would reduce welfare dependency and raise the living standards of lone mothers in the longer term.

This contrasts with the effects of welfare benefit programmes like Income Support, which tend to reduce future earning potential by reducing experience in paid employment. Moffitt and Rangarajan (1989) found a negative effect of AFDC receipt over the previous five years on current wages of 20 per cent, but the effect falls off rapidly beyond five years. They also find that the wage depressing effects are larger for more educated women.

Thus, Income Support may have longer-term effects on lone mothers' pay and employment, and conversely policies that improve lone mothers' chances of taking employment have favourable impacts that go beyond the immediate impacts on their welfare dependency and living standards.

As Moffitt (1990) points out, however, training programmes are unlikely to be a panacea for the problem of one-parent families' low incomes, because the earnings increase is not that large. Nevertheless, such programmes do provide an additional tool for reducing welfare dependency and improving the incomes of one-parent families. Child care subsidies are the other important tool.

CONCLUSION

The number of one-parent families has grown dramatically, and it appears that there is little that policy can do to reduce their number. Child care and training policies offer the best hope for improving their living standards while reducing dependency on welfare benefits. Better enforcement of the child support responsibility of the absent parent should also be an important component of policy towards one-parent families. We should probably not expect dramatic changes in lone parents' welfare dependency or poverty, but such policies could make a substantial improvement.

NOTES

2 ONE-PARENT FAMILIES IN INDUSTRIALISED COUNTRIES: AN OVERVIEW OF TRENDS

1 A formal and more complex model of the incidence of lone parenthood is presented in the next chapter.

2 The proportion of births that are outside marriage is $R/(1+R)$, where R is the ratio of illegitimate to legitimate births, and $R = f_i u/f_1(1-u)$, where f_i is the illegitimate birth rate (per unmarried woman), f_1 is the legitimate birth rate (per married woman), and u is the proportion of women of childbearing age who are not married.

3 All of these patterns also exist when mothers are partitioned by the age of the youngest child (less than five years compared with aged 5–16).

4 'One-parent families' in the *Family Expenditure Survey* are identified as households with one adult and one or more dependent children. Year-to-year fluctuations in one-parent families' relative income reflect sampling error, owing to relatively small samples of such households.

5 Equivalent income is calculated using the following equivalence scale: married couple = 1; one adult = 0.6; each child = 0.23. Calculated from McClements (1977).

6 Based on author's analysis of the 1980 *Women and Employment Survey*; see Martin and Roberts (1984). There are 249 lone mothers in the survey in 1980, of which 63 worked full-time and 52 worked part time.

7 Author's analysis of *Women and Employment Survey*.

3 MODELLING THE DYNAMICS OF ONE-PARENT FAMILIES

1 *The General Household Survey* has collected marriage and birth histories since 1979, but its lack of employment history data makes analyses like those in Chapters 5, 7 and 8 impossible. It could, however, be used to estimate the simple transition rates of this chapter, but it has not been used in this way.

2 While there are undoubtedly instances in which unmarried, childless women marry a man with children (that is $P_{14}>0$, $P_{54}>0$), these cannot be identified with the WES data, because the birth history, which is used in relation to a woman's marriage history to identify one-parent families, refers to a woman's *own* children. I know of no source from which the importance of such marriages can be inferred, but they are probably of insufficient importance in aggregate to make it safe to ignore them in this analysis. Similarly, instances in which custody of the

children is with the father (that is, $P_{45}>0$), cannot be identified; father's custody is, however rare.

3 The Markov chain represented by the transition matrix C is made up of one *absorbing chain* represented by matrices Q and R and one *regular chain* represented by the transition matrix P. P is the *minimal set* and the single *ergodic set* while Q is a *transient set*.

4 Marriage is the 'absorbing state' since everyone is assumed to marry.

5 The median duration in the Markov model is given by $-\log(0.5)/p_{24}$.

4 AN ECONOMIC MODEL OF MARRIAGE AND MARITAL SEARCH

1 This is not 'wealth' in the traditional sense, although couples with more resources would usually be able to acquire more of these home commodities.

2 For readers not interested in the mathematical derivation of the model, a summary is given at the end of this section.

3 The next four sections derive hypotheses concerning the impacts of changes in the parameters. For readers not interested in the mathematical derivations, a summary of the predictions of the model is given in a separate section on the bottom of page 49.

4 Evidence in Main (1985) and Joshi and Newell (1986) suggests work experience acquired earlier (say, before the first birth or before marriage) may have a smaller effect on earning capacity than that acquired more recently.

5 ENTRY TO LONE PARENTHOOD: ANALYSIS OF MARITAL DISSOLUTION AND PRE-MARITAL BIRTHS

1 Beyond ten years, only women becoming mothers in the 1960s could be at risk of dissolution.

2 In each case the hazard rate is the total number of dissolutions divided by the total months of exposure to risk during a twelve-month period, which is a maximum likelihood estimate of the hazard rate.

3 In the analyses of marital dissolution and pre-marital births (which follows later in the chapter), there are 211,882 and 156,975 months of exposure respectively. Furthermore, it is difficult to estimate the heterogeneity distribution when there are non-repeated events, such as those analysed here.

4 When D replaces the trend variable in the first model of table 5.2, its coefficient (and standard error) is 0.410 (0.179), with a chi-square value of 5.25. The model chi-square is, however, lower than the first model of table 5.2 (77.30).

5 The chi-square values for the test that these two coefficients are different from zero are 4.98 and 0.16 respectively. The full sets of parameter estimates are shown below in table 5.5.

6 While the coefficient on this dummy variable is positive, it never exceeds its standard error in the various specifications.

7 There is some evidence that the relationship between the number of children and the dissolution risk exhibits an inverted J-shape, with the risk being higher for mothers of one than for mothers of three or more children. But the coefficient associated with this large family category is never significantly different from zero; even in a model with neither a work status nor experience variable, the coefficients (and standard errors) associated with two children and three or more children are −0.386 (0.169) and −0.223 (0.206), the latter being statistically insignificant ($\chi_1^2 = 1.17$).

8 The coefficient of this work experience variable is not significantly different from zero at significance levels below 0.05. Occupational status at motherhood does not come anywhere near having a significant influence on the risk of dissolution; thus it is omitted from the models.

9 There was some evidence that women whose highest educational attainment is 'O-levels' face a lower risk of dissolution than women with higher or lower qualifications. But such a relationship is difficult to interpret.

10 Because the coefficients of the other variables in the model hardly change, they are not shown in table 5.3.

11 The duration categories associated with these variables are 12–23 months since the birth of the first child, 24–35 months, 36–49 months, 50–63 months, 64–79 months, 80–98 months, 99–120 months, 121–149 months, and 150 or more months. The omitted category is eleven or less months. As noted earlier, the categories were constructed so that each contains about 10 per cent of all months of exposure. Also, the chi-square values for the log of duration in the models in table 5.2 are 0.10 and 0.15 respectively. The inclusion of the log of duration in the model implicitly assumes that duration has a Weibull distribution. When trend variables are included in the model, there is never any evidence of Weibull duration dependence.

12 A model replacing the variable indicating whether a woman had a birth in the previous year with a dichotomous variable for the first year after becoming a mother produces similar results (a risk 43 per cent lower), but the model chi-square is lower (99.93) than that of model 3.

13 The square of the age at marriage is dropped from the equation because collinearity with age at marriage made it impossible to estimate either variable's parameter precisely.

14 The test is analogous to the one for changes over time in the marital dissolution hazard in equation (5.2), where 1968 replaces 1971 in the definition of D and the interaction term is $D(y-67)$. When these two variables are included in the models in table 5.6, they are jointly (and individually) insignificant. Even when welfare benefits, the unemployment rate and women's relative pay are excluded from the model and D is included along with year of exposure, the coefficient of D is positive and statistically insignificant ($\chi_1^2 = 1.98$).

15 Young women in neither education nor a job were rare in the WES data. Only 5 per cent of the months of exposure were contributed by women neither in employment nor education.

16 A model that includes the linear trend along with the three macro variables was also estimated. The coefficient on year is -0.02, but its chi-square value is only 0.10, while the coefficients of the three macro variables are similar to those in the first model in table 5.6.

17 See models 8, 9 and 10 in Appendix table 5A.1. Model 8 only includes a time trend along with the relative pay variable. The time trend is highly significant ($\chi^2_1 = 17.27$), but the coefficient of women's relative pay is not statistically significant at levels below 0.15 ($\chi^2_1 = 1.84$). In models 9 and 10, the coefficient of relative pay is less than its standard error. Similar results are found for women's average real hourly pay, when it replaces women's pay relative to men's. Its estimated positive coefficient makes even less economic sense.

18 Appendix table 5A.1 presents various model specifications with women's relative pay. It is also worth noting that the high standard error of the coefficient of the unemployment rate in model 1 could just reflect collinearity with the other two macro variables.

19 Furthermore, model 10 in Appendix table 5A.1, which includes only unemployment and women's relative pay, shows a strong unemployment effect.

20 This contrasts with its statistically significant coefficients in the first and third models and in models 6 and 7 in Appendix table 5A.1. In a model in which the only macro variable is real welfare benefits, its coefficient (and standard error) is 5.909 (1.129).

21 Such a trend is also apparent in model 9, which includes women's relative pay along with the trend.

22 The American study referred to earlier (Leibowitz *et al.*, 1986) indicated that pregnant girls were significantly more likely to have the baby and remain single if they *would be* eligible for welfare benefits, and Plotnick (forthcoming) finds that a higher welfare benefit (AFDC) guarantee increases the probability of an out-of-wedlock birth by the age of nineteen among the United States white population.

23 Real welfare benefits increased by 62 per cent between 1960 and 1980, and the unemployment rate increased from 1.5 to 5.8 per cent.

6 LONE PARENTS' EMPLOYMENT AND WELFARE BENEFITS

1 During the last two years of our study, the Supplementary Benefit system offered a 'tapered disregard' of 50 per cent of earnings between £4 and £20 per week, after which the 100 per cent tax rate applied. At women's median hourly wage, the range of working hours covered by the tapered disregard in 1981 was 2–9 hours per week (2–8 in 1982), and in our sample covering 1973–82, 21 per cent of lone mothers in employment earned less than £20 per week. The analysis of Hanoch and Honig (1978) raises the possibility that the segment of the budget constraint with the 50 per cent tax rate is not effective. Our empirical analysis below is consistent with the ineffectiveness of that segment for most women.

2 Child benefit is paid to all mothers and varies with the number of

children, and One Parent Benefit is a fixed amount paid to one-parent families.

3 Both are drawn for the tax and benefit system prevailing in mid–1979, for a mother with one child aged under five facing fixed money costs of employment (FC) of £4 per week (which are disregarded in calculating SB payments) and receiving £5 per week in non-labour income other than state benefits (Z^*).

4 Hausman's empirical analysis (1980, pp.190–91) also indicates that the analagous first segment of the budget constraint arising from AFDC, where lone mothers receive the AFDC maximum payment, is irrelevant because working only a few hours does not cover the fixed costs of working.

5 For simplicity, we also ignore fixed time costs of employment when ignoring the earnings disregards.

6 In terms of chart 6.1, higher Z shortens the horizontal portion of the budget constraint, reducing 'breakeven hours' E^* and making it more likely that a woman takes a job.

7 See Blinder and Rosen (1985); it is indeed a 'notch' with a linear tax. Higher C raises the level of the kink in the budget constraint at 24 hours in chart 6.1, making it more likely that a woman chooses to work.

8 The peculiarities of the formula relating benefit entitlement to the ages and the number of children can also help identify a benefit effect, but it is a weak source of identification compared with variation over time. Also, the effect of the ages and number of children among women with $Z>B$ provides estimates of their effects independent of any effects through benefit entitlement. Thus, comparison of these with child effects estimated for women with $Z<B$ would suggest whether estimates of the impact of benefit entitlement is capturing effects of children independent of benefits or whether the impacts of children are capturing effects of benefits. The sample of women with $Z>B$ is, however, relatively small, making these estimates less precise than those in the larger sample. For further discussion of the problem of identifying benefit effects in behavioural models see Heckman and Robb (1985) and Moffit (1989).

9 Lone parent families living in other households cannot be identified with the data, and the data only gives detailed information on the household head. Furthermore, even if we had information on one-parent families within other households, it would not be possible to determine how income was shared within the household. Other information indicates that about one-fourth of lone mothers live in households with other people.

10 Estimates of 'take-up' of SB indicate that 89 per cent of lone parents whose low earnings and other income made them eligible for SB in 1977 received it (*Social Security Statistics, 1980,* table 34.38). It may appear that, because we do not take account of payment of housing costs by SB, a much larger percentage of employed lone mothers have total income below their SB entitlement, but this ignores the fact that

employed lone mothers with low income would also obtain help with their housing costs through rent and rates allowances.

11 The availability of rent and rates allowances to families eligible for FIS is ignored. These would increase their virtual non-labour income and make their marginal tax rate even higher. Some families ineligible for FIS may also receive these allowances. As noted earlier however, there is insufficient information in the data to model these allowances related to housing costs.

12 While the coefficient of the unemployment rate is not statistically significant in the equation for non-eligibles, the imprecision of the estimate may be due to the relatively small sample.

13 Only a few women in the group not eligible for benefits had a child aged less than one. The parameter estimate for this variable was extremely unstable, so the categories were grouped. They were not, however, grouped in the likelihood ratio test of the hypothesis that only the parameters associated with B and Y_i differed between the two groups of mothers.

14 Estimating the same specification for married mothers from the 1980 *Women and Employment Survey* indicates that their probability of employment is also not significantly affected by the number of children, once the age of the youngest child is taken into account. Walker (1990) also finds that the age of the youngest child, but not the number of children, affects lone mothers' probability of employment.

15 The magnitudes of the parameters of the linear and quadratic age terms indicate that the probability of employment increases up until about age 31 and then declines.

16 The first adjustment entailed dividing his coefficients by 1.434, and the second entailed multiplying his coefficients by $\pi/R3$ (see Maddala, 1983, p.22).

17 Unless stated otherwise, all comparisons are between models analogous to the specification in column 1 of table 6.1.

18 Moffitt's model implies that the derivative of the difference between utilities on (v_1) and off (v_0) welfare with respect to the guarantee is $\delta^2\gamma/(\beta-\delta H_1)$, where δ and β are the coefficients of non-wage income and the wage respectively in a linear hours of work function ($\beta\geqslant0$, $\delta\leqslant0$), H_1 is hours worked on welfare and γ is a measure of 'variable welfare stigma' ($\gamma>0$). The probability of welfare participation is $F(\bar{v}_1-\bar{v}_0)$, where $F(\cdot)$ is the normal distribution function and $\bar{v}_1-\bar{v}_0$ is the systematic (non-stochastic) part of the utility difference at the means. The elasticity of this probability with respect to the guarantee is equal to $(\delta^2\gamma/(\beta-\delta H_1)f(\bar{v}_1-\bar{v}_0)G/P$, where $f(\cdot)$ is the normal density function, G is the mean of the guarantee and P is the mean proportion of female-heads on welfare.

19 Note he does not take the 'virtual income approach' to estimating the effect of FIS.

20 In addition to the coefficient of the SB guarantee (discussed above), the coefficient of wages is the minor exception to this. It ranged from

0.0715 in the model excluding regional and year dummies to 0.0867 in the model including both of these. As real wages vary across time and region, it is not surprising that its coefficient shows some sensitivity to the inclusion of these dummies.

21 The value of the critical benefit taper depends on a woman's preferences as well as her benefit entitlement and the initial earnings disregard.

22 Similarly, a likelihood ratio test also indicates that the 25 parameters in column 2 do not differ significantly between the two periods ($\chi^2_{25}=17.5$).

7 EMPLOYMENT DYNAMICS AMONG LONE PARENTS

1 Fixed hours makes income maximisation equivalent to utility maximisation.

2 $\lim_{\varepsilon \to 0} o(\varepsilon)/\varepsilon = 0$.

3 The estimation method amounts, in practice, to making months of 'exposure to risk' of a transition, rather than women, the observations. Characteristics of a woman and her family are 'attached' to each month of exposure contributed by her, as are macro-level variables that vary with calendar time. The likelihood functions are given in Ermisch and Wright (1991, Appendix 1).

4 The likelihood to be maximised comes from integrating out the ε_k, as described in Ermisch and Wright (1991, Appendix 1). Recall that a woman may contribute a number of spells of employment and non-employment.

5 It is a model of *job search* rather than *turnover* because it assumes that once a job is accepted it will be held forever. The theoretical analysis becomes intractable if this assumption is relaxed, because non-stationarity in future spells influences the optimal strategy in the present spell.

6 The SB scheme replaced National Assistance in 1966; in our data, 82 per cent of exposures to risk of entry to full-time employment and 85 per cent of exposures to risk of full-time exits occur since 1965.

7 As the previous chapter showed, as many as 10 per cent of women have sufficient non-labour income to make them ineligible for SB when not employed; as expected, SB entitlement has no effect on their probability of employment. Furthermore, the absolute value of the coefficient of SB entitlement is biased toward zero when other non-labour income is omitted from the logit equation.

8 The FIS scheme has been available since 1971.

9 A higher benefit scale (or 'guarantee' in Gottschalk's terminology) does not affect the cost of job search (it raises the opportunity cost of search by the same amount that it offsets the out-of-pocket costs), but the benefit of search declines because low wages, which keep the woman eligible for benefits, are made more attractive by the higher benefit scale, while higher wages are unaffected.

10 About 15 per cent of employed lone parents received FIS in the late 1970s.

11 For studies covering short periods of calendar time (for example, Lancaster, 1979), it is probably safe to ignore such increases. But our period covers a long period, 1948–80, when real benefit levels increased by a large amount.

12 It also reflects differences in housing costs, but we cannot measure these.

13 A better treatment of the competing risks of entering either full-time or part-time employment from non-employment would model the two transitions together. This was done for the model without unobserved heterogeneity using a multinomial logit specification. The estimated parameters were very close to those in the first column of table 7.2. More generally, remarriage could also be treated as a competing risk, but at least under the assumptions of the multinomial logit model and no unobserved heterogeneity, my experience is that the results are very similar to those that treat competing transitions as censoring. Thus, because treating transitions involving part-time employment (or remarriage) as censored is simpler for computations, this method was used to estimate the parameters. It is also worth nothing that direct movements between full-time and part-time employment are relatively rare in the data.

14 Another source of true, negative duration dependence could be the expectation of increasing real wages and welfare benefits over the spell, which, as noted earlier, van den Berg (1990) shows could produce an increase in the reservation wage over the spell.

15 For exits from full-time employment a simple dichotomy between women aged above and below 25 represented this best, while for part-time employment a continuous representation of age worked best.

16 As Appendix table 7A.1 shows, welfare benefits do not have a statistically significant effect on part-time transitions in this constrained model. Confinement of the effect of benefits to full-time employment transitions is very plausible, because the supplementary benefit system is likely to entail a high level of 'breakeven hours' for most lone mothers (see previous chapter).

17 As the earlier discussion of non-stationarity suggests, the macro variables w_s and B_{ks} are not stationary time series, and their trends over time make them strongly correlated with one another. This can make it difficult to obtain very precise estimates of the impacts of these variables on employment transitions. It also may make the estimated effect of any one variable strongly dependent on which of the other macro variables are included in the equation.

18 The unemployment rate never had a statistically significant influence on the transition rates. As before (table 7.2), the business cycle indicator only affects entries to full-time employment, and its estimated impact varies little with the other macro variables included in the equation.

19 While the human capital wage appears to have a significant positive

effect on exits from part-time jobs in constrained model 1, the restriction in this specification is rejected (see Appendix table 7A.1).

20 As Appendix table 7A.1 shows, the restriction in this specification is accepted for exits from part-time employment, with a perverse negative sign on breakeven hours.

21 The different sample periods do not appear to account for the difference. The dynamic analysis covered the period 1948–80 while the analysis in the previous chapter covered 1973–82, but similar results are obtained when the dynamic analysis in this chapter is restricted to months of exposure to risk occurring during 1973–80.

22 The transition rate from out of employment to part-time employment is estimated to depend only on a woman's human capital wage, duration out of employment and calendar year. Movements from full-time to part-time employment are rare, and a constant rate has been estimated for this transition.

23 The much smaller effects of the business cycle than higher wages on duration out of employment reflects the finding that the business cycle only affects the entry rate to full-time employment, while the potential wage affects the part-time entry rate as well.

8 THE DURATION OF LONE PARENTHOOD

1 As noted in earlier chapters, months of lone parenthood, rather than women, become the observations in the estimation method. Characteristics of a woman and her family are 'attached' to each month of lone parenthood contributed by her, as are environmental variables that vary annually.

2 The other coefficients change very little when expanding or contracting the sample to these different time periods.

3 The likelihood to be maximised comes from integrating out the ε_i: see Appendix I of Ermisch and Wright (1991).

4 It is noteworthy that when we estimate a clearly mis-specified model, including only age at marital dissolution in X, the estimated residual variance is large and four times its standard error, and the coefficient of age increases in size from -0.07 to -0.08 when ε_i is added to the model.

5 Because the impact of the number of children on the benefit–wage ratio varies over time, the average durations for large families and for marriages ending before 1971 are computed from the model in table 8A.1, which excludes the benefit–wage ratio.

6 The statistically insignificant employment status effect has been ignored.

9 PROSPECTS AND POLICIES

1 There is some British evidence (Kiernan 1986), discussed later in the chapter, that suggests that women whose parents divorce are more likely to divorce themselves. The evidence is only for one birth cohort,

and it is not possible to quantify the impact of such intergenerational effects on the prospects for divorce rates. They would only begin to act with force, however, from around the turn of the century; they suggest an acceleration in divorce during the first decade of the next century.

2 Recall that this proportion is not sensitive to the estimates of the other transition rates. The calculation is carried out by scaling the particular transition rate in table 3.1b by the proportionate change in the comparable demographic rate between 1971 and 1988. In particular, the remarriage rate halved while the divorce rate increased by a factor of 2.17 between 1971 and 1988.

3 In all of these British intergenerational studies, the children are from the 1946 birth cohort.

4 The empirical analysis in Chapter 8 indicated that higher welfare benefits *increased* remarriage rates and *reduced* the duration of lone parenthood significantly (see tables 8.2 and 8.4). As this estimated effect is difficult to interpret and of questionable validity, it is ignored in assessing the effects of welfare benefits on the number of one-parent families. Taking the result literally, the size of the effect relative to the impact of welfare benefits on the creation of never-married mothers implies that higher welfare benefits would *reduce* the relative number of one-parent families.

5 This estimate is based on the coefficient of the dummy variable for whether their marriage ended after 1971 or not in the model excluding the welfare benefit–wage ratio (table 8A.1 of Chapter 8).

6 Changing the FIS scales would also affect the proportion of lone mothers who would face a broad range of hours in which they could receive FIS, but there is no way of modelling this change with the data used here. It is assumed that the same 30 per cent of mothers would receive FIS if they take a job, and this is also assumed for the simulation of the effect of higher maintenance payments below.

7 The calculations assume that additional employed lone mothers are paid the median wage and work 25 hours per week, and it ignores changes in FIS expenditure.

8 Note that because child support is taxed at 100 per cent for lone parents on Income Support (formerly Supplementary Benefit), higher child support must reduce welfare dependency if it is to improve the living standards of lone parents on Income Support.

9 Only 6 per cent of AFDC recipients were employed in 1987; thus, AFDC receipt usually means being out of employment as well.

10 As the wage predicted for a woman is for full-time employment, her predicted *hourly* wage is approximately her predicted weekly wage divided by 35 (hours per week). That is what is assumed in the calculation of the effect of an hourly subsidy.

REFERENCES

Allison, P.D. (1982), 'Discrete-time methods for the analysis of event histories', *Sociological Methodology 1982.*

Bamford, C. and Dale, A. (1988), General Household Survey Time Series 1973–1982, Guildford, Surrey, Department of Sociology, University of Surrey.

Becker, G.S. (1973), A theory of marriage: Part I, *Journal of Political Economy*, 81, no. 46.

—— (1981), *A Treatise on the Family*, Cambridge, Mass, Harvard University Press.

Becker, G.S., Landes, E.M. and Michael, R.T. (1977), 'An economic analysis of marital instability', *Journal of Political Economy*, 85.

Berg, G.J. van den (1990), 'Nonstationarity in job search theory', *Review of Economic Studies*, 57.

Bishop, J. (1980), 'Jobs, cash transfers and marital instability: a review and synthesis of the evidence', *Journal of Human Resources*, 15.

Blanc, O. (1985), 'Les ménages en Suisse. Quelques aspects de leur évolution de 1960 à 1980 à travers les statistiques du recensement', *Population*, no. 2.

Blank, R.M. (1985), 'The impact of state economic differentials on household welfare and labor force behaviour', *Journal of Public Economics*, 28(1).

Blinder, A.S. and Rosen, H.S. (1985), 'Notches', *American Economic Review*, 75.

Boulier, B.L. and Rosenzweig, M.R. (1984), 'Schooling, search, and spouse selection: testing economic theories of marriage and household behavior', *Journal of Political Economy*, 92.

Bumpass, L. and McLanahan, S. (1989), 'Unmarried motherhood: Recent trends, composition and black–white differences', *Demography*, 26.

Burdett, K., Kiefer, N.M. and Sharma, S. (1985), 'Layoffs and duration dependence in a model of turnover', *Journal of Econometrics*, 28.

Cain, G. and Wissocker, D. (1988), 'Marital breakups in the Seattle-Denver income maintenance experiment: a different conclusion', Institute for Research on Poverty, Discussion Paper no. 870–888, Madison, University of Wisconsin.

Cherlin A. and McCarthy, J. (1985), 'Remarried couple households: Data from the June 1980 Current Population Survey', *Journal of Marriage and the Family*, 47.

Cogan, J.F. (1981), 'Fixed Costs and Labor Supply', *Econometrica*, 49.

Danziger, S., Jakubson, G., Schwartz, S. and Smolensky, E. (1982), 'Work and welfare as determinants of female poverty and household headship', *Quarterly Journal of Economics* 97.

Department of Health and Social Security (1984), *Abstract of Statistics for Index of Retail Prices, Average Earnings Social Security Benefits and Contributions*, London, Department of Health and Social Security, Branch HQ SR8A, April.

Duncan, G.J. and Hoffman, S.D. (1985), 'A reconsideration of the economic consequences of marital dissolution', *Demography* 22.

Easterlin, R.A. (1980), *Birth and Fortune, The Impact of Numbers on Personal Welfare*, London, Grant McIntyre.

Ermisch, J.F. (1981), 'Economic opportunities, marriage squeezes and the propensity to marry: an economic analysis of period marriage rates in England and Wales', *Population Studies*, 35.

—— (1986), 'The economics of the family: applications to divorce and remarriage', Discussion Paper no. 140, London, Centre for Economic Policy Research.

—— (1988), 'Economic influences on birth rates', *National Institute Economic Review*, 126, November.

—— (1990), 'Demographic aspects of the growing number of one parent families', Paris, OECD.

Ermisch, J.F. and Wright, R.E. (1988), 'Differential returns to women's human capital in full-time and part-time employment', Discussion Paper in Economics, no. 14, London, Birkbeck College.

—— (1991), 'Employment dynamics among British single mothers', *Oxford Bulletin of Economics and Statistics* (forthcoming).

Faessen, W.B.M. (1988), 'Eenoudergezinnen, 1 januari 1987', *Maandstatistiek van de Bevolking*, 36, August.

Garfinkel, I., Robins, P.K., Wong, P. and Meyer, D.R. (1990), 'The Wisconsin Child Support Assurance System', *Journal of Human Resources*, 25(1).

Glick, Paul (1984), 'Les ménages aux Etats-Unis, 1960, 1970, 1982', *Population*, no. 4–5.

Glick, P.C. and Lin, S–L. (1986), 'Recent changes in divorce and remarriage', *Journal of Marriage and the Family*, 48.

Gottschalk, P. (1988), 'The impact of taxes and transfers on job search', *Journal of Labor Economics*, 6.

Griffith, J.D., Koo, H.P. and Suchindran, C.M. (1984), 'Childlessness and marital stability in remarriages', *Journal of Marriage and the Family*, 46.

Groeneveld, L.P., Tuma, N.B. and Hannan, M.T. (1980), 'The effect of negative income tax programs on marital dissolution', *Journal of Human Resources*, 15.

Hannan, M.T., Tuma, N.B. and Groeneveld, L.P. (1977), 'Income and marital events: evidence from an income-maintenance experiment', *American Journal of Sociology*, 82.

Hanoch, G. and Honig, M. (1978), 'The labor supply curve under income maintenance programs', *Journal of Public Economics*, 9.

Haskey, J. (1984), 'Social class and socio-economic differentials in divorce in England and Wales', *Population Studies*, 38.

Haskey, J. (1986), 'One-parent families in Great Britain', *Population Trends*, 45.

—— (1989), 'One-parent families and their children in Great Britain: numbers and characteristics', *Population Trends*, 55.

Haskey J. and Kiernan, K. (1989), 'Cohabitation in Great Britain – characteristics and estimated numbers of cohabiting partners', *Population Trends*, 58.

Hausman, J.A. (1980), 'The effects of wages, taxes and fixed costs on woman's labor force participation', *Journal of Public Economics*, 14.

Heckman, J.J. (1979), 'Sample selection bias as a specification error', *Econometrica*, 47.

Heckman, J.J. and MaCurdy, T. (1980), 'A life cycle model of female labor supply', *Review of Economic Studies*, 47.

Heckman, J.J. and Robb, R. (1985), 'Alternative methods for evaluating the impact of interventions', in Heckman, J.J. and Singer, B. (eds.), *Longitudinal Analysis of Labor Market Data*, Cambridge, Cambridge University Press.

Heckman, J.J. and Singer, B. (1984), 'Econometric duration analysis', *Journal of Econometrics*, 24.

Hoem, B. and Hoem, J.M. (1988), 'Dissolution in Sweden: the break-up of conjugal unions to Swedish women born in 1936–60', Working Paper, Stockholm, Section of Demography, University of Stockholm.

Hoem, J. and Rennermalm, B. (1985), 'Modern family initiation in Sweden: experience of women born between 1936 and 1960', *European Journal of Population*, no. 1.

Hoffman, S.D. and Duncan, G.J. (1986), 'Remarriage and welfare choices of divorced women, unpublished manuscript, University of Delaware, Department of Economics.

—— (1988a), 'A comparison of choice-based multinomial and nested logit models: the family structure and welfare use decisions of divorced or separated women', *Journal of Human Resources*, 23.

—— (1988b), 'Multinomial and conditional logit discrete-choice models in demography', *Demography*, 25.

Honig, M. (1974), 'AFDC income, recipient rates, and family dissolution', *Journal of Human Resources*, 9.

Hutchens, R.M. (1979), 'Welfare, remarriage and marital search', *American Economic Review*, 69.

Joshi, H. (1984), 'Women's participation in paid work: further analysis of the Women and Employment Survey', Research Paper no. 45, London, Department of Employment.

Joshi, H. and Newell, M–L (1986), 'Pay differentials and parenthood: analysis of men and women born in 1946', Report to the Department of Employment.

Keeley, M.C. (1977), 'The economics of family formation', *Economic Inquiry*, 15.

Kemeny, J.G. and Snell, J.L. (1960), *Finite Markov Chains*, London, D. Van Nostrand Company.

Kiernan, K. (1986), 'Teenage marriage and marital dissolution: a longitudinal study', *Population Studies*, 40.

Killingsworth, M.R. (1983), *Labor Supply*, Cambridge, Cambridge University Press.

Koesoebjono, S. (1986), 'Evolution des ménages aux Pays-Bas', *Population*, no. 2.

Lam, D. (1988), 'Marriage markets and assortative mating with household public goods', *Journal of Human Resources*, 23.

Lancaster, T. (1979), 'Econometric methods for the duration of unemployment', *Econometrica*, 47.

Lancaster T. and Nickell, S. (1980), 'The analysis of reemployment probabilities for the unemployed', *Journal of the Royal Statistical Society A*, 143.

Leibowitz, A., Eisen, M. and Chow, W.K. (1986), 'An economic model of teenage pregnancy decision-making', *Demography*, 23.

Levy, F. (1979), 'The labor supply of female heads or AFDC work incentives don't work too well', *Journal of Human Resources*, 14.

Lippman, S.A. and McCall, J.J. (1976), 'The economics of job search: a survey', *Economic Inquiry*, 14.

Lommerud, K.E. (1989), 'Marital division of labor with risk of divorce; the role of 'voice' enforcement of contracts', *Journal of Labor Economics*, 7.

McClements, L. (1977), 'Equivalence scales for children', *Journal of Public Economics*, vol. 8.

McLanahan, S.S. (1988), 'Family structure and dependency: early transitions to female household headship', *Demography*, 25.

McLanahan, S.S. and Bumpass, L.L. (1988), 'Intergenerational consequences of marital disruption', *American Journal of Sociology*, 94.

Maddala, G. (1983), *Limited Dependent and Qualitative Variables in Econometrics*, Cambridge, Cambridge University Press.

Main, B. (1985), 'Women's earnings: the influence of work histories on rates of pay', Discussion Paper, Edinburgh, Department of Economics, University of Edinburgh.

Martin, J. and Roberts, C. (1984), *Women and Employment: A Lifetime Perspective*, London, HMSO.

Michael, R.T. (1973), 'Education in nonmarket production', *Journal of Political Economy*, 81, part 1.

Mincer, J. (1978), 'Family migration decisions', *Journal of Political Economy*, 86.

Moffitt, R. (1983), 'An economic model of welfare stigma', *American Economic Review*, 73.

—— (1986), 'The econometrics of piecewise-linear budget constraints: a survey and exposition of the maximum likelihood method', *Journal of Business and Economic Statistics*, 4.

—— (1988), 'The effect of the U.S. welfare system on marital status', Paper presented at the International Union for the Scientific Study of Population's Seminar on the Family, the Market and the State in Ageing Societies, Sendai, Japan.

—— (1989), 'Demographic behaviour and the welfare state: econometric issues in the identification of the effects of tax and transfer programs', *Journal of Population Economics* 1.

—— (1990), 'Incentive effects of the U.S. welfare system: a review', University of Wisconsin, Institute for Research on Poverty, Special Report No. 48, March.

Moffitt, R. and Rangarajan, A. (1989), 'The effect of transfer programmes on work effort and human capital formation: evidence from the US', in Dilnot, A. and Walker, I. (eds.), *The Economics of Social Security*, Oxford, Oxford University Press.

Mortensen, D.T. (1970), 'Job search, the duration of unemployment and the Phillips curve', *American Economic Review*, 60.

—— (1982), 'Property rights and efficiency in mating, racing and related games', *American Economic Review*, 72.

Mott, F.L. and Moore, S.F. (1983), 'The tempo of remarriage among young American women', *Journal of Marriage and the Family*, 45.

Mroz, T.A. (1987), 'The sensitivity of an empirical model of married women's hours of work to economic and statistical assumptions', *Econometrica*, 55(4).

Murphy, M.J. (1984), 'Fertility, birth timing and marital breakdown: a reinterpretation of the evidence', *Journal of Biosocial Science*, 16.

—— (1985), 'Demographic and socio-economic influences on recent British marital breakdown patterns', *Population Studies*, 39.

Nilsson, T. (1985), 'Les ménages en Suede', *Population*, no. 2.

Office of Population Censuses and Surveys (1981), *The General Household Survey*, London, HMSO.

Peters, H.E. (1986), 'Marriage and divorce: informational constraints and private contracting', *American Economic Review*, 76.

—— (1988), 'Retrospective versus panel data in analyzing lifecycle events', *Journal of Human Resources* 23.

Plotnick, R. (forthcoming), 'Welfare and out-of-wedlock childbearing: evidence from the 1980s', *Journal of Marriage and the Family*.

Richards, T., White, M.J. and Tsui, A.O., (1987), 'Changing living arrangements: a hazard model of transitions among household types', *Demography*, 24.

Robins, P.K. (1986), 'Child support, Welfare dependency, and poverty', *American Economic Review*, 76.

Roll, J. (1989), *Lone Parent Families in the European Community*, London, Family Policy Studies Centre.

Roussel, L. (1986), 'L'évolution récente de la structure des ménages dans quelques pays industriels', *Population*, no. 6.

Sardon, J-P. (1986), 'Evolution de la nuptialité et de la divortialité en Europe depuis la fin des années 1960', *Population*, no. 3.

Schwartz, K. (1983), 'Les ménages en Republique féderale d'Allemagne (1961, 1972, 1981)', *Population*, no. 3.

Steinberg, D. (1989), 'Induced work participation and returns to experience for welfare women: evidence from a social experiment', *Journal of Econometrics*, 41.

Wadsworth, M.E.J. (1979), *Roots of Delinquency: Infancy, Adolescence and Crime*, Oxford, Martin Robertson.

Wadsworth, M.E.J. and Maclean, M. (1986), 'Parents' divorce and children's life chances', *Children and Youth Services Review*, 8.

Walker I. (1990), 'The effects of income support measures on the labour market behaviour of lone mothers', *Fiscal Studies*, 11.

Weale A. *et al.* (1986), *Lone Mothers, Paid Work and Social Security*, London, Bedford Square Press.

Weiss, Y. and Willis, R.J. (1985), 'Children as collective goods and divorce settlements', *Journal of Labor Economics*, 3.

Wright, R.E. and Ermisch, J.F. (1988), 'Gender discrimination in the British labour market: a reassessment', Discussion Paper no. 278, London, Centre for Economic Policy.

Wright R.E. and Hinde, A. (1991), 'The dynamics of female labour force participation in Great Britain', *European Journal of Population (forthcoming)*.

INDEX

THE NATIONAL INSTITUTE OF ECONOMIC
AND SOCIAL RESEARCH
PUBLICATIONS IN PRINT

published by
THE CAMBRIDGE UNIVERSITY PRESS
(available from booksellers, or in case of difficulty from the publishers)

ECONOMIC AND SOCIAL STUDIES

XIX *The Antitrust Laws of the USA: A Study of Competition Enforced by Law*
By A. D. NEALE and D. G. GOYDER. 3rd edn. 1980. pp. 548. £35.00 net.

XXI *Industrial Growth and World Trade: An Empirical Study of Trends in Production, Consumption and Trade in Manufactures from 1899–1959 with a Discussion of Probable Future Trends*
By ALFRED MAIZELS. Reprinted with corrections 1971. pp 563. £22.50 net.

XXV *Exports and Economic Growth of Developing Countries*
By ALFRED MAIZELS, assisted by L. F. CAMPBELL-BOROSS and P. B. W. RAYMENT. 1968. pp. 445. £20.00 net.

XXVII *The Framework of Regional Economics in the United Kingdom*
By A. J. BROWN. 1972. pp. 372. £22.50 net.

XXVIII *The Structure, Size and Costs of Urban Settlements*
By P. A. STONE. 1973. pp. 304. £18.50 net.

XXIX *The Diffusion of New Industrial Processes: An International Study*
Edited by L. NABSETH and G. F. RAY. 1974. pp. 346. £22.50 net.

XXXI *British Economic Policy, 1960–74*
Edited by F. T. BLACKABY. 1978. pp. 710. £40.00 net.

XXXII *Industrialisation and the Basis for Trade*
By R. A. BATCHELOR, R. L. MAJOR and A. D. MORGAN. 1980. pp. 380. £25.00 net.

XXXIV *World Inflation since 1950. An International Comparative Study*
By A. J. BROWN assisted by JANE DARBY. 1985. pp. 428. £35.00 net.

XXXV *Unemployment: A Problem of Policy*
By G. D. N. WORSWICK. 1991. pp. 297. £27.50 net.

XXXVI *Macroeconomic Policy in Britain 1974–87*
By ANDREW BRITTON. 1991. pp. 378. £30.00 net.

OCCASIONAL PAPERS

XXV *The Analysis and Forecasting of the British Economy*
By M. J. C. SURREY. 1971. pp. 120. £8.50 net.

XXVI *Mergers and Concentration in British Industry*
By P. E. HART, M. A. UTTON and G. WALSHE. 1973. pp. 190. £11.50 net.

XXVII *Recent Trends in Monopoly in Great Britain*
By G. WALSHE. 1974. pp. 156. £10.50 net.

XXVIII *Cyclical Indicators for the Postwar British Economy*
By D. J. O'DEA. 1975. pp. 184. £12.50 net.

XXIX *Poverty and Progress in Britain, 1953–73*
By G. C. FIEGEHEN, P. S. LANSLEY and A. D. SMITH. 1977. pp. 192. £12.95 net.

XXX *The Innovation process in the Energy Industries*
By G. F. RAY and L. UHLMANN. 1979. pp. 132. £9.50 net.

XXXI *Diversification and Competition*
By M. A. UTTON. 1979. pp. 124. £10.50 net.

XXXII *Concentration in British Industry, 1935–75*
By P. E. HART and R. CLARKE. 1980. pp. 178. £22.50 net.

XXXIV *International Industrial Productivity*
By A. D. SMITH, D. M. W. N. HITCHENS and S. W. DAVIES. 1982. pp. 184. £15.00 net.

THE NATIONAL INSTITUTE OF ECONOMIC AND SOCIAL RESEARCH

publishes regularly

THE NATIONAL INSTITUTE ECONOMIC REVIEW

A quarterly analysis of the general economic situation in the United Kingdom and overseas with forecasts eighteen months ahead. The last issue each year usually contains an assessment of medium-term prospects. There are also in most issues special articles on subjects of interest to academic and business economists.

Annual subscriptions, £65.00 (home) and £80.00 (abroad), also single issues for the current year, £17.00 (home) and £25.00 (abroad), are available direct from NIESR, 2 Dean Trench Street, Smith Square, London, SW1P 3HE.

Subscriptions at a special reduced price are available to students and teachers in the United Kingdom and Irish Republic on application to the Secretary of the Institute.

Back numbers and reprints of issues which have gone out of stock are distributed by Wm. Dawson and Sons Ltd., Cannon House, Park Farm Road, Folkestone. Microfiche copies for the years 1959–88 are available from EP Microform Ltd., Bradford Road, East Ardsley, Wakefield, Yorks.

Published by
HEINEMANN EDUCATIONAL BOOKS
(distributed by Gower Publishing Company and available from booksellers)

DEMAND MANAGEMENT
Edited by MICHAEL POSNER. 1978. pp. 256. £18.50 net.

BRITAIN IN EUROPE
Edited by WILLIAM WALLACE. 1980. pp. 224. £12.95 (paperback) net.

THE FUTURE OF PAY BARGAINING
Edited by FRANK BLACKABY. 1980. pp. 256. £31.00 (hardback), £8.95 (paperback) net.

INDUSTRIAL POLICY AND INNOVATION
Edited by CHARLES CARTER. 1981. pp. 250. £26.50 (hardback), £9.95 (paperback) net.

THE CONSTITUTION OF NORTHERN IRELAND
Edited by DAVID WATT. 1981. pp. 233. £24.00 (hardback), £10.50 (paperback) net.

SLOWER GROWTH IN THE WESTERN WORLD
Edited by R. C. O. MATTHEWS. 1982. pp. 182. £26.50 (hardback), £10.95 (paperback) net.

NATIONAL INTERESTS AND LOCAL GOVERNMENT
Edited by KEN YOUNG. 1983. pp. 180. £25.00 (hardback), £10.95 (paperback) net.

EMPLOYMENT, OUTPUT AND INFLATION
Edited by A. J. C. BRITTON. 1983. pp. 208. £36.00 net.

THE TROUBLED ALLIANCE, ATLANTIC RELATIONS IN THE 1980s
Edited by LAWRENCE FREEDMAN. 1983. pp. 176. £25.00 (hardback), £8.95 (paperback) net.

(Available from Heinemann and from booksellers)
THE UK ECONOMY
By the NIESR. 1990. pp. 96. £3.75 net.

Published by
GOWER PUBLISHING COMPANY
(Available from Gower Publishing Company and from booksellers)

ENERGY SELF-SUFFICIENCY FOR THE UK
Edited by ROBERT BELGRAVE and MARGARET CORNELL. 1985. pp. 224. £22.50 net.

THE FUTURE OF BRITISH DEFENCE POLICY
Edited by JOHN ROPER. 1985. pp. 214. £24.00 net.

ENERGY MANAGEMENT: CAN WE LEARN FROM OTHERS?
By GEORGE F. RAY. 1985. pp. 131. £22.50 net.

UNEMPLOYMENT AND LABOUR MARKET POLICIES
Edited by P. E. HART. 1986. pp. 230. £30.00 net.

NEW PRIORITIES IN PUBLIC SPENDING
Edited by M. S. LEVITT. 1987. pp. 136. £26.00 net.

POLICYMAKING WITH MACROECONOMIC MODELS
Edited by A. J. C. BRITTON. 1989. pp. 285. £29.50 net.

HOUSING AND THE NATIONAL ECONOMY
Edited by JOHN ERMISCH. 1990. pp. 158. £29.50 net.

Printed in the United States
By Bookmasters